The Canterbury and York Society
GENERAL EDITOR: A. K. McHARDY
M.A., D.Phil.

DIOCESE OF SALISBURY

T0339308

The Register of

Thomas Langton

BISHOP OF SALISBURY

1485-93

EDITED BY

D. P. WRIGHT

Haileybury

Privately Printed for
the Canterbury and York Society
1985

PART CXLVII   VOL. LXXIV

DEDICATED TO THE MASTER

AND FELLOWS OF

SIDNEY SUSSEX COLLEGE, CAMBRIDGE.

FIRST PUBLISHED 1985

© CANTERBURY AND YORK SOCIETY

ISSN. 0262 - 995X

This volume is published with
the help of a grant from
the British Academy.

Details of previous volumes available from the
Hon. Treasurer of the Society, St. Anthony's Hall, York YO1 2PW

CONTENTS

INTRODUCTION

Thomas Langton

On 6 October 1485, six weeks after the battle of Bosworth, Henry VII granted to Peter Courtenay, bishop of Exeter and keeper of the privy seal, the lands and revenues of the bishopric of Salisbury forfeited to the king because of the 'many rebellions' of Thomas, bishop of Salisbury. (1) Moreover, Henry gave Courtenay custody of the bishop of Salisbury himself, so that the administration of the diocese – especially the bishop's extensive patronage – could be expedited 'by the counsel, assent, and advice of the said bishop'.(2) Thus Henry VII had arrested the bishop of Salisbury, placed him in the custody of the keeper of the privy seal, and suspended him from the plenary exercise of his temporal powers. Courtenay too had been imprisoned, by Richard III, for his implication in the treason of the duke of Buckingham in 1483, and had shortly thereafter gone overseas into exile with Henry Tudor; soon after Bosworth, on 8 September 1485, Henry rewarded him with the privy seal. Another bishop who was on the wrong side in this episode, Stillington of Bath and Wells, suffered imprisonment at Windsor from 1487 until his death in 1491. What is extraordinary about the case of Langton is the fullness of his rehabilitation – to the extent that he was nominated by Henry for the archbishopric of Canterbury fifteen years later in 1500.

We can infer from his will that Thomas Langton was born at Appleby in Westmorland; the date of his birth is less certain, but it can have been no earlier than 1430, for he is described as an M.A. of Cambridge during the academic year 1456-7, and he was a fellow of Pembroke Hall already in 1462-3 when he was senior proctor of the university. (3) He vacated his fellowship in 1464 to begin studying at Padua; but he soon returned to Cambridge, perhaps because of

1 PRO, C82/3/44, delivered 11 October 1485; printed in Materials for a History of the Reign of Henry VII, ed. William Cambell [Rolls Series, No. 60 (1873)], Vol. I, p.81.

2 He would be able, apparently, to exercise his episcopal functions – including his patronage – without enjoying freedom of movement; cf. the imprisonment of Robert Stillington, bishop of Bath and Wells, from 1487 to 1491 (Knecht, Robert J., 'The Political and Intellectual Activities of Cardinal John Morton and his Episcopal Colleagues', University of London M.A. Thesis, May 1953, pp.353-4).

3 Here and elsewhere in this biographical note, all detail not otherwise acknowledged derives from Emden, [A.B., A Biographical Register of the University of] Cambridge [to 1500 (1963)], pp.252-3.

shortage of funds, (4) for he was admitted B.Th. and dispensed from residence in 1465-6. By 1468 he had resumed his studies in Padua; and from Padua he moved to Bologna where he took his D.Cn.L on 15 February 1473. (5) During this second, longer stay in Italy, 1468-73, Langton may have met his future warder Peter Courtenay; he undoubtedly met the Benedictine monk William Selling, later prior of Christ Church, Canterbury, to whom Langton became life-long friend and legal advisor. It was possibly in Italy that Langton earned his second doctorate, that in theology, which he obtained before 1476. There are, unfortunately, scant details of the more than twenty years that Langton spent in his studies.

We cannot tell how he financed his education – although, as suggested, he may have experienced some embarrassments; it is unlikely that he drew on the resources of the church. Under papal constitution cum ex eo a scholar possessed of a benefice could obtain license to reside in a university where he might stay for up to seven years without proceeding to holy orders higher than the subdiaconate. (6) However, Langton's first known benefice was the parish church of Seaham, Durham, of which he was rector in May 1473 when he obtained papal dispensation to hold an incompatible benefice – a dispensation to plurality of which he does not appear to have taken advantage for five years at least. His movements are unknown until 1476 when he came to court as a royal chaplain and embarked on his career as a diplomat. From this moment ecclesiastical preferments showered on Langton. In November 1477 he became a canon of the collegiate church of Crediton, in Exeter diocese but resigned his canonry the following February to accept the treasurership of Exeter cathedral; both of these benefices he owed to the bishop of Exeter, but one at least, and probably both, came ultimately from the king. (7) The royal patronage

---

4   PRO, C.1/59/252 (Early Chancery Proceedings); discussed by Scofield, C.L., The Life and Reign of Edward IV, Vol.II, pp.448-9; however, there is no evidence to support her remark that 'Langton . . . who, so far as we know, had no need to fly from his creditors, probably found money enough to buy a number of manuscripts'.

5   Langton is described as 'Doctor of Decrees' already in 1464, ibid., but the document referring to him as such belongs to c.1474-80.

6   Liber sextus decretalium (ap. Corpus juris canonici, ed. E. Friedberg, Vol. II), I.vi.34.

7   Langton wrote to Selling, from London, 27 February 1478: 'My Lord of Excytyr gaf me this other weke a dignyte in his churche of Excytyr that is worth as I am credibly enformyd ix. li. and better clerly by yere. Yesterday he sent his servant to me and shewyd how that the Kyng had wryttyn to hym for a prebend . . .', Literae Cantuarienses. The Letter Books of the Monastery of Christ Church, Canterbury, ed. J. Brigstocke Sheppard [Rolls Series, No.85 (1887-9)], Vol. 3, p.300.

is no less apparent in Langton's appointment to a canonry and prebend
worth £20 p.a. in Wells cathedral in January 1478. We do not know
whether he still held the rectory of Seaham in January 1479 when the
king gave him the rectory of Pembridge in Herefordshire, but Langton
was an indubitable pluralist from 1 July 1480 when he was instituted
as rector of All Hallows, Bread Street, London, which was in the
collation of the archbishop of Canterbury. By virtue of a dispensation from Sixtus IV to hold three incompatible benefices, (8)
Langton was given the rectory of All Hallows, Grace Church (Lombard)
Street, London, by his friend William Selling, prior of Christ Church,
Canterbury, in May 1482; while in October 1479 Selling had granted
Langton the advowson of another benefice in the gift of the prior and
convent of Christ Church, Canterbury, the rectory of St Leonard,
Eastcheap, which Langton gave to his nephew, Christopher Bayngrige. (9)
Langton also obtained a canonry and prebend worth more than £16 p.a.
in Lincoln cathedral from Bishop Russell, the keeper of the privy seal,
and later chancellor under Richard III. In 1483 Langton was promoted
to the bishopric of St Davids by Edward V, on the advice of the
protector, Richard duke of Gloucester; and early in 1485 he was
translated to the more valuable see of Salisbury by Richard III.

Langton's experience of travel on the continent as a student
doubtless proved invaluable at the outset of his diplomatic career.
Edward IV first sent him to Spain in November 1476 to seek a confirmation of the existing treaty between England and Castile, and to
discuss a possible marriage between the Prince of Wales (then aged six)
and the Infanta Isabella, daughter of Ferdinand of Aragon and Isabella
of Castile. A year later Langton went to France to dissuade Louis XI
from his proposed attack on Burgundy; (10) it was at this time that
Langton also settled some business for the prior of Christ Church,

8   Registrum Thomae Bourgchier, Cantuariensis Archiepiscopi, A.D.
    1454-1486, ed. F.R.H. DuBoulay (Canterbury and York Society, liv,
    1957), p.353.

9   Ibid., p.338.

10 Despite the difficulty over Langton's being styled 'Doctor', Emden
    (op.cit.) accepts Rymer's attribution to Langton of a French
    embassy in 1467 (Rymer, Thomas, Foedera, Conventiones, Litterae,
    et cujuscunque generis Acta Publica . . . 1101-1654, 1704-35,
    Vol. XI, p.591); this document is identical with Rymer, Vol.XII,
    p.50 (30 Nov. 1477); of the other envoys commissioned with Langton,
    John Howard is not known to have been styled 'Lord Howard' until
    1470, and Richard Tunstall, a distinguished Lancastrian, was not
    captured and pardoned by the Yorkists until 1468 and still accepted
    office during the readeption (Scofield, op.cit., pp.459, 544); the
    1467 embassy must be rejected.

Canterbury. (11) In August 1478 Langton was empowered to conclude with the king of France the betrothal of Edward IV's eldest daughter to the dauphin. These negotiations were protracted for some two years by Louis XI's delays in paying the ransom of Margaret of Anjou, and then his refusal to start payment of Princess Elizabeth's dowry. During the last years of his reign, Edward IV employed Langton on missions concerning relations with Maximilian, duke of Austria and later emperor, and Louis XI. Upon the accession of Richard III, Langton become royal proctor to the Roman curia to swear obedience to the pope on behalf of Richard; about the same time, Richard empowered him to negotiate a truce with Charles VIII, the new king of France.

When Langton was not on embassy, he was busy at court. In 1478 Edward IV caused certain 'Orders and Regulations set down for the Government of the Household' to be carried to the chancery for exemplification 'by our trusty and rightwell beloved clark and councillor, Master Thomas Langton'. (12) He accompanied Richard III on his progress in 1483; when, on arriving at Canterbury, the king declined the gift of a purse offered to him, it was given to Langton '_propter suas multiplices benevolentias erga Civitatem Cantuariam._'(13) Langton himself eulogised Richard in a letter to the prior of Christ Church: 'He contents the people wher he goys best that ever did prince; for many a poor man that hath suffred wrong many days have be relevyd and helpyd by hym and his commands in his progresse. And in many grete citeis and townis were grete summis of mony gif hym which he hath refusyd. On my trouth I lykyd never the condicions of ony prince so wel as his; God hathe sent hym to us for the wele of us al . . .' (14)

Langton probably visited his benefices in London when he was in the capital; but he would have hired a curate to take the services. Whether or not he ever visisted the remote diocese of St Davids after

11 _Literae Cantuarienses_, op.cit., Vol. 3, pp.293-4.

12 PRO, C.81/1386/8 (Warrants under the Signet); the text of the warrant is printed in translation in Myers, A.R., ed., _English Historical Documents, IV, 1327-1485_ (1969), pp.438-9, and discussed by Scofield, op.cit., Vol. II, p.217 (where, however, the PRO reference is incorrect). Scofield notes that the PRO copy of the 'Orders and Regulations' derived from the Provost of Queen's College, Oxford, in the late seventeenth century; Langton was Provost of Queen's College, 1487-97.

13 _Literae Cantuarienses_, op.cit., Vol. 3, p.xxvii.

14 _Christ Church Letters. A Volume of Medieval Letters relating to the affairs of the Priory of Christ Church Canterbury_, ed. J.B. Sheppard (Camden Society, new series xix, 1877), p.46.

his promotion to the episcopate we cannot tell, because his St Davids register has not suvived. Fewer Welshmen figure in his Salisbury register than in that of his successor Blyth, and this suggests that Langton's relationship with his diocese of St Davids was distant. Probably he employed a vicar-general to administer the diocese and used a suffragan to deputise for him in his spiritual functions. We do not know whether Langton was present at Bosworth Field; he was not conspicuous in his new diocese of Salisbury during the four months prior to Bosworth and we may suppose that he was, instead, with the king. The day on which the privy seal warrant was sealed, 6 October 1485, granting custody of Langton's person and lands to the bishop of Exeter, Langton was reported to be at Bisham, near Maidenhead, in Berkshire; his register describes him as 'being at that time impeded by business' (412), and he commissioned both a vicar-general and a suffragan to carry out his administrative and spiritual functions (416, 416). One month later, on 6 November, a privy seal warrant was sealed granting Langton a full pardon and restitution of his lands and revenues as bishop of Salisbury; (15) and another month after that, on 6 December, Giovanni Gigli wrote to the pope that 'antequam has clauderem intellexi dominos Batenses [Stillington] et Sarisbruenses [Langton] esse liberatos, amissis omnibus bonis, quod etsi antea intellexissem non scripsi quia pro certo non habebam; ambo omnibus sunt exosi et non immerito.' (16) By the end of November Langton was exercising his episcopal patronage (27), presumably now unimpeded; and early in the new year he could be found at his manor at Edington, near Westbury, in Wiltshire. During his tenure of Salisbury, Langton moved among the episcopal residences of Edington, Salisbury, Sherborne, Sonning (near Maidenhead, in Berkshire), and Ramsbury (near Marlborough) for which he seems to have had a preference. He visited London rarely, using the bishop's house in Fleet Street, and then usually only in obedience to a summons to parliament or convocation. His known movements are set out in the itinerary (Appendix B).

Langton apparently did not employ a suffragan to hold ordinations in the diocese of Salisbury after 1485, but himself officiated, usually on every canonical date: the four Ember Saturdays, Sitientes Saturday (the eve of Passion Sunday), and Holy Saturday, until his translation

15   PRO, C.82/4/31; Langton is said to have forfeited his temporalities on 21 August 1485; the warrant for pardon and restitution, having effect from 1 November 1485, was delivered on 8 November but not apparently recorded on the Patent Rolls.

16   Materials, op. cit., Vol. I, pp.198-9.

to Winchester in June 1493. (17) Although he did employ a vicar-general, who presided over the consistory court, Langton was himself fully occupied in the day-to-day administration of his diocese. He was assiduous in his efforts to eradicate the 'Lollard-type' heresy which surfaced first in 1486 in Berkshire, and which, probably late in 1490, elicited Langton's monition to the curates of Newbury, Speen, Shaw, and Thatcham, for the denunciation of known heretics and traitors in those parishes (467); this in turn resulted in the celebrated Newbury heresy trials of 1491 (484-504), discussed below.

In December 1487 Langton had been elected Provost of Queen's College, Oxford; the mastership of an Oxford or Cambridge college at this time tended to be filled by an ecclesiastic too occupied eslewhere to interfere significantly with the actual administration of the college, but well-enough placed at court to exercise himself, if necessary, on the college's behalf. This is perhaps the earliest indication that Langton had made his peace with the new king, Henry VII. After having been excluded from Henry's first parliament in 1485, Langton was summoned to the next, which met in November 1487, and to all subsequent parliaments until his death. In the same month (November 1487) he was appointed to the commission of the peace for Wiltshire, and to all subsequent commissions during his tenure of the see of Salisbury. (18) 'But, perhaps for health reasons, Langton never regained the diplomatic eminence which he had enjoyed under Edward IV and Richard III, though he was appointed once to treat with De Puebla (the Spanish ambassador in Westminster), and, in February 149[6], was one of the guarantors of the Intercursus Magnus.' (19) In November 1494 Langton was one of the seven bishops among the forty members of the king's great council. (20)

17 The ordination lists for September 1486 to April 1489 and for 6 and 27 March 1490 do not survive, but the advance through clerical orders of those ordained by Langton before and after March 1490 suggests that he may have celebrated ordinations on one or both of those occasions too; if the ordinations were in London - away from his registrar, who seems to have remained in the diocese - the lists could have been mislaid.

18 C.P.R., 1485-94, p.504.

19. Knecht, op.cit., p.354; on the contrary, Langton seems to have been vigorously healthy until three days before his death.

20. Ibid., pp.173-4; nonetheless, his name was mentioned in the disclosure of a plot to assassinate Henry VII in the interest of Perkin Warbeck in March 1496 (ibid., p.354); the king, however, evidently discounted the report.

The most convincing proof that Langton had gained the confidence of Henry VII was his translation, early in 1493 to the see of Winchester, the wealthiest see in England, valued at nearly three times as much as Salisbury. While bishop of Winchester Langton moved, as before, from one episcopal manor to another: from Wolvesey Palace (adjacent to the cathedral close as well as to the College), to Bishop's Waltham, to Southwark. The Henrician antiquary Leland describes Waltham as 'a right ample and goodly maner place motid aboute and a praty brooke renning hard by it. This maner place hath beene of many bisshops building. Most part of the 3. partes of the base court was buildid of brike and timbre of late dayes by Bisshop Langton. The residew of the inner part of the house is al of stone.' (21) Waltham was Langton's favourite residence, perhaps for reasons obvious to anyone who has passed through the estate on the road between Winchester and Portsmouth. As in the diocese of Salisbury, Langton was fully occupied in carrying out his episcopal functions in his new see, although his activity cannot be judged so immediately by reference to the regular, personal celebration of ordinations; Langton is known to have ordained on only six occasions during his tenure of Winchester, employing a suffragan for all other canonical occasions down to Holy Saturday 1500. He remained alert to the dangers of heresy, prosecuting three or four cases in 1496 and another in 1499. He continued to shun the court; he appears to have visited his residence in Southwark only about once a year, often only when summoned, and otherwise drew no nearer to the capital than Farnham in Surrey. (22) He did, however, serve on commissions of the peace for Hampshire and Surrey from 1494 until his death. (23) When Cardinal Morton died in the autumn of 1500, Henry VII sent to the monks of Christ Church, Canterbury, for them to elect their friend Langton as their next archbishop, an election which, we may suppose, they were happy to make, on 22 January 1501. (24) But on 24 or 25 January Langton fell ill with the plague, and on 27 January 1501 he was dead.

In his will, (25) dated 25 January, he committed his soul to

21 The Itinerary of John Leland in or about the Years 1535-1543, ed. Lucy Toulmin Smith (1964), Vol. I, p.185 (Part III, fo. 83).

22 Hampshire Record Office, Reg. Langton (Winchester).

23 C.P.R. 1485-94, pp.500, 502; C.P.R., 1494-1509, pp.657, 660.

24 John Le Neve: Fasti Ecclesiae Anglicanae 1300-1541, Vol. IV, ed. B. Jones, p.5.

25 Sede Vacante Wills: A Calendar of Wills Proved before the Commissary of the Prior and Chapter of Christ Church, Canterbury, during Vacancies in the Primacy. . ., ed. C. Eveleigh Woodruff (Kent Arch- aeological Society, Records Branch, Vol. III, 1914), pp.105-12.

Almighty God, the Blessed Virgin Mary, and the whole court of Heaven, and his body to be buried in Winchester cathedral near to the shrine of St Swithun. (26) The text runs to more than one hundred items. His money legacies amount to upwards of £2,000, including the provision of six scholars for the space of twenty years to study in scienciis liberalibus et theologia in Queen's College, Oxford, each of them to have six marks a year. He cancelled the debt of £364 due him from the prior and convent of Winchester cathedral on condition that a brother of that cathedral should daily in perpetuity celebrate a mass for the salvation of his soul and those of his parents and friends. The value of some of his benefactions is quite impossible to calculate – for instance, 12d. to every friar priest of the four mendicant orders both in the city of Winchester and in London. To his well-off friends he left not money, but some keepsake. Thus, Richard Foxe, bishop of Durham, who was to be his successor at Winchester, received two gold rings, one his episcopal ring and the other of the Order of the Garter. (27)

There are two other features of Langton's life which may be fruitfully discussed: his interest in learning, and his nepotism. Langton's foundation, in his will, of six exhibitions in Queen's College, Oxford, of which he had been provost, is but one of more than a dozen benefactions touching one or other of the universities – which is exactly what one might have expected of a man who derived so much pleasure and comfort from his great learning. He has left us no published works. We know that he owned a book of canon law now in the British Library; it is possible that he owned two other manuscripts in the British Library, one a volume of Justinian, and the other called La Bible historiaus (28) – not a surprising, if scant, collection for a lawyer and a theologian. We read in his will, 'lego Ricardo Pace (29) scolari meo Bononie studenti pro exhibicione sua pro septem annis in studio pro quolibet anno x li, lxx li.' Pace remembered his bene-factor in his book De Fructu qui ex Doctrina Percipitur Liber, in which he wrote: 'the science of music also demands her place, particularly from me, whom she distinguished when a boy, among other boys. For Thomas Langton, whose manu-minister I was, noticing my advance in music far

---

26 For Langton's place of burial see Emden, Cambridge, p.353, his sumptuous monumental brass was mutilated during the Interregnum.

27 He became chancellor of the Order of the Garter while bishop of Salisbury; Wood, Anthony à, Athenae Oxonienses, ed. P. Bliss, 1813-20, Vol. I, p.550.

28 Emden, Cambridge, p.353.

29 The future diplomat and dean of St Paul's; see Wegg, Jarvis, Richard Pace: a Tudor diplomatist (1932).

beyond my years, would pronounce and assert (being perhaps biased in my favour by his love) "This boy's talents are born for higher things." And soon afterwards (paucos post dies) he sent me to Italy, to Padua University, then at the top of its fame, to study Letters, and generously provided for the annual expenses, for he befriended all learned men exceedingly, and in his time was another Maecenas, rightly remembering (as he often said), that it was for learning that he had been promoted to the rank of bishop . . . And he valued the Literary Humanities so highly that he provided for the teaching of them to boys and youths in his own private school (domestica schola). And most of all he delighted in hearing the boys repeat to him in the evening what they had learned that day from the schoolmaster. And in this examination he who did well was nicely complimented, and given something he wanted. For that best of masters had always on his lips the saying that worth thrives on praise. And if a boy seemed dull, but willing, he did not treat it as a fault, but with kindness urged him on, that diligence might strive with nature, quoting the example of others who had succeeded under similar circumstances.' (30)

Another beneficiary of Langton's will was Master Machell, a scholar in Cambridge University. (31) Langton's relations were named 'Machell' - his sister Elizabeth had married Rouland Machell - and 'Blynkensop' - his sister Joan had married a Blynkensop - and 'Crakenthorp' and 'Baynbrige' - another sister had married a Baynbrige - and 'Colynson', as well as 'Langton'. For those of his nephews who chose to enter the church, he provided well. He gave at least four benefices, including the valuable archdeaconry of Surrey, to his nephew Christopher Baynbrige, the future bishop of Durham, archbishop of York, cardinal, and resident English ambassador to the Curia. He gave the archdeaconry of Dorset to his nephew Robert Langton, who was the author of a book published in 1522 recounting his inter- minable pilgrimages on the continent. Langton installed his nephews Edmund and Robert Blynkensop in rectories; along with Alexander Blynkensop (whose precise relationship with Langton is difficult to establish) they would appear to have been of lesser intellectual abilities than either Baynbrige or Robert Langton, and their benefices are accordingly of lesser value. Another Langton, Ralph, who held at least two benefices in the diocese of Salisbury and who died in 1492, may have been a cousin of the bishop. One must guard against con- demning this nepotism which was a regular feature of medieval life; and

30 Ibid., pp.4-5; Langton's 'private school' was probably at Wolvesey
    Palace.

31 His Christian name is unknown. On Langton's family, see Brown, R.
    Percival, 'Thomas Langton and his Tradition of Learning', in
    Transactions of the Cumberland and Westmorland Antiquarian and Arch-
    aeological Society, new series, Vol.xxvi (1926), pp.150-246; cf.
    emendatory note by C. Moor, 'Crackenthorp of Newbiggin', ibid.,
    Vol.xxxiii (1933), p.55.

in all fairness it should be pointed out that both Baynbrige and Robert Langton were already beneficed in the diocese of Salisbury when Thomas Langton became bishop there. These two intelligent and well-trained clerics would have been advanced by any wise bishop.

The Manuscript

Thomas Langton's Salisbury register is a well-preserved volume of 127 parchment folios, with paper flyleaves, bound (or re-bound) probably in the eighteenth century. Until recently it could be consulted in the Wren Hall in the Close at Salisbury, but it has now been moved, in common with other diocesan records, to the Wiltshire Record Office at Trowbridge. The evenly cut folios measure 40 x 28 cm.; there are seven gatherings of eight folios (A-D, G-I), two of twelve folios (E, L), two of ten folios (M, N), one of four (F), one of eighteen (J), and one of fourteen (O), and there is one half folio on its own (K). There are probably two different hands in the register, remarkably alike, one of which adds to slight calligraphic idiosyncrasy a preference for the ampersand when 'or' (usually <u>seu</u>, sometimes <u>aut</u>, rarely <u>vel</u>) is required for sense. Further identification of the hands would be largely guesswork. (32)

Folios 1-48 (gatherings A-F) contain institutions to benefices, together with the vicar-general's commission (Fo. 1) and a contemporary <u>index locorum</u> (Fos. 47v-48v). The second part of the register is numbered separately, the forty-ninth folio in the volume being No. 1, but irregularly, lacking folios numbered 17, 45, 46, and 77. The present edition preserves the original numeration of the two parts, but carries (in brackets) after Fo. 48 a continuous, definitive numeration. In the second part, Fos. 1(49) - 79(127) contain miscellaneous <u>acta</u>, including a number of heresy cases with depositions in English. The second part also has a contemporary index, Fo. 80(128), which was probably added when the volume was first bound, for the index is to be found on the first folio of the last gathering (O) which, but for an intruding English entry from 1502 (<u>562</u>: Fo. 81r), is given over entirely to ordination lists (Fos. 82-93). Since ordination lists for 1485 do not survive, it seems reasonable to suppose that the first two folios of the last gathering were left blank to record them subsequently. However, ordination lists are also missing from May 1486 to June 1489. (33)

32 It is probable that M. John Wely, notary public, who is described as the bishop's registrar (<u>485</u>, <u>487</u>, <u>494</u>, <u>498</u>, <u>502</u>, <u>504</u>), had a hand in the register; but he neither referred directly to himself nor did he sign the register. Wely was a beneficiary (described as 'my servant') and witness of Langton's will (<u>Sede Vacante Wills</u>, <u>op.cit</u>., pp.108, 112).

33 See n.17 above.

In addition to the entries' marginal headings (which in this edition have been ignored unless they contain place-name variants or other significant additions to the entries), other notes have been added in the margins in a minute, contemporary hand. More than half of these additional notes consist of nothing more than the abbreviation for 'nihil', and others record sums, which almost certainly refer to the fruits of the vacancy; one probably incomplete note (280) records merely 'pro fructibus vacationis' but no sum. In a few instances the marginal notes are illegible, usually because bound in or cut off when the register was bound.

There is no reason to doubt the dating of the entries in the register, although there are a few obvious errors: in one case (491) the scribe seems to have been looking at a calendar for the wrong year. A few of the marginal notes draw attention to the faulty chronological sequence of some institutions.

Langton's vicar-general, Laurence Cokkys, held a particularly full commission (1) and deputised for Langton throughout his episcopate, but chiefly from June 1485 to June 1487 and from October 1492 to January 1493, when the bishop may have been overseas. In the register Cokkys is accorded various styles: 'vicar-general' or 'vicar-general in spiritualities' (3, 6-16, 18-25, 366, 369-72, 376) or 'custos spiritualitatis' (4), which together with a few entries for which a vaguer or perhaps no authority for Cokkys's action is recorded (5, 17, 367-8) cover the chief periods of Cokkys's deputisation (as above) during which the bishop did not himself act; 'commissary-general' or 'commissary' is the common form for the remainder of Cokkys's activity (32-3, 35-8, 46, 48-50, 52-9, 67, 69-70, 73-7, 82-4, 86, 92-4, 96-8, 100-2, 106-9, 111). Cokkys, who was born in the diocese, was given a canonry and prebend in Salisbury cathedral, his first preferment in the diocese, by bishop Beauchamp in 1478; he was commissioned vicar-general by Langton's successor Blyth, and after Blyth's death was official of the spiritualities sede vacante, 19 September 1499 to 19 March 1500. (34)

The register's taxation material is tantalisingly full; comparison of the lists of impoverished benefices (440-2, 544-6, 552-4) with the Valor Ecclesiasticus (35) of 1535 reveals apparently inexplicable discrepancies of valuation. Similarly, the fullness and continuous nature of the ordination lists from June 1489 to June 1492 render them susceptible to the sort of analysis recently carried out on York ordinations, 1340-1530; (36) a cursory sampling of the Salisbury

---

34 Emden, Oxford I, pp.457-8.

35 Valor Ecclesiasticus, temp. Henrici VIII, auctoritate regia institutus, ed. J. Caley and J. Hunter (1810-34), Vol. II.

36 Moran, Jo Ann Hoeppner, 'Clerical Recruitment in the Diocese of York, 1340-1530: Data and Commentary', The Journal of Ecclesiastical History, Vol. 34, No. 1 (January 1983), pp.19-54.

ordinations suggests strikingly different conclusions. (37) However,
detailed analysis of such material should await the appearance of
further late-fifteenth-century registers.

The heresy detections (419-20, 459-60, 476, 484-504) have long
been known through the work of Dr J.A.F. Thomson. (38) Of the
seventeen persons detected only nine confessed expressly to disbelief
in transubstantiation (419, 486, 490, 501, 503), one of whom admitted
to having held an alternative belief for forty years past (419), and
two of whom held a belief identified half a century later with that of
the radically reformed Church of England - namely that the sacrament
is but a commemoration of Christ's Passion (490, 501). (39) One other
confessed to believing that priests in deadly sin may not consecrate
nor bless water; she was, however, apparently orthodox in her under-
standing of transubstantiation (459). The range of irregular beliefs
extends from identifiable heterodoxies (that baptism is unnecessary
for children of Christian parents, that the soul dies with the body,
and that the priesthood was not ordained by God, but that the only
sacrament so ordained was matrimony: 484); to the frankly arcane
(that the Lord's Prayer is the prayer of the devil: 459; that St Peter
never was a priest but a little before his death, and that Simon
Magus gave him his tonsure: 486; that all the churches in Christendom
and all those who adhere to them should be set in the middle of Hell;
499). Although there is no evidence of hostility to particular
clergy, (40) the commonest element is anti-clericalism (that the
priesthood teaches false doctrine, that the sacrament of penance is
unnecessary for salvation: 484, 486; that the church is but a synagogue
and house of merchandising, that the priests be but scribes and
pharisees 'dissaving' people: 486, 488; that images of saints ought
not to be worshipped nor pilgrimages made: 484, 486, 495, 497, 501,

37 Salisbury ordinations 1408-17 are published in The Register of
    Robert Hallum, Bishop of Salisbury, 1407-17, ed. Joyce M. Horn
    (Canterbury and York Society, lxxii, 1982), pp.158-95; the
    proximity of Oxford must be taken into account in any analysis of
    clerical recruitment in Salisbury diocese.

38 The Later Lollards 1414-1520 (1965), chiefly pp.74 ff.

39 492 and 497 also refer to the sacrament of the altar.

40 On the contrary, the deposition of Philip Browne (419) suggests
    almost friendly exchange between heretic and clergy: 'whereas by
    the exhortation of divers men, as well by my curate of Hinton as
    by Master Richard Birde, parson of More, and most especially by
    the predication of the worshipful father John, the abbot of
    Abingdon, in the church of Standlake in Lincoln diocese, proving
    by divers arguments and reasons my opinions to be false and
    contrary to the faith, I was for the time of half a year next
    following that sermon made in good belief of the sacrament of the
    altar . . .'

503). There is even a touch of chiliasm in two depositions (488, 497), one of which substantiates the claim that priests are the disciples of the Anti-Christ 'as it shall openly appear in the coming of Enoch and Elias', with the suggestion that within ten years' time all Lollards and heretics 'the which have received grace shall preach openly' (488). Three confessed to possessing suspect books (484, 486, 488). There is no evidence of the authorities employing a fixed agenda of questions, but their apparent interest in tracing the dissemination of heretical beliefs led to poignant detail ('whensoever was any preaching or teaching of the word of God in the pulpit, I would contrary it at alehouse': 499).

These detections from the diocese of Salisbury are significant because the Thames Valley and Newbury area, the locus of most of them, was a notorious centre of Lollardy, (41) and because the bishop was both resident and keenly interested in expunging heresy. (42) The number of cases is extremely small; the area is largely limited to a corner of this large diocese; and the register gives the impression that the investigations by the authorities were thorough — the bishop even going to the length of writing to the bishop of the neighbouring diocese of Winchester to apprehend one of the heretics who had escaped across the diocesan boundary. (43)

Pensions

In a short article published during the last war, Professor Kathleen Major described and discussed a number of 'Resignation Deeds in the Diocese of Lincoln' which came to light when she was calendaring the Lincoln Diocesan Archives preparatory to their removal to a safe place for the duration of the war. (44) Of 172 resignations by deed during the years 1504-33, fifty-two were conditional upon receiving a pension, and some of the pensions were probably onerous to the new incumbent. Professor Major never claimed that these 172 were either the total (improbable in a diocese with about 2,000 benefices over a period of thirty years) or even a representative sample of the total number of resignations. Nevertheless these statistics have been used to support the view that the financial plight of the parish priest was worsened by these 'often crippling' pensions which were 'extremely common by

41 Cf. Thomson, op.cit., Chap. III.

42 Thomson comments that from Langton's episcopate 'the pace of prosecutions increased', ibid., p.74; Langton personally presided at all but two of the prosecutions (495-60, 499-500).

43 Hampshire Record Office, Reg. Courtenay (Winchester), Fos. 26-7, discussed by Thomson, op.cit.,pp.77-9.

44 Bulletin of the Institute of Historical Research, XIX (1942-3), pp.57-65.

the end of the Middle Ages.' (45) The evidence of Langton's Salisbury register suggests that this view should be revised.

Of 405 benefices in the diocese of Salisbury filled between 1485 and 1493, just under half (197) had fallen vacant for some reason other than the death of the incumbent (see Table I). (46) Of these, twenty-eight were subject to exchange – although not invariably specified as such by the registrar – twenty of them parochial benefices and eight prebendal. (47) This 'exchange rate' accords well with nearly contemporaneous evidence reported elsewhere. (48) Only 8% (15/197) of all resigned or exchanged benefices were cumbered with pensions; of these only one was non-parochial (discussed below). Of parochial benefices alone, 9% (14/155) were subject to pensions. While there can be no certainty that all, or even most, pensions were recorded by the registrar, the evidence of bishop Blyth's Salisbury register (1493-9) (49) and bishop Langon's Winchester register (1493-1501) (50) supports the conclusion that perhaps 8-10% of all resigned or exchanged benefices were cumbered with pensions. Pensions were not therefore 'extremely common' but rather rare, affecting only perhaps 4% of all benefices. (51)

Moreover, it was the poorer benefice in which the parish·priest upon his resignation might hope – although the possibility was remote – for a pension from the income of the new incumbent. Of the fourteen parochial benefices cumbered with pensions (see Table II), three were valued at 12 marks or below for the purpose of exemption from taxation. Nearly all the pensions granted were in a range suitable for a meagre retirement economy: all but two were for £4 or less; half

45 Heath, Peter, The English Parish Clergy on the Eve of the Reformation (London, 1969), pp.146, 183: 'very few churches escaped' the burden of a pension, ibid., p.147.

46 Including 236: 'death or resignation'

47 Including among 'prebendal' one 'collegiate': 78.

48 Heath, op.cit., pp.44-5.

49 Wiltshire Record Office: 11 pensions ex 127 benefices resigned or exchanged.

50 Hampshire Record Office: 10 pensions ex 114 benefices resigned or exchanged.

51 The incidence of pensions in the diocese of York, 1480-1500 (The Register of Thomas Rotherham, Archbishop of York, 1480-1500, Vol.I, ed. Eric E. Barker (Canterbury and York Society, lxix, 1976), was higher, 8-9% (82/975 vacancies), but the point stands: these pensions were not 'extremely common'; the difference of incidence is probably related to local custom and conditions.

were for 5 marks or less. (52) The encumbrance of Steeple Ashton
vicarage with a £10 pension was exceptional: M. William Lane, the
incoming vicar, had obtained papal dispensation to hold an incompatible benefice with his nearby church of Poulshot (53) (it is not
inconceivable that he could have personally served both churches,
less than five miles apart by road); however, M. William resigned
Poulshot nine months after receiving Steeple Ashton to accept another
preferment in Berkshire (323-4), and it is tempting to imagine the
handsomely pensioned former vicar continuing to serve the cure at
Steeple Ashton. The pension of 5 marks p.a. for seven years against
the income of the church of West Dean is also exceptional: M. John
Morgan was instituted on 25 November 1485 (26) but Richard Balteswell
resigned the benefice on 30 January 1488 (145), receiving a pension.
Was there a dispute over possession of this church? or is this an
indication of the registrar's lack of thoroughness? In the absence
of any record of bishop Woodville's activity or of the ensuing
vacancy, it is difficult to tell. Balteswell used his pension as
sufficient title to have himself ordained priest by December 1491
(573-4, 579), and his intention to take holy orders may explain why
there was a fixed term of seven years. It is harder to explain why
the incoming rector, M. John Denbye, was interested in West Dean,
since the church was valued at 12 marks or less (544, 552); but M.
John did not reside (552). (54) The third exceptional case (205) is
that of the sole pension encumbering a prebendal benefice: M. Ralph
Langton, who may have been a kinsman of the bishop, resigned the
prebend of Grantham Australis on 23 March 1489 in consideration of a
pension of £10 p.a. until he should have gained title and admission
to another prebend in the cathedral; this he did not achieve until 23
January 1492 (333). The case appears to be one of disputed title,
resolved by a 'resignation'.

Editorial Practice

All entries in the register have been assigned consecutive numbers and
are normally given in calendar form, apart from entries in English,
chiefly the lollard depositions. Material and notes supplied by the
editor are placed in brackets; the foliation of the register is
described above. All dates between 1 January and 24 March have been
altered to new style. Place names are given in the modern form, but
variant forms occurring in the manuscript are preserved in the Index
of Persons and Places. Surnames are given as in the manuscript and
variants brought together also in the Index. In literal transcripts

52 In the diocese of York, 1480-1500 (ibid.), the average pension was
    11 marks, but half were 8 marks or below, and a third were 6
    marks or below.

53 Calendar of Papal Letters, 1492-1503, No. 489.

54 He had dispensation to plurality, 2 September 1488, and again 1491-
    2 (ibid., XV, No. 241, 1467).

all abbreviations have been expanded; the symbol for '-s', '-es',
'-is', or '-ys' has always been rendered '-ys'. Academic degrees
are given in the forms preferred by Emden. (55) Unless otherwise
stated, the institution entries include a memorandum of mandate for
induction by the appropriate archdeacon or his official, though in
the case of Salisbury cathedral canonries and prebends, admission is
by the dean (or president) and chapter of Salisbury; in the case of
exchanges where institution is made to a benefice in another diocese,
induction to that benefice is reserved to the bishop of that diocese.

Acknowledgements

I should like to thank Miss Pamela Stewart, archivist of the former
Salisbury Diocesan Record Office, and her successors in the
Wiltshire Record Office, Trowbridge, for their generous assistance.
Dr A.K. McHardy, the Society's General Editor, has been inexhaustibly
patient in seeing this edition through many permutations; her wise
judgements and solicitous care have eliminated numerous errors; she is
not, of course, responsible for any that may remain. My colleague
Kenneth Bartlett kindly drew the map of Salisbury diocese. The
preparation of the original draft of this edition was made possible
by the granting of a sabbatical leave by the Master and Governors of
Haileybury College; during that leave I was nurtured by the friendship
and counsel of the Master and Fellows of Sidney Sussex College,
Cambridge, to whom I respectfully dedicate this work.

D.P.W.

55 Emden, <u>Cambridge</u>, pp.xxviii-xxix.

Table I: Types of Benefices Resigned or Exchanged

Parochial		Non-parochial					
<u>R</u>.	<u>V</u>.	<u>Chapel</u>	<u>Chantry</u>	<u>Prebend</u>	<u>College</u>	<u>Hospital</u>	<u>Other</u>
106	49	5	5	26	1	3	2*

* one archdeaconry; on portion of tithes.

Table II: Pensions

<u>No</u>.	<u>Benefice</u>	<u>Retiring Incumbent</u>	<u>Incoming Incumbent</u>	<u>Amount</u>
145	West Dean*	Richard Balteswell	M. John Denbye MA	5 marks
146	Swyre	Edward Ryde	Luke Mouncell	4 marks
158	Melbury Osmond*	Robert Gawler	Thomas Kymer	33s.4d.
181	Ramsbury v.	James Coterell	Thomas Wylkynson	40s.
205	Grantham australis prebend	Ralph Langton	Robert Day	£10, until adm. to another.[1]
215	Cheselbourne	Thomas Porter	M. John Osplete MA	8 marks
223	Farnborough	M. Michael Carvenell	William Haynes	5 marks
250	Inkpen*	William Bray	Hugh Fylell	46s.8d.
253	Long Crichel	M. Edward Underwode	Robert ap David	4 marks until promoted
292	Steeple Ashton v.	M. Thomas Waget	M. William Lane	£10
315	Stapleford v.	William Marshall	John Lynde	£3
320	Sherston v.	Thomas Strobull	M. Robert Burton	£3.19s.8d[2]
322	Coleshill v.	John Bentley	Lewis Davy	£4
325	Milborne St Andrew v.	Richard Moore	Thomas Childe	£3.6s.8d
331	Blandford St Mary	M. Thomas Dokelby	M. John Atwell MA	6 marks

* valued at 12 marks or below for taxation

1   Ralph Langton obtained the prebend of Bitton, 23 January 1492
    (<u>333</u>)

2   This pension was still being paid to Strobull in January 1499
    (W.R.O., Register Blyth, fo. 31v).

Abbreviations

adm.	admission	ind.	inductor; induction
archbp.	archbishop	kt.	knight
archd.	archdeacon	M.	Master
BA	Bachelor of Arts	mand.	mandate
BCL	Bachelor of Civil Law	MD	Doctor of Medicine
BCnL	Bachelor of Canon Law	ms.	the manuscript
BC & CnL	Bachelor of Civil and	MTh	Master of Theology
	Canon Law	OC	Carmelite Order
Ben.	Benedictine	OCarth	Carthusian Order
bp.	bishop	OCist	Cistercian Order
BTh	Bachelor of Theology	OClun	Cluniac Order
B.V.M.	Blessed Virgin Mary	OFM	Franciscan Order
cath.	cathedral	OGilb	Gilbertine Order
ch.	church	OP	Dominican Order
chapl.	chaplain	OSA	Augustinian Order
Cist.	Cistercian		(canons)
cl.	clerk	OSB	Benedictine Order
Clun.	Cluniac	p.a.	per annum
coll.	college; collegiate	Prem.	Premonstratensian
conv.	convent	P.R.O. C81, C82/ Public Record
C.P.R.	Calendar of Patent Rolls		Office, warrents for
DCL	Doctor of Civil Law		the Great Seal Series,
DCnL	Doctor of Canon Law		Series II.
DC & CnL	Doctor of Civil and	r.	rector
	Canon Law	res.	resignation
dim.	having a letter dimissory	tons.	having a first
dioc.	diocese		tonsure
Dom.	Dominican	Trin.	Trinitarian
DTh	Doctor of Theology	v.	vicar
gent.	gentleman	vac.	vacant
Gilb.	Gilbertine		
HBC.	Handbook of British		
	Chronology, ed. E.B.		
	Fryde & F.M. Powicke,		
	2nd ed., (London, 1961)		

THE REGISTER OF THOMAS LANGTON

(Fol. 1) REGISTRUM REVERENDI IN CHRISTO PATRIS ET DOMINI DOMINI THOME LANGTON PERMISSIONE DIVINA SARESBURIENSIS EPISCOPI INCEPTUM (blank in ms.) DIE MENSIS MAII ANNO DOMINI MILLESIMO CCCCmo LXXXmo Vto INDICCIONE TERCIA PONTIFICATUS SANCTISSIMI IN CHRISTO PATRIS ET DOMINI NOSTRI DOMINI INNOCENCII DIVINA PROVIDENCIA PAPE OCTAVI ANNO PRIMO.

1   Commission of Thomas, bp. of Salisbury, to M. Laurence Cokkys DCnL canon of Salisbury cath., to be official principal of the consistory and, in the bp.'s absence from his dioc., vicar-general in spiritualities, having authority to determine all cases and business, both instance and ex officio, pertaining to the bp.'s diocesan jurisdiction, and to institute to benefices. Sonning, 14 June 1485.

2   (Fo. 1v) Institution of John ap Herry, chapl., in the person of M. Richard Hill, his proctor, to Holy Trinity ch., Dorchester, vac. by death of John Wykys; patron, King Richard III. Shaftesbury, 31 May 1485.

3   Institution of John Taylor, priest, to Foxley ch. (in arch-deaconry of Wiltshire), vac. by death of Thomas Geffray; patron, John Mody, armiger, lord of the manor of Foxley. (Ind. omitted). 12 July 1485 .

4   Institution of William Heworth, chapl., to Minety vicarage, vac. by res. of John Taylor; patron, M. Hugh Pavy, archd. of Wiltshire. Salisbury, the canons' house within the close, 12 July 1485.

5   Institution of George Bury, acolyte, to a moiety of Shillingstone ch., vac. by death of Thomas Ogan; patron, John Haselden, armiger. (F. 2) 18 July 1485.

6   Institution of John Shipton, chapl., to Up Cerne ch., vac. by death of William Martyn; patron, John Storton, kt., lord Stourton. 26 July 1485.

7   Institution of Richard Foster, chapl., to Rowde vicarage, vac. by res. of John Sclatter; patron, abbot and conv. of Stanley. 17 August 1485.

8   Institution of M. Thomas Hedlay BCL to St Mary's chapel, Atworth, vac. by res. of George Bewshyn, cl., r. or keeper; patron,

William Bewshyn, _armiger_. 24 August 1485.

9 (Fo. 2v)   Institution of Thomas Noresse BA to Castle Combe ch.,
   vac. by death of M. William Sheryff; patron, John Scrope, _armiger_.
   15 September 1485.

10 Institution of Geoffrey Morgan, chapl., to Oaksey ch., vac. by
   death of Richard Tokyll; patrons, prior and conv. of Monkton
   Farleigh. 21 September 1485.

11 Institution of William George, chapl., to St Mary's chantry in
   Lambourn ch., vac. by death of William Yarreby; patron,
   John Estbury, _armiger_. Salisbury, the close, 26 September 1485.
   (Marginal: 'Usque huc pro primo termino parte institut')

12 Institution of M. Edward Willoughby to Berwick St John ch., vac.
   by death of M. John Emwell; patrons, Cecily, abbess, and conv. of
   Wilton. Salisbury, the close, 10 October 1485.

13 (Fo. 3) Institution of Thomas Thomson, chapl., to Stapleford
   vicarage, vac. by death of M. John Wolfe; patrons, prior and conv.
   of Easton. 10 October 1485.

14 Institution of Elisha Banaster, priest, to Gussage All Saints
   vicarage, vac. by res. of Robert Scrayton; patron, William Aiscugh,
   archd. of Dorset. 11 October 1485.

15 Institution of William Coyn, chapl., to Ham ch., vac. by death of
   M. John Preston BCnL; patron, William, bp. of Winchester.
   15 October 1485.

16 Institution of William Budde, chapl., to St Mary's vicarage,
   Reading, vac. by death of M. John Burde _alias_ Brydd; patrons,
   abbot and conv. of Reading. 21 October 1485.

17 (Fo. 3v) Institution of Robert Fosse, chapl., to Chitterne St
   Mary vicarage, vac. by death of Thomas Staunborne; patrons,
   M. William Ive, chancellor and president of the chapter of
   Salisbury, and the chapter of Salisbury. 26 October 1485.

18 Institution of M. William Walton MA to Wytham ch., vac. by death
   of M. William Petir; patron, Richard Harecourte, kt. 27 October
   1485.

19 Institution of Edward Roberd, chapl., to Radipole ch., vac. by
   death of Edward Englisshe; patrons abbot and conv. of Cerne.
   27 October 1485.

20 Institution of M. Edward Chayne DC & CnL to Stalbridge ch., vac.
   by death of M. John Emwell; patrons, abbot and conv. of Sherborne.
   4 November 1485.

21 (Fo. 4) Institution of Thomas Sterr MA to Holwell ch., vac. by
   death of M. David Geffray; patrons, abbot and conv. of Cirencester.
   5 November 1485.

22 Institution of M. Thomas Bowdon MA to New Windsor vicarage, vac.
   by death of William Hether; patrons, abbot and conv. of Waltham.
   5 November 1485.

23 Institution of William Bochell, chapl., to Batcombe ch., vac. by
   death of Thomas Elmelay; patrons, John Cheyne, Robert Stowell,
   Henry Hull, John Byconyll, and John Kendall, feoffees of Humphrey,
   (Stafford), late earl of Devon, lord of the manor of Batcombe.
   9 November 1485.

24 Institution of M. Robert Gente BCnL to Langton Herring ch., vac.
   by res. of James Cokkys; patrons, John Wrowghton, armiger, and
   Margaret his wife. Salisbury, the close, 10 November 1485.

25 (Fo. 4v) Institution of M. John Michell MA to Castle Eaton ch.,
   vac. by res. of M. Edward Cheyne; patron, John Zouche, kt.,
   Lord Zouche. 22 November 1485.

26 Institution of M. John Morgan DCnL to West Dean ch., vac. by death
   of M. John Emwell; patron Richard Harecourt, kt. 25 November 1485.

27 Collation to M. Geoffrey Elys of a canonry and the prebend of
   Coombe and Harnham in Salisbury cath., vac. by death of M. John
   Emwell. (Mand. adm. omitted.) 29 November 1485

28 Institution of Stephen Mathu, chapl., to East Lulworth vicarage,
   vac. by death of John Robynson; patrons, prior and conv. of Merton.
   29 November 1485.

29 Institution of M. Stephen Saunders, chapl., notary public, to
   St Katharine's chantry or chapel in the churchyard of St Edmund's

collegiate church, (Fo. 5) Salisbury, vac. by death of John Moren; patrons, abbot and conv. of Abbotsbury. Ind.: provost of St Edmund's Coll. 29 November 1485.

30 Institution of William Say, chapl., to Corsley ch., vac. by death of M. Richard Gartham; patron, Robert Ley of Corsley, armiger. 5 December 1485.

31 Institution of John Lane, chapl., to Bradpole vicarage, vac. by res. of (John) Sylke; patrons, abbess and conv. of Syon. 15 December 1485.

32 Institution of M. Richard Toppe BC & CnL to Steeple ch., vac. by res. of M. William Jonis BCnL; patron, Cecily, duchess of York. 23 December 1485. (Marginal: 'Usque huc computum cum domino apud Edingdon')

33 (Fo. 5v) Institution of John Oder, chapl., to Swanage vicarage, vac. by death of Thomas Merefeld; patron, M. Edmund Martyn DC & CnL, r. of Swanage. 24 December 1485.

34 Institution of M. Laurence Cokkys DCnL to Winterbourne Bassett ch., vac. by res. of M. Richard Toppe; patrons, prior and conv. of Lewes. Ind.: arch. of Dorset (rectius Wiltshire). 4 January 1486.

35 Institution of Richard Page, chapl., to Urchfont vicarage, vac. by death of Thomas Million; patrons, abbess and conv. of Nunnaminster, Winchester. Salisbury, the close, 18 January 1486

36 Institution of M. Lewis John BC & CnL to Chilton ch., vac. by death of John Attewell, last chapl. (sic); patrons, abbot and conv. of Abingdon. Bradenstoke priory, 20 January 1486.

(Fo. 6) SEPTIMO DIE MENSIS FEBRUARII MUTATUR ANNUS TRANSLACIONIS DOMINI DE ANNO PRIMO IN ANNUM 2m.

37 Institution of Henry Palmer, chapl., to Moreton ch., vac. by death of Robert Pepyr; patron, James Frampton, armiger. 18 February 1486.

38 Institution of Robert Grenehode, chapl., to Lytchett Matravers ch.,

vac. by death of M. Thomas Campyon; patron, William (fitz Alan), earl of Arundel. 18 February 1486.

39 Collation to M. Richard Fox DCL of a canonry and the prebend of Grantham Australis (<u>Rectius</u> Grantham Borealis) in Salisbury cath., (1) vac. by res. of M. Christopher Baynebrige. Edington, 7 February 1486.

40 (Fo. 6v) Collation to Christopher Baynebrig, cl., of a canonry and the prebend of Chardstock in Salisbury cath., vac. by res. of M. Ralph Hethcottys. Edington, 7 February 1486.

41 Collation to M. John Doget DCnL of the chancellorship and prebend of Brixworth in Salisbury cath., vac. by death of M. William Ive DTh. 8 February 1486.

42 Mand. ind. of M. John Doget in the prebend of Brixworth, Lincoln dioc., to John (Russell), bp. of Lincoln. Edington, 10 February 1486. (Marginal: 'Note the form when the prebend is in another dioc.')

43 (Fo. 7) Collation to M. Ralph Hethcottys BCnL of a canonry and the prebend of Bitton in Salisbury cath., vac. by res. of M. John Doget. Ind. in his prebend: bp. of Worcester. Edington, 8 February 1486. (Marginal: <u>Nihil</u>)

44 Collation to M. William Elyott BCL of a canonry and the prebend of Bishopstone is Salisbury cath., vac. by res. of M. Richard Fox DCL. Edington, 5 March 1486. (Marginal: <u>Nihil</u>)

45 Institution of John Lee, priest, to Winterborne Steepleton ch., (in archdeaconry of Dorset) vac. by death of the last r.; patron, Cecily, duchess of York. (Ind. omitted.) Edington, 10 March 1486.

46 Institution of M. Edmund Martyn DC & CnL to Chaldon Herring or East Chaldon ch., vac. by death of John Powerstoke; patrons, abbot and conv. of Bindon, as is clear from the inquisition made on the bp.'s authority. 22 March 1486. (Marginalia illegible.)

1 Emden, <u>Cambridge</u>, p.240.

(Fo. 7v) HIC MUTATUR ANNUS DOMINI DE ANNO MILLESIMO &c LXXXmo
Vto IN ANNUM DOMINI MILLESIMUM CCCC OCTUAGESIMUM SEXTUM.

47 Institution of John Elyot, chapl., to Swanage ch., vac. by res. of
    M. Edmund Martin; patron, William (fitz Alan), earl of Arundel.
    Edington, 27 March 1486.

48 Institution of Thomas Holder, chapl., to Mildenhall ch., vac. by
    death of John Davyson; patrons, John Mompesson, Thomas Tropnell,
    John Mervyn, and John Tewke, co-feoffees of Robert Hungerforde,
    kt., Lord Hungerford, Heytesbury, and Homet, as is clear from the
    inquisition made at Mildenhall. 5 April 1486.

49 Institution of M. John Stokys MA to Milton ch., vac. by res. of
    M. William Sylke DCnL; patrons, abbot and conv. of Abingdon.
    11 April 1486.

50 Institution of William Gobarde, chapl., to Church Knowle ch., vac.
    by death of Roger Howton; (Fo. 8) patron, Cecily, duchess of York.
    12 April 1486.

51 (Intruded in a different hand at the bottom of Fo. 7v) Collation
    to M. Christopher Baynbryg, cl., of a canonry and the prebend of
    Horton in Salisbury cath., vac. by consecration of M. Robert Morton
    to the bishopric of Worcester. (Mand. adm. omitted.) Woodford,
    11 April 1486.

52 Institution of John Newman, chapl., in the person of John Whitacre,
    his proctor, to Tarrant Hinton ch., vac. by res. of M. John Stokys;
    patrons, abbess and conv. of Shaftesbury. 13 April 1486.

53 Institution of Thomas Glowceter, chapl., to St Mary Major ch.,
    Wallingford, vac. by res. of M. Lewis John; patrons, prior and
    conv. of Wallingford. 17 April 1486.

54 Institution of Gilbert Wilkyns, chapl., to a moiety of Child
    Okeford ch., vac. by res. of John Lloyde; patron, John Trencharde,
    armiger. 19 April 1486.

55 Institution of Edward Grynall, chapl., to Winterborne Zelston
    ch., vac. by death of John Weste; patron Nicholas Grynall, armiger,
    of Northamptonshire. 21 April 1486.

56 (Fo. 8v) Institution of M. Geoffrey Ellis BCL to Enborne ch., vac. by death of John Milverton; patron, John Cheyne, kt., as appears from inquisition taken. 22 April 1486.

57 Institution of M. David Miles BCnL to St Peter's ch., Wareham, vac. by res. of William Jokyns; patrons, prior and conv. of Sheen. 11 April (sic) 1486.

58 Institution of Henry Rawlyn, cl., to Urchfont prebend, vac. by death of M. William Ive DTh; patrons, abbess and conv. of Nunnaminster, Winchester. 12 May 1486. (Marginal: lx)

59 Institution of M. Thomas Assheborne BCL to Shaw ch., vac. by res. of M. William Combe; patrons, warden, fellows, and scholars of St Mary's Coll., Winchester. 12 May 1486. (Marginalia illegible.)

60 Collation to Robert Attekynson, chapl., of Pusey ch., vac. by death of the last r. Sonning, 12 May 1486. (Marginalia illegible.)

61 (Fo. 9) Collation to Thomas Rope, priest, of a canonry and the prebend of Axford in Salisbury cath., vac. by res. of Robert Day. Salisbury, the Leadenhall in the close, 24 April 1486. (Marginal: Nihil)

62 Collation to Robert Day, chapl., of a canonry and the prebend of Ratfyn in Salisbury cath., vac. by res. of M. Henry Sutton. Salisbury, the close, 24 April 1486. (Marginal: Nihil)

63 Collation to M. Henry Sutton MD of a canonry and the prebend of Chisenbury and Chute in Salisbury cath., vac. by res. of Thomas Rope. Salisbury, the close, 24 April 1486. (Marginal: l)

64 Institution of Morgan Sawell to Hannington vicarage, on an exchange of benefices with Ralph Karon; patrons, dean and canons of Lanchester Coll.; and institution of Ralph Karon to East Shefford ch., on the above exchange of benefices with Morgan Sawell; (Fo. 9v) patron, Richard Feteplas, armiger. Sonning, 22 May 1486. (Marginal: Nihil)

65 Collation to M. Richard Hill BCnL, dean of the Chapel Royal, of a canonry and the prebend of Beminster Secunda in Salisbury cath., vac. by dimission of M. Edward Cheyne, dean-elect of Salisbury.

Mand. adm.: <u>locumtenens</u> and chapter of Salisbury. 19 May 1486.

66 Institution of M. Owen Morgan MA to St Leonard's ch., Wallingford,
    vac. by death of M. John Bewpyll; patrons, prior and conv. of
    St Frideswide, Oxford. Sonning, 3 June 1486.

67 Institution of Thomas Mareis, chapl., to the chantry of
    St Michael de Mowndes in Bridport ch., vac. by res. of John Kelnar;
    patron, William Wykys, r. of Bridport. 5 June 1486.

68 (Intruded in a different hand at the bottom of Fo. 9v) Collation
    to M. Robert Langton, cl., of the archdeaconry of Dorset, vac. by
    death of M. William Ascough. Mand. for installation to dean and
    chapter of Salisbury. Sonning, 25 June 1486.

69 (Fo. 10) Institution of M. John Bostoke, canon residentiary of
    Salisbury cath., to Melksham vicarage, vac. by death of
    M. John Baker; patrons, <u>locumtenens</u> and chapter of Salisbury.
    20 June 1486.

70 Institution of John Brice, chapl., to Melbury Sampford ch., vac.
    by res. of William Gedney; patron, William Brownyng, <u>armiger</u>.
    30 June 1486.

71 Collation to M. Richard Kelsay BCL of the subdeanery of Salisbury
    cath., vac. by death of M. William Branche. Ind.: dean and his
    <u>locumtenens</u> and chapter of Salisbury. Sonning, 11 July 1486.
    (Marginal: <u>Nihil</u>)

72 Collation to Robert Day, chapl., of St Peter's ch., Marlborough,
    vac. by res. of Adrian de Bardys. Sonning, 20 July 1486.
    (Marginal: <u>Nihil</u>)

73 (Fo. 10v) Institution of John Belche, chapl., to Pentridge ch.,
    vac. by res. of John Anderton; patrons, abbot and conv. of
    Tewkesbury. 15 July 1486.

74 Institution of Robert Sherarde, chapl., to Rampisham ch., vac. by
    death of John Taberer; patron, Thomas (Butler), earl of Ormund,
    lord of the manor, as is clear from inquisition taken.
    2 August 1486. (Marginal: <u>1x</u>)

75 Institution of John Stephins, chapl., to John Sewarde's chantry in
    Holy Trinity ch., Dorchester, vac. by res. of John Sampson;
    patrons, royal bailiffs in the borough of Dorchester. 2 August
    1486.

76 Institution of William Mitton, chapl., to Upton Lovell ch., vac.
    by res. of M. Richard Kelsay; patron, Henry Lovell, kt., Lord
    Morley, as is clear from inquisition made. 8 August 1486.

77 (Fo. 11) Institution of M. Thomas Beweshyn BCL to Orcheston
    St George ch., vac. by death of M. William Branche; patron,
    William (fitz Alan), earl of Arundel, kt. 25 August 1486.

78 Institution of M. John Lane DTh to Lutterworth ch., Lincoln dioc.,
    on an exchange of benefices with John Vernham; patron, Thomas
    (Grey), marquess (of Dorset), Lord Ferrers of Groby, Harington,
    Bonville, and Astley; and institution of M. John Vernham to
    Shottesbrooke Coll., on the above exchange of benefices with
    John Lane, warden or keeper; patrons, William Gybson of Leicester
    and Robert Swettok of Ashwell, Lincoln dioc., for this time as is
    clear from letters of the said M. John Vernham, William Rawlyns,
    John Swan, and Humfry Belecher, feoffees of William Trussel, kt.,
    deceased. Sonning, 5 August 1486. (Marginal: <u>Nihil</u>)

79 (Fo. 11v) Institution of M. William Burges BCnL to Winterborne
    Steepleton ch., vac. by res. of Richard Hancok; patron, Cecily,
    duchess of York. Sonning, 27 August 1486. (Marginalia, probable
    reading: <u>Nihil</u>)

80 Institution of Thomas Empster, chapl., to Sulham ch., vac. by res.
    of William Ringesall; patrons, William Twyneo, <u>armiger</u>, and
    Margaret his wife. Sonning, 1 September 1486. (Marginalia (?),
    <u>Nihil</u>)

81 Institution of William Vowell, chapl., to Holy Trinity ch.,
    Wareham, vac. by res. of Nicholas Gybault; patrons, abbot and conv.
    of Sherborne. Salisbury, M. John Doget's house in the close,
    12 September 1486.

82 (Fo. 12) Institution of Alexander Anne, chapl., to Fittleton
    ch., vac. by death of Thomas Moressh; patron, Edward Darell,
    <u>armiger</u>, son and heir of George Darell, kt., deceased.
    26 September 1486.

83 Institution of M. Thomas Holes BCL to Dinton ch., vac. by res.
    of Simon Bowyer _alias_ Brynfyre; patrons, abbess and conv. of
    Shaftesbury. Salisbury, 17 September 1486.

84 Institution of John Clarke, chapl., to Newton Toney ch., vac.
    by death of John Harris; patron, Thomas Weste, kt., Lord de la
    Warr. Salisbury, 17 September 1486.

85 Institution of M. Richard Joyce MA to Sunningwell ch., vac. by
    death (Fo. 12v) of William Trevillyan; patrons, abbot and conv.
    of Abingdon. Fleet Street beside London, 12 October 1486.
    (Marginal: _Nihil_)

86 Institution of John Skypton, chapl., to Holy Trinity ch.,
    Shaftesbury, vac. by res. of William Jonis, r. or chaplain;
    patrons, abbess and conv. of Shaftesbury. 13 October 1486.
    (Marginalia, probable reading: 'They write as if they present to
    a chaplaincy, notwithstanding which I write otherwise, for.it is
    a parish church having the cure of souls committed to it.')

87 Admission of presentation of John Davyd, r·. of St Teilo's ch.,
    Crunwear, St David's dioc., to Hamstead Marshall ch., on an
    exchange of benefices (with M. John Tudir BCnL): patron,
    King Henry. Mand. to Hugh, bp. of St David's to investigate the
    exchange, specifically reserving induction &c. Fleet Street,
    18 October 1486.
    (This exchange was effected on 17 November 1486: The Episcopal
    Registers of the Diocese of St David's, 1397-1518, ed.
    R.F. Isaacson (Cymmrodorion Record Series, 6, 1917), Vol. 2,
    pp.476-8: 'M. John David _alias_ Kidwely, priest'.)

88 Institution of Christopher Notte, chapl., to Biddlestone ch., vac.
    by death of Henry Palmer; patrons, prior and conv. of Monkton
    Farleigh. 19 October 1486. (Marginal: _Nihil_)

89 (Fo. 13) Collation to Robert Pevesay MA of the succentorship of
    Salisbury cath., vac. by death of John Tykyll. 20 October 1486.

90 Mand. for installation of Robert Pevesay in the succentorship of
    Salisbury cath. and his ind. in Ebbesborne Wake ch., annexed
    thereto, to dean of Salisbury or his _locumtenens_. Dated &c (_sic_).
    (Marginal, in nineteenth or twentieth-century hand, written over
    pencil erasure: 'Ebisborne'.)

91 Institution of John Denby MA to Melbury Osmond ch., vac. by res.
    of Nicholas Watson, on an exchange with the v. of the prebendal
    ch. of Chute which Denby held; patron, William Brownyng, _armiger_.
    Ramsbury, 29 September 1486. (Marginal: _Nihil_)

92 (Fo. 13v) Institution of Walter Barbour MA to Codford St Peter
    ch., vac. by res. of William Crampelay, _de facto_ but not _de jure_
    incumbent; patrons, Katherine Hastings, widow of William Hastings,
    kt., Lord Hastings, and Edward Hastings, kt., Lord Hastings,
    executors of William, both by reason of the grant of custody of
    the lands and tenements of George (Talbot), earl of Shrewsbury, to
    the said William by letters patent of Edward IV, and by reason of
    the recovery of the presentation of that ch. in the _curia regis_
    against John Audley, kt., Lord Audley, and William Cramplay afore-
    said. 1 December 1486.

93 Institution of Thomas Blewette, chapl., to Remenham ch., vac. by
    death of John Wortys; patrons, William Husee, chief justice of
    England, and Edmund Mounteforde, kts., John Hewes, _armiger_,
    Henry Assheborne, gent., and Thomas Blewet, as is clear from
    inquisition made. 16 December 1486. (Marginalia illegible.)

94 Institution of Richard Bullok BCnL to Lydiard Tregoze ch., vac.
    by death of John Hille; patron, Oliver Saymour, _armiger_, Lincoln
    dioc., as is clear from inquisition taken. 17 December 1486.

95 (Fo. 14) Institution of John Curtayse, chapl., to Melksham
    vicarage, vac. by res. of M. John Bostoke; patrons, _locumtenens_
    and chapter of Salisbury. Woodford, 11 December 1486.

96 Institution of Richard Dusavir, chapl., to Askerswell ch., vac. by
    res. of John Peverell; patron, Robert Gray, _armiger_. Ind.: archd.
    of Wiltshire (_rectius_ Dorset). 12 December 1486.

97 Institution of M. Robert Wykys MA, chapl., to Whaddon ch., vac. by
    res. of John Curteys; patron, Nicholas Beauchamp, kt. 15 January
    1487.

98 Institution of John Haton, chapl., to Teffont Evias ch., vac. by
    death of William Lovell; patron, Walter Hungerfforde, lord of
    Teffont. Mand. for induction after inquisition into the right of
    patronage of the said Walter Hungerforde. 27 January 1487.

99 (Fo. 14v) Institution of William Brome, chapl., to Swindon

11

vicarage, vac. by res. of William Camyll; patrons, prior and conv. of Southwick. 28 February 1487.

100   Institution of Thomas Burley, chapl., to Long Bredy ch., vac. by res. of M. John Ryse; patrons, abbot and conv. of Cerne. 23 March 1487.

HIC MUTATUR ANNUS DOMINI DE ANNO MILLESIMO &c. LXXXVIto IN ANNUM DOMINI MILLESIMUM QUADRINGENTESIMUM OCTUAGESIMUM SEPTIMUM.

101   Institution of William Ludwell, chapl., to Frome St Quintin ch., vac. by death of John Vagge; patrons, abbot and conv. of Tewkesbury. 29 March 1487.

102   Institution of Thomas Strobull, chapl., to Sopworth ch., vac. by res. of Thomas Davell; patrons, prior and conv. of Monkton Farleigh. Woodford, 7 ('December' struck out) April 1487.

103   Institution of M. Thomas Dokelby BCnL to (Fo. 15) Blandford St Mary ch., vac. by res. of M. Robert Legge alias Palyngton; patrons, prioress and conv. of Clerkenwell. Woodford, 24 April 1487. (Marginalia illegible.)

104   Institution of Nicholas Skaylehorne, chapl., to Uffington vicarage, vac. by death of John Stanford; patrons, abbot and conv. of Abingdon. 24 April 1487.

105   Institution of M. James Vaughan BCL to Godmanstone ch., vac. by res. of Nicholas Holande; patron, John Trencharde, armiger. Woodford, 11 April 1487.

106   Institution of John Arthur, chapl., to Chilton Foliat ch., vac. by death of Thomas Holme; patron for this turn by reason of a grant made to him, Thomas Waryn. Mand. for induction after inquisition into the right of patronage of the said Thomas Waren. 27 April 1487.

107   Institution of John Botyll, chapl., to Compton Chamberlayne vicarage, vac. by death of William Snowdon; patron, William Elyot, provost of St Edmund's Coll., Salisbury. 2 May 1487.

108   (Fo. 15v) Institution of John Sympmyngys, chapl., to

Leigh Delamere ch., vac. by res. of Roger Leyfonde (probable reading); patron, Thomas Nores, gent. Mand. for induction after inquisition into the right of patronage of the said Thomas Nores. 4 May 1487.

109 Institution of M. David Irlande MA to Hinton Martell ch., vac. by death of William Syngle; patron, dean of the royal (free) chapel of Wimborne. Mand. for induction after inquisition into the title of the said dean. 5 May 1487.

110 Institution of William Marshall to Stapleford vicarage, vac. by death of Thomas Thompson; patron for this turn by reason of a grant by the prior and conv. of Easton dated 24 May 1487, M. Laurence Cokkys DCnL. 27 May 1487.

111 Institution of John Gilbert, chapl., to Fifehead Magdalen vicarage, vac. by death of John Clareys; patrons, abbot and conv. of Bristol. 9 June 1487.

112 Institution of M. Richard Smyth, in the person of M. Bartholomew Underwode, proctor, to Codford St Mary ch., vac. by death of Richard Benet; patron, William Calthrop, kt. 16 June 1487.

113 (Fo. 16) Institution of Thomas Laurence, chapl., to Bradford Abbas ch., vac. by res. of Richard Wyggynton; patrons, abbot and conv. of Sherborne. Ramsbury, 29 June 1487.

114 Institution of Nicholas Taverner, chapl., to Askerswell ch., vac. by death of Richard Dewsaver; patron, Robert Grey, armiger. Ind.: arch. of Wiltshire (rectius Dorset). Ramsbury, 12 July 1487.

115 Institution of Robert Barker, chapl., in the person of John Wely, to Bower Chalke vicarage, vac. by res. of William Baase; patrons, provost and scholars of King's Coll., Cambridge. 31 July 1487.

116 Institution of John Pymbarde, chapl., to the chantry in St Mary's ch., Reading, for King Edward I, Thomas Colney, William Catour, and all the faithful departed, vac. by death of Richard Tenante; patron, John Langham, mayor of Reading. 7 August 1487.

117 (Fo. 16v) Collation to Robert Wulfe, chapl., of Chitterne All Saints vicarage, vac. by death of John Baker. Ramsbury, 8 August

1487. (Marginal: <u>Nihil</u>)

118 Institution of M. William Thomas BCnL to St Mary's ch., in Brede
Street, Wilton, vac. by death of John Walker; patrons, abbess
and conv. of Wilton. Ramsbury, 8 August 1487.

119 Institution of John ap Lothyum, chapl., to Milston ch.; patron,
Jasper (Tudor), duke of Bedford and earl of Pembroke, as adjudged
by the report of M. Nicholas Gotfrith BC & CnL and M. Alexander
Cator BC & CnL, commissioned 21 July 1487 to inquire into the
right of patronage, by reason of the forfeiture of William
Berkeley of Stoke by which the said duke obtained from the king
among others the manor of Milston, as appears by letters of
indenture between William Berkley and Anne his wife, John Mateij
junior and Joan his wife, and John his son, letting to farm
under the seal of the said duke. 21 August 1487.

120 Institution of M. Richard Ewlawe, chapl., to Hatford ch.;˙patron,
Henry Doget, found to be true patron by reason of a concession to
him by John (de la Pole), duke of Suffolk, patron for this turn,
by commission dated 28 July 1487 to M. William Jonys BC & CnL and
M. David Parsons BC & CnL. 23 August 1487.

121 (Fo. 17) Institution of John Lokkesley, chapl., to Blunsdon St
Andrew ch., vac. by death of John Hoy, last chapl.; patron,
John Ferys, <u>armiger</u>. Mand. for induction after inquisition into
the right of patronage of the said John Ferys. Ramsbury, 24
August 1487.

122 Collation to John Bryan, abbot of Bindon, of Tyneham ch., a
benefice usually governed by secular clerks and by no means
regulars, vac. by death of M. Thomas Mone, and falling to the
bp.'s collation because of the fault of the prior and conv. of
Tortington, who presented to that church John Martyn, chapl.,
unfit to hold an ecclesiastical benefice with cure because of
the disability and intolerable defect which he has suffered in
his sight. (Undated.)
(See 449 for a papal dispensation to John, abbot of Bindon.)

123 Institution of M. Ralph Hethcotys BCnL to Buckland ch., vac. by
death of M. Adam Marlande; patrons, r. and conv. of Edington.
Ramsbury, 25 August 1487. (Marginal: <u>Nihil</u>)

124 Institution of David Santt, chapl., to Catmore ch., vac. by res.
of Reginald Mutte; patron, Brother Robert Egilsfelde, perceptor

of Beverley, in his capacity as <u>locumtenens</u> for Brother John
Weston, prior of the Hospital of St John of Jerusalem in England.
13 September 1487.

125 Collation to John Hewlet, chapl., of Brixton Deverill ch., vac.
by res. of M. John Leche. 17 September 1487.

126 (Fo. 17v) Institution of M. Robert Saunders MA to West Wittenham
ch., vac. by res. of M. Thomas Symon; patrons, r. and fellows of
Exeter Coll., Oxford. 25 September 1487.

127 Institution of Robert Gawlare, cl., to Melbury Osmond ch., vac.
by res. of M. John Denby; patron, William Brownyng, <u>armiger</u>.
4 October 1487.

128 Institution of M. William Atwater MA to Piddlehinton ch., vac. by
death of M. William Wither; patrons, provost and coll. of Eton.
5 October 1487.

129 Institution of Thomas Fox, chapl., to Tubney ch. or chapel, vac.
by res. of M. William Chypnam; patrons, president and scholars of
Magdalen Coll., Oxford. Ramsbury, 6 October 1487.

130 Institution of Richard Hancok, chapl., to Sydling St Nicholas
vicarage, vac. by death of Thomas Lardener (probable reading);
patrons, abbot and conv. of Milton. Ramsbury, 11 October 1487.

131 (Fo. 18) Institution of John Akers, chapl., to Harwell vicarage,
vac. by res. of M. William Hulverdale; patrons, Stephen Bereford,
dean of the royal free chapel in Wallingford castle, and the coll.
or fellows of the chapel there. 26 October 1487.

132 Institution of William Symson, chapl., to Stanton St Quintin ch.,
vac. by res. of Thomas Sutton MA; patron, Alice, Lady Fitzhugh,
relict of Henry Fitzhugh. Ramsbury, 28 October 1487.

133 Institution of M. Henry Mompesson BC & CnL to Mildenhall ch., vac.
by res. of Thomas Holder; patrons, John Mompesson, Thomas
Tropnell, John Mervyn, and John Touke, co-feoffees of Robert
Hungerford, kt., lord of Hungerford, Heytesbury, and Homet, for
this turn by reason of the feoffment. Ramsbury, 28 October 1487.

134 Institution of Thomas Clerke, chapl., to Denchworth ch., vac. by
     death of Richard Curteys; patrons, abbot and conv. of Bruern.
     Sonning, 30 October 1487.

135 Institution of M. Richard Newporte BCL to Long Bredy ch., vac. by
     death of John Haselwiche; patrons, abbot and conv. of Cerne.
     9 November 1487. (Marginal: Nihil)

136 (Fo. 18v) Institution of John Dygton, chapl., to Allington ch.,
     vac. by death of M. Gilbert Lye; patron, Richard Walop, armiger,
     of Farleigh Wallop, Winchester dioc. 20 November 1487.

137 Institution of Thomas Morley, chapl., to Blunsdon St Andrew ch.,
     vac. by death of John Lokley; patron John Ferreis, armiger.
     28 November 1487.

138 Institution of William Balle, chapl., to Sydling St Nicholas
     vicarage, vac. by res. of Richard Hancoke; patrons, abbot and
     conv. of Milton. Woodford, 2 January 1488.

139 Institution of John Leyott, chapl., to Fifield Bavant ch., vac.
     by res. of Robert Barkar; patrons, prioress and conv. of Dartford.
     Woodford, 5 January 1488.

140 Collation to Robert Wulfe, chapl., of Boscombe ch., vac. by res.
     of M. Richard Newporte. Ramsbury, 26 January 1488. (Marginal:
     Nihil)

141 Collation to M. Robert Langton, cl., of a canonry and the
     prebend of Charminster and Bere in Salisbury cath., vac. by death
     of Robert Bothe. 30 January 1488. (Marginal: Nihil)

142 (Fo. 19) Collation to M. John Forster MA of a canonry and the
     prebend of Fordington and Writhlington in Salisbury cath., vac.
     by the acceptance of another prebend in that ch., by Robert
     Langton. 30 January 1488.

143 Collation to M. Edward Willoughby MA of a canonry and the prebend
     of Grantham Borealis in Salisbury cath., vac. by the acceptance
     of another prebend in that ch. by M. John Forster. 30 January
     1488.

144 Mand. ind. of above Willoughby in his prebend to John (Russell),
    bp. of Lincoln. Dated &c. (sic; marginalia illegible.)

145 Institution of M. John Denbye MA to West Dean ch., vac. by res.
    of Richard Balteswell, cl.; patron, Katherine Harecourte.
    Pension to retiring r.: 5 marks p.a. for seven years. 30
    January 1488. (Marginal: Nihil)

HIC MUTATUR ANNUS TRANSLACIONIS DOMINI TERTIUS IN ANNUM QUARTUM.

146 (Fo. 19v) Institution of Luke Mouncell, chapl., to Swyre ch.,
    vac. by res. of Edward Ryde; patron, King Henry. Pension to
    retiring r.: 4 marks p.a. Ramsbury, 15 February 1488.

147 Institution of M. John Phelipes BCL to Swanage ch., vac. by death
    of John Elyot; patron, Thomas (fitz Alan) earl of Arundel. 24
    February 1488.

148 Institution of M. Edward Wylloughby to Chilmark ch., vac. by
    death of Nicholas Blakemore; patrons, abbess and conv. of Wilton.
    4 March 1488.

149 Institution of Henry Crokkar, chapl., to West Overton vicarage,
    vac. by res. of M. Robert Preston; patrons, prior and conv. of
    Winchester. 6 March 1488.

150 Institution of John Massy, chapl., to Odstock ch., vac. by death
    of M. Nicholas Gotfrith; patron, William Gerbarde, armiger.
    7 March 1488.

151 Institution of M. Richard Estmonde DTh to Broughton Gifford ch.,
    vac. by death of M. Nicholas Gotfrith; patrons, abbess and conv.
    of Shaftesbury. 13 March 1488.

152 (Fo. 20) Institution of Walter Dudston, chapl., to Finchampstead
    ch., vac. by death of William Mytton; patron for this turn,
    John Perkyns, armiger. Mand. for induction after inquisition into
    the right of patronage of the said John Perkyns. 15 March 1488.

153 Institution of Edward Hawtre, chapl., to the chapel cure of St
    John the Baptist in East Hendred manor, vac. by res. of M. Thomas
    Lee DTh, last keeper or r.; patron, John Eyston, armiger. 17
    March 1488.

154 Institution of William Vasse, chapl., to Langton Herring ch., vac. by death of M. Robert Gente; patrons, John Wroughton senior and Margaret his wife. 17 March 1488.

155 Institution of John Estmonde, cl., to the free chapel or portion of Haxton, vac. by dimission of John Wroughton, last portioner or keeper; patrons, John Sapcote, kt., and Elizabeth his wife, late wife of Fulk Bourgchier, late Lord FitzWarin. Mand. for induction after inquisition into the right of patronage for this turn of the said John and Elizabeth. 20 March 1488.

HIC VIDELICET VICESIMO QUINTO DIE MENSIS EIUSDEM MUTATUR ANNUS DOMINI MILLESIMUM CCCCmus OCTUAGESIMUS SEPTIMUS IN ANNUM DOMINI MILLESIMUM CCCCmum OCTUAGESIMUM OCTAVUM.

156 Institution of Gilbert Lancaster. chapl., to Stratton St Margaret vicarage, vac. by res. of M. Sampson Aleyn; patrons, warden, scholars, and brothers of Merton Coll., Oxford, the bp.'s. nomination having first been made to them. Salisbury, 5 April 1488.

157 (Fo. 20v) Institution of M. Philip Morgan to Chieveley vicarage, vac. by death of Hugh Lynell; patrons, abbot and conv. of Abingdon. Ramsbury, 18 April 1488.

158 Institution of Thomas Kymer, chapl., to Melbury Osmond ch., vac. by res. of Robert Gawler; patron, William Brownyng, armiger. Pension to retiring r.: 33s.4d p.a. 29 April 1488.

159 Institution of William Hawardyn, chapl., to Barford St Martin ch., vac. by res. of M. Humfry Hawardyn; patron for this turn, John Mompesson, armiger, by virtue of letters patent of William Lucy, lord of the manor of Compton Chamberlayne, patron, granting the right of presentation to that ch. to the same Mompesson for life. Ramsbury, 12 May 1488.

160 Institution of John Esterfeld, cl., to Newbury ch., vac. by res. of M. Christopher Twynyho; patrons, prior and conv. of Witham. 7 June 1488.

161 Institution of Thomas Goldesmyth, chapl., to Charlton vicarage, vac. by res. of John Thacham; patrons, prior and conv. of Ivychurch. 8 June 1488.

162 (Fo. 21) Institution of Maurice Deremonte, chapl., to Buckhorn Weston ch., vac. by death of Thomas Waren; patron, William Stourton, Lord Stourton. Mand. for induction after inquisition into the right of the said William Stourton. 12 June 1488.

163 Institution of M. John Coldale DTh to Buckland vicarage, vac. by res. of M. Ralph Hethcote; patrons, r. and conv. of Edington. 7 July 1488. (Marginal: <u>Nihil</u>)

(Marginal 'B' next to <u>163</u> and 'A' next to <u>166</u> corrects faulty chrono-logical order.)

164 Institution of Jerome Sperkefeld, chapl., to Aldermaston vicarage, vac. by death of William Porte; patrons, warden, chapls., and brothers of the hospital of St Julian called God's House, Southampton. 7 July 1488.

165 Institution of Thomas Clerke, chapl., to Padworth ch., vac. by res. of Jerome Sperkfeld; patrons, warden, chapls., and brothers of the hospital of St Julian called God's House, Southampton. 7 July 1488. (Marginal: <u>Nihil</u>)

166 Collation to Robert Day, chapl., of Eaton Hastings ch., vac. and falling to the bp.'s collation this turn by lapse. 6 July 1488. (Marginal: <u>Nihil</u>)

167 (Fo. 21v) Collation to Thomas Langporte, chapl., of Great Chalfield ch., falling to the bp.'s collation this turn by lapse. Ramsbury, 23 July 1488.

168 Institution of Richard Waren, chapl., in the person of Richard Dale, proctor, to the portion of the tithes of Woolley, vac. by dimission of William Hanyngton, last keeper or co-portioner; patrons, abbess and conv. of Nunnaminster, Winchester. 24 July 1488. (Marginal: 'This portion is situated next to Poughley priory in Chaddleworth parish'.)

169 Institution of Edmund Wilkynson, chapl., to Ham ch., vac., by res. of William Coyne; patron, Peter, bp. of Winchester. 28 July 1488.

170 Institution of Thomas Gowrton, chapl., to Chilton ch., vac. by res. of M. Lewis John; patrons, abbot and conv. of Abingdon. 28 July 1488.

171 Institution of Gervase Ketyll, chapl., to Glanvilles Wooton chantry, vac. by death of John Browne; patron, John Ley, armiger. 29 July 1488.

172 Collation to Robert Harryson, chapl., of Huish ch., vac. and falling to the bp.'s collation this turn by lapse. 2 August 1488. (Marginal: Nihil)

173 (Fo. 22) Institution of Thomas Smyth, chapl., to Melcombe Horsey ch., vac. by res. of Henry Thorp; patron, Richard Turges, armiger. Ramsbury, 4 August 1488.

174 Institution of Roger Rostragyn, chapl., to Hammoon ch., vac. by death of Thomas Whittok; patron, John Trenchard, armiger. 10 August 1488.

175 Institution of William Leystone, chapl., in the person of Henry Wilkynson, his proctor, to Chisledon vicarage, vac. by death of Hugh Baker; patrons, abbot and conv. of Hyde by Winchester. 12 August 1488.

176 Institution of Walter Dudston, chapl., to Hurley vicarage, vac.; patrons, prior and conv. of Hurley. 20 August 1488.

177 Institution of Thomas Blacked, chapl., to Donhead St Andrew ch., vac. by res. of John Howse; patrons, abbess and conv. of Shaftesbury. Ramsbury, 1 September 1488.

178 Institution of Thomas Blakden, chapl., to Manningford Abbots ch., vac. by res. of Roger Fabell; patrons, abbot and conv. of Hyde by Winchester. 2 September 1488.

179 (F. 22v) Collation to Thomas Hedley, chapl., of Little Chalfield ch., vac. and falling to the bp.'s collation this turn by lapse. 27 September 1488.

180 Institution of M. William Morland, cl., in the person of Hugh Morland, his proctor, to Binfield ch., vac. by death of M. (blank); patron for this turn, John (Morton), archbp. of Canterbury, by a concession to him as bp. of Ely together with John Brown, cl., John Broune, gent., and others, of the next only presentation by the abbot and conv. of Cirencester, patrons. Ramsbury, 29 September 1488.

181 Institution of Thomas Wylkynson, chapl., to the vicarage of the parish or prebendal ch. of Ramsbury, vac. by res. of James Coterell; patron, Adrian de Bardys. Pension to Coterell: 40s p.a. for life. 4 October 1488. (Marginal: <u>Nihil</u>)

182 Institution of Thomas Brenfyre, chapl., to Wootton Bassett vicarage, vac. by death of John Wynsley; patrons, abbot and conv. of Stanley. 7 October 1488.

183 Institution of M. Thomas Warner BCL to Wytham ch., vac. by death of M. Thomas Walton; patron, Katherine Harecourte, relict of Richard Harecourte, kt., lord of Wytham. Mand. for induction after inquisition into the right of patronage for this turn. 7 October 1488. (Marginal: '3d. for the cure of the vicarage of Chaddleworth.')

184 (Fo. 23 Institution of M. John Rokysburgh MA to Allington ch., vac. by death of John Dygton; patron, Richard Walop, <u>armiger</u>. 21 October 1488.

185 Institution of M. Thomas Henbury, chapl., to Sulham ch., vac. by res. of Thomas Empstar; patrons, William Twynyho, <u>armiger</u>, and Margaret his wife. 31 October 1488.

186 Institution of M. Robert Beke, chapl., to the vicarage of the parish or prebendal ch., of Fontmell Magna, vac. by res. of William Wright; patron, Christopher Twynyho, prebendary of Fontmell. London, 10 November 1488.

(Marginal 'b' next to <u>186</u> and 'a' next to <u>188</u> corrects faulty chrono-logical order.)

187 Institution of John Elys, chapl., to Silton ch., vac. by res. of Henry Payn; patron, Matilda Preston, widow. (N.d.)

188 Collation to Christopher Bayly, chapl., of Bremhill vicarage, vac. by res. of William Hoper. 4 November 1488.

189 Institution of Robert Borde, chapl., to Godmanstone ch., vac.; patrons, William Browne and Christina his wife. 12 November 1488.

190 Institution of Richard Bordeall <u>alias</u> Bourdell, chapl., to North

Poorton ch., vac. by res. of Thomas Pavy; patrons, John Cheyne, kt., and Margaret his wife. 14 November 1488.

191 (Fo. 23v) Institution of M. John Hosplete, chapl., to Gussage St Michael ch., vac. by death of John Newman; patrons, prior and conv. of Sheen. 4 December 1488.

192 Institution of Thomas Knethill, chapl., to Tockenham ch., vac. by res. of Thomas Lee; patron, Cecily, duchess of York. 12 December 1488. (Added: 'Commission for inquisition &c.')

193 Institution of Thomas Wythleye, chapl., to Manningford Bruce ch., vac. by the acceptance of another benefice by Thomas Boyer; patron, Thomas Coksey, kt. 18 December 1488.

194 Institution of William Ketylton, chapl., to the custody of the hospital of St John the Baptist in St Martin's parish, Shaftesbury, vac. by res. of M. John Osplete, last keeper; patrons, abbess and conv. of Shaftesbury. 18 December 1488.

195 Institution of Richard Hardy, chapl., to the chantry of St Michael (de Mowndes), Bridport, vac. by res. of Thomas Marys; patron, William Wykes, r. of Bridport. 22 December 1488.

196 Institution of William Palmer, chapl., to Everleigh ch., vac. by res. of M. Thomas Smyth; patrons, abbess and conv. of Wherwell. 31 December 1488.

197 Institution of William Banyster, chapl., to Damerham vicarage, vac. by death of William Blakden; patrons, abbot and conv. of Glastonbury. 2 January 1489.

198 (Fo. 24) Institution of John Kewys, chapl., in the person of M. John Wely, notary public, his proctor, to St Michael's ch., Wareham, vac. by death of Hugh Fyssher; patrons, prior and conv. of Sheen. 2 January 1489.

199 Institution of M. Robert Beke, chapl., to Sutton Waldron ch., vac. by res. of William Wright; patron, John Audley, kt., Lord Audley. London, 14 January 1489.

HIC VIDELICET DECIMO DIE FEBRUARII MUTATUR ANNUS TRANSLACIONIS DOMINI
QUARTUS IN ANNUM QUINTUM.

200 Institution of M. John Westley to Rushall ch., on an exhange of
     benefices with M. John Thwaytis; patron Edward Hastings, kt.,
     Lord Hastings, Botreaux, and Hungerford; and institution of
     M. John Thwaytys to Langton Matravers ch., on the above exchange
     of benefices; patron, Thomas (fitz Allan), earl of Arundel. 10
     February 1489.

201 Collation to M. Thomas Mades, cl., of a canonry and the prebend
     of Chardstock in Salisbury cath., vac. Mand. adm.: dean and his
     locumtenens and the chapter of Salisbury. 20 February 1489.
     (Marginal; Nihil)

202 Institution of M. William Thirlowe to New Windsor vicarage, on an
     exchange of benefices with George Garde; patrons, abbot and conv.
     of Waltham; and institution of M. George Garde to Leigh ch.,
     London dioc., acting by commission granted by Thomas (Kempe), bp.
     of London; patron, Thomas (Butler), earl of Ormond and Lord
     Rochford. (1)   13 March 1489.

203 (Fo. 24v) Institution of Robert Day, chapl., to Welford ch., vac.
     by death of John Westlake; patrons, abbot and conv. of Abingdon.
     Ramsbury, 22 March 1489. (Marginal: Nihil)

204 Collation to M. Richard Toppe BC & CnL of St Peter's ch.,
     Marlborough, vac. by res. of Robert Day. Ind.: chapls. in that
     ch. 22 March 1489. (Marginal: Nihil)

205 Collation to Robert Day, chapl., of a canonry and the prebend of
     Grantham Australis in Salisbury cath., vac. Ind. in his prebend:
     bp. of Lincoln. Pension of £10 p.a. to Ralph Langton, cl.,
     resigned prebendary, until the said Ralph gains title and adm.
     to another prebend in Salisbury cath. 23 March 1489 (Marginal:
     Nihil)
     (See no. 333)

HIC VIDELICET VICESIMO QUINTO DIE MENSIS MARCII MUTATUR ANNUS DOMINI
MILLESIMUS QUADRINGINTESIMUS OCTUAGESIMUS OCTAVUS IN ANNUM DOMINI
MILLESIMUM QUADRINGINTESIMUM OCTUAGESIMUM NONUM.

1   On the style 'Lord Rochford' see Complete Peerage, rev. edn., Vol.
     X (1945), p.132, note (d).

206 (Fo. 25) Institution of Richard Townsend, chapl., to Winterbourne
Stoke vicarage, vac. by death of John Westrope; patrons, prior
and conv. of Sheen. 27 March 1489.

207 Institution of John Abendon, chapl., to Blunsdon St Andrew ch.,
vac.; patron, John Tame, <u>armiger</u>, for this turn by reason of
the donation of the advowson of that ch. by William Luke in the
right of his wife Alice, patron. 28 March 1489.

208 Collation to M. Thomas Holes BCL of a canonry and the prebend of
Ratfyn in Salisbury cath., vac. Ramsbury, 1 April 1489.

209 Institution of David Lawson, chapl., to Winterborne Abbas ch.,
vac. by res. of John Gent; patrons, abbot and conv. of Cerne.
4 April 1489.

210 Institution of John Menger, chapl., to Pilsdon ch., vac.; patron,
William Hody, kt. Salisbury, 17 April 1489.

211 Institution of Christopher Lambarde, cl., to the free chapel of
St Nicholas de Burglen (Porton; modern corruption, 'Birdlime')
in Idmiston parish, vac. by dimission of Roger Uffenham, last
keeper; patron John Chawsey of Stratford Toney. 28 April 1489.

212 Collation to M. William Russell DCnL of a canonry and the
prebend of Wilsford and Woodford in Salisbury cath., vac. by
death of M. Henry Sharpe. 28 April 1489.

213 (Fo. 25v) Institution of John Garet, chapl., to Somerford
Keynes vicarage, vac. by res. of Robert Philipis; patrons, prior
and conv. of Merton. 1 May 1489.

214 Institution of John Kymer, chapl., to West Chelborough ch., vac.
by res. of Martin Gulbey; patron, William Kymer. Cerne, 7 May
1489.

215 Institution of M. John Osplete MA to Cheselbourne ch., vac. by
res. of Thomas Porter; patrons, abbess and conv. of Shaftesbury.
Pension to retiring r. upon supplication by his proctor,
M. Richard Newporte BCL: 8 (<u>octo</u> written over erasure) marks p.a.
7 May 1489.

216 Institution of Edmund Blynkynsop, cl., to Witherston free chapel, vac. by res. of M. Thomas Holes, last keeper; patrons, abbot and conv. of Abbotsbury. Abbotsbury, 10 May 1489. (Marginal: <u>Nihil</u>)

217 Institution of William Wilton, cl., in the person of M. Ralph Store, notary public, to Marnhull ch., vac. by res. of M. William Boket; patrons, abbot and conv. of Glastonbury. 16 May 1489.

218 (Fo. 26) Institution of Peter Esshing, chapl., to Wooton Fitzpaine ch., vac. by res. of John Genys; patron, Thomas (fitz Alan), earl of Arundel. Ramsbury, 1 June 1489.

219 Institution of M. Richard Colyns MA to Longbridge Deverill vicarage, vac. by death of Robert Westwode; patrons, abbot and conv. of Glastonbury. 4 June 1489.

220 Institution of John Lagowche, chapl., to Frome Vauchurch ch., vac. by death of Thomas Benvile; patron for this turn, Lady Elizabeth Colyshull. Mand. for induction after inquisition into the right of patronage by which the said Elizabeth presents this turn by reason of a consensus among Robert de Browkys, Eleanor Twynehow, and the said Elizabeth, heirs of the Lord Humphrey Stafford, late earl of Devon, who last presented. 12 June 1489.

221 Institution of Robert Goddysgrace, chapl., to Teffont Evias ch., vac. by death of John Hatton; patron, Walter Hungerford, kt. 13 June 1489.

222 Institution of John Bargh, cl., to Sturthill free chapel, vac. by death of M. John Sparwell, last keeper; patron, John Newburgh, <u>armiger</u>. 17 June 1489.

223 Collation to William Haynes, chapl., of Farnborough ch., vac. and falling to the bp.'s collation this turn by lapse. Pension to M. Michael Carvenell, retiring r.: 5 marks p.a. for life. 29 June 1489.

224 (Fo. 26v) Commission to Richard Lichefeld DCnL, canon residentiary of St Paul's cath. and official and keeper of the spiritualities of the city and diocese of London <u>sede vacante</u>, to institute, after enquiry, M. Richard Baldry, v. of Walden, London dioc., to Bishops Cannings vicarage, to which he has been presented by the dean and chapter of Salisbury, patrons, on an exchange of benefices with M. John Leche, reserving profession of

obedience to the bp. of Salisbury. Commission dated Bisham,
21 June 1489; profession of obedience, by proctor Thomas Jonson,
and institution dated 17 August 1489.

225 Institution of M. John Bostoke, canon residentiary of Salisbury
cath., to Okeford Fitzpaine ch., patrons, Guy Fayrfax and
Edward Berkeley, kts., and John Goryng, _armiger_, feoffees of
Henry (Percy), late earl of Northumberland. Ramsbury, 25 July 1489.

226 Institution of M. John Bayly, cl., to the collegiate ch., or
wardenship of Shottesbrooke, vac. by death of M. John Vernham,
last keeper or warden; patrons, John Swane, alderman of the city
of London, and Humphrey Belcher, gent., feoffees of William
Trussell, kt., during the minority of Edward Trussell, son and
heir to that William deceased, on the nomination of John Dane, kt.,
guardian or keeper of the said Edward during his minority. 4 August
1489.

227 Institution of William Hayward, chapl., to Melbury Sampford ch.,
vac. by death of John Bryce; patron, William Brownyngs, gent.
6 August 1489.

228 Collation to M. John Gylys, cl., of a canonry and the prebend of
Major pars altaris in Salisbury cath., vac. by death of M. William
Bolton. Ramsbury, 11 August 1489.

229 (Fo. 27) Institution of Richard Forster to Clyffe Pypard vicarage
on an exchange of benefices with William Higges; patrons, abbess
and conv. of Lacock; and the institution of William Higges to
Rowde vicarage on the above exchange; patrons, abbot and conv. of
Stanley. 12 August 1489.

230 Collation to Roger Edmond, chapl., of Tidmarsh ch., vac. and
falling to the bp.'s collation this turn by lapse. 24 August 1489.

231 Institution of William Wykwike, chapl., to Wootton Bassett ch.,
vac. by death of Thomas Brenfyre; patrons, abbot and conv. of
Stanley. 28 August 1489.

232 Institution of Walter Seyntlo, chapl., to North Wraxall ch., vac.
by death of John Mason; patron for this turn, Thomas Yonge,
armiger. Mand. for induction after inquisition into the right of
patronage for this turn as parcel of the manor of North Wraxall,
which was demised in three parts, two of which parts are held by

Thomas Yonge, in the right of which he presents two out of three times, and the third part by William Huse, kt., keeper of the son and heir of Simon Blount, in the right of which he presents every third time. 5 September 1489.

233 (Fo. 27v) Institution of John Stevynton, chapl., to Wingfield ch., vac. by death of Robert Longe; patrons, abbot and conv. of Keynshaw. 8 September 1489.

234 Institution of John Shaper, chapl., to West Chelborough ch., vac. by res. of John Kymer; patron, William Kymer. Ramsbury, 29 September 1489.

235 Institution of Richard Jamys, chapl., to the chantry in Glanvilles Wootton ch., vac. by res. of Gervase Ketyll; patron, John Ley, armiger. 4 October 1489.

236 Institution of Walter Crosse, chapl., to Wootton Fitzpaine ch., vac. by death or res. of Peter Essyng; patron, Thomas (fitz Alan), earl of Arundel. 5 October 1489.

237 Institution of Thomas Strong, cl., to Hilmarton vicarage, vac. by death of (blank); patrons, prior and conv. of Bisham. 6 October 1489.

238 Institution of Robert Elyot, chapl., to Stourton ch., vac. by death of John Edmond; patrons, John Cheyne, kt., and Margaret his wife, Lady Stourton. 10 October 1489.

239 Institution of Owain Watson, chapl., in the person of M. Michael Skyllyng, his proctor, to Bishopstone vicarage, vac. by res. of Robert Elyot; patron, M. John Pierson, r. of that ch. (Fo. 28) Ind.: arch. of (Salisbury). 12 October 1489.

240 Institution of John Hawkyns, chapl., to Barkham ch., vac. by res. of John Welles; patron, Eleanor Bullokys, widow. London, 20 October 1489.

241 Institution of M. Edmund Martyn DC & CnL to Athelhampton free chapel, vac. by death of M. John Sparwell, last keeper; patron, William Martyn, armiger. London, 25 October 1489.

242 Institution of M. John Arundell to Sutton Courtenay ch., vac. by
death of M. Thomas Pashe; patrons, dean and canons ('canons'
erased) and chapter of the royal free chapel of St George in the
castle of Windsor. London, 14 November 1489.

243 Institution of M. Alexander Cator to Norton Bavant vicarage on an
exchange of benefices with John Dracott; patrons, prioress and
conv. of Dartford; and institution of John Dracott, acting on a
commission from John (Russel), bp. of Lincoln, to Grasby ch.,
Lincoln dioc., on the above exchange with Alexander Cator; patron,
John Welles, Viscount Welles. 16 November 1489.

244 (Fo. 28v) Institution of M. Richard Topp BCnL to St Nicholas ch.,
Abingdon, vac. by death of M. Thomas Stephyns; patrons, abbot
and conv. of Abingdon. London, 27 November 1489.

245 Institution of Henry Shan, chapl., to St Martin's ch., Wareham,
vac. by death of William Byrte; patrons, prior and conv. of
Sheen. 30 November 1489.

246 Collation to M. John Arundell, cl., of a canonry and the prebend
of Beminster Secunda in Salisbury cath., vac. by the consec-
ration of M. Richard Hylle to the bishopric of London.
30 November 1489. (Marginal: Nihil)

247 Collation to M. William Higham DTh of a canonry and the prebend
of Durnford in Salisbury cath., vac. by the acceptance of another
prebend in that ch. by M. John Arundell. 1 December 1489.
(Marginal: Nihil)

248 Institution of Nicholas Inglesshent, chapl., to Steeple ch., vac.
by res. of M. Richard Topp; patron, Cecily, duchess of York.
16 December 1489.

249 Institution of M. William Fynymor MA to the ch. or free chapel of
Tubney, vac. by death of M. Thomas Fox, last keeper or r.;
patrons, warden and fellows of Magdalen Coll., Oxford. Ramsbury,
8 January 1490.

250 (Fo. 29) Institution of Hugh Fylell, chapl., to Inkpen ch., vac.
by res. of William Bray; patron, John Trenchard, armiger. Pension
to Bray: 46s. 8d p.a. for life. Ramsbury, 11 January 1490.
(Marginal: Nihil)

251 Institution of Edward Robardes to Winterborne Abbas ch., on an exchange of benefices with David Lawson; patrons, abbot and conv. of Cerne; and institution of David Laweson to Radipole ch. on the above exchange with Edward Robardes; patrons, abbot and conv. of Cerne. 16 January 1490.

252 Institution of Thomas Hobbis, chapl., to Tollard Royal ch., vac. by death of Robert Kempe; patron, Richard Beauchampe, kt. 29 January 1490.

HIC MUTATUR ANNUS TRANSLACIONIS DOMINI QUINTUS IN ANNUM SEXTUM TRANS-LACIONIS SUAE.

253 (Fo. 29v) Institution of Robert ap David, chapl., to Long Crichel ch., vac. by res. of Edward Underwode; patron, John Chayne, kt. Pension to Underwode until he be promoted to another benefice with or without cure, 4 marks p.a. London, 21 February 1490.

254 Institution of Thomas Pendelton, chapl., to Latton vicarage, vac. by death of William Odyngesley; patrons, abbot and conv. of Cirencester. 6 March 1490.

255 Institution of Robert Snowe, chapl., to Englefield ch., vac. by death of William Mawrice; patron, Thomas Englefeld, gent. 10 March 1490.

256 Institution of Geoffrey Austen, chapl., to Kintbury vicarage, vac. by death of Eli ap Richard; patrons, prioress and conv. of Amesbury. 11 March 1490.

257 Collation to John Sonner, chapl., of Wasing ch., vac. and falling to the bp.'s collation by lapse. 17 March 1490.

258 Institution of John Whithorne, chapl., to Letcombe Bassett ch., vac. by death of Gilbert Huddeston; patron for this turn, Thomas Kyngeston, armiger. 18 March 1490. (Marginalia illegible.)

259 (Fo. 30) Collation to Thomas Philippis, chapl., of the sub-deanery of Salisbury cath., vac. by death of M. Richard Kelsey. Mand. for installation and induction to dean and his locumtenens and chapter of Salisbury. London, 23 March 1490. (Marginal: Nihil)

260 Institution of M. Mathew Delamar, chapl., to West Overton
vicarage, vac. by res. of Henry Crokker; patrons, prior and conv.
of Winchester. 27 March 1490.

261 Institution of Thomas Childe, chapl., to Woodsford ch., vac. by
death of John Tesdale; patrons, abbot and conv. of Cerne.
30 March 1490.

(Marginal 'B' next to 261 and 'A' next to the new year date corrects
faulty chronological order.)

HIC MUTATUR ANNUS DOMINI MILLESIMUS CCCC LXXXIXus IN ANNUM DOMINI
MILLESIMUM QUADRINGENTESIMUM NONAGESIMUM.

262 Institution of John Ball, chapl., to the chantry of St Michael de
Mowndes, Bridport, vac. by res. of Richard Hampton; patron,
William Wyke, r. of Bridport. 2 April 1490.

263 (Fo. 30v) Collation to M. William Byrley MA of Hilton vicarage,
vac. by death of (blank). Ramsbury, 6 April 1490.

264 Institution of M. John Doget DCnL to Winterborne Zelston ch., vac.
by death of Edward Grenall; patron, Nicholas Grenall. Salisbury,
the palace, 27 April 1490.

265 Institution of M. Geoffrey Warburton to Ditchampton ch., on an
exchange of benefices with Richard Hauson, chapl.; patron,
Thomas Mylborne, kt.; and institution on commission from John
(Morton), archbp. of Canterbury, of Richard Hawson, in the
person of Richard Hauson (sic), cl., his proctor, to Balinghen
ch., Therouanne dioc., on the above exchange; patron, King Henry.
Sherborne castle, 29 April 1490.

(Marginal '+.b.' next to 265 and '+.a.' next to 267 corrects faulty
chronological order.)

266 (Fo. 31) Institution of M. Roger Lancastre MA in the person of
Thomas Kyrkby, literate, his proctor, to Portesham vicarage, vac.
by death of Thomas Churchill; patrons, abbot and conv. of
Abbotsbury. Sherborne castle, 29 April 1490. (Marginal: Nihil)

267 Institution of John Warlond, chapl., in the person of M. John

Wely, notary public, his proctor, to Canford Magna vicarage, vac.
by res. of William Michell; patrons, prior and conv. of Bradenstoke.
Sherborne castle, 28 April 1490.

268 Institution of Robert Harthorn, chapl., to Warfield vicarage, vac.
by death of Henry Medewe; patrons, prior and conv. of Hurley.
Sherborne castle, 2 May 1490.

269 Collation to M. John Bostok BCnL of a canonry and the prebend of
Durnford in Salisbury cath., vac. by death of M. William Higham.
Sherborne castle, 4 May 1490.

270 (Fo. 31v) Collation to Richard Payn, cl., of a canonry and the
prebend of Minor pars altaris in Salisbury cath., vac. by the
acceptance of another prebend by M. John Bostok. Sherborne
castle, 5 May 1490. (Marginal: _Nihil_)

271 Institution of William Temset, chapl., to Market Lavington
chantry (_sic_), vac.; patron, Richard Beauchamp, kt. Sherborne,
11 May 1490.

272 Institution of M. Richard Spenser, chapl., to Swayne's chantry in
St Thomas's ch., Salisbury, vac. by death of Simon Tayllour;
patrons, dean and chapter of Salisbury. Ind.: subdean of
Salisbury. Sherborne, 17 May 1490.

273 Institution of John Gryce, chapl., to Langley Burrell ch., vac. by
death of William Devenyshe; patron, Edmund Mody, gent., for this
turn by a grant from Edward Burgh, kt., as of the right of Anne, his
wife. Sherborne castle, 10 June 1490.

274 Institution of John Alford, cl., to Rollestone ch., vac. by res.
of Nicholas Alyn; patron, Robert Eglesfeld, preceptor of Beverley,
in remotis agente locumtenens of brother John Kendale, prior of
the Hospital of St John of Jerusalem in England. Sherborne
castle, 27 June 1490.

275 (Fo. 32) Institution of Gervase Ketyll, chapl., to St Michael the
Archangel chapel, Norridge, vac. by death of Thomas Taillour;
patron, John Ley, _armiger_. Sherborne castle, 2 July 1490.

276 Institution of M. Walter Wilde BCnL to Sturminster Newton
vicarage, vac. by res. of M. Thomas Goldewegge; patrons, abbot and

conv. of Glastonbury. Sherborne castle, 29 July 1490.

277 Institution of Richard Scotte, chapl., to Wootton Rivers ch., vac.
by res. of Richard Bampton; patron, John Seymour, armiger.
Composition for the fruits of that church during vacancy, 40s.
Sherborne, 14 August 1490. (Marginal: xv)

278 Institution of M. Robert Wykys MA to Lacock vicarage, vac. by
death of (blank); patrons, abbess and conv. of Lacock.
Chardstock, 20 August 1490.

279 Collation to William Smyth, chapl., of Burstock vicarage, vac. by
death of Michael Bartholomei. 27 August 1490. (Marginal: Nihil)

280 (Fo. 32v) Collation to M. William Hewster MA of Cholsey
vicarage, vac. and falling to the bp.'s collation this turn by
lapse. Composition for fruits during vacancy (no details).
12 September 1490. (Marginal: pro fructibus vacationis)

281 Institution of John Cleve, chapl., to Whaddon ch., vac. by res.
of M. Robert Wykys; patron, Richard Beauchamp, kt. Ramsbury,
15 September 1490.

282 Institution of William Hymner, chapl., to Froxfield vicarage, vac.
by death of William Morgan; patrons, prior and conv. of Easton.
Ramsbury, 18 September 1490.

283 Institution of Robert Monke, chapl., to St Martin's ch.,
Shaftesbury, vac. by res. of Thomas Grivville; patrons, abbess
and conv. of Shaftesbury. 26 September 1490.

284 Collation to John Sharp, chapl., of Holy Trinity chantry,
Hungerford, vac. by death of John Harrison. Ind.: (blank).
Ramsbury, 30 September 1490. (Marginal: Nihil)

285 (Fo. 33) Institution of William Horseman, chapl., to Baverstock
ch., vac. by death of William Randolffe; patrons, abbess and conv.
of Wilton. Ramsbury, 4 October 1490. (Marginal: Nihil)

286 Institution of John Odlande, chapl., to Godmanston chantry in
St Thomas's ch., Salisbury, vac. by death of Edward Gamlyn;
patrons, Edward Chayne, dean, and chapter of Salisbury. Ind.:

dean and chapter of Salisbury. Ramsbury, 13 October 1490.

287 Institution of John Ferrour, chapl., to Chicklade ch., vac. by
     res. of John Odlande; patron, Margaret, daughter and heir of
     John Rigge, cousin and next heir of Joan Barre, late wife of
     John Barre, deceased. Ramsbury, 8 November 1490.

288 Collation to M. John de Giglis DC & CnL, in the person of
     M. Richard Bosquyet BCnL, his proctor, of a canonry and the
     prebend of Fordington and Writhlington in Salisbury cath., vac.
     by res. of M. John Forster. Ramsbury, 13 November 1490.
     (Marginal: Nihil)

289 Collation to M. Richard Newporte BCL of a canonry and the prebend
     of Major pars altaris in Salisbury cath., late that of M. John de
     Giglis. Ramsbury, 26 November 1490. (Marginal: Nihil)

290 (Fo. 33v) Institution of Robert Borde, chapl., to Winterborne
     Abbas ch., on an exchange of benefices with Edward Robert;
     patrons, abbot and conv. of Cerne; and institution of Edward
     Robert to Godmanstone ch., on the above exchange of benefices with
     Robert Borde; patrons, William Broune and Christina his wife.
     Ramsbury, 3 December 1490.

291 Commission, dated 10 September 1490, to M. John Westlay, commis-
     sary-general in the archdeaconry of Salisbury, to make inquisition
     into the right of patronage of Great Cheverell ch., vac. by death
     of John Maydeman, and the right of Christopher Tropnell to
     present Christopher Notte, chapl., and into the morals and
     holiness of the said presentee; certificate of the inquisition
     finding Christopher Tropnell to be true patron by reason of a
     charter or grant by Margaret, Lady Hungerford and Botreaux, late
     wife of Robert, late Lord Hungerford, kt., John Chayne and John
     Mervyn, armigeri, made to Thomas Tropnell, father of the said
     Christopher Tropnell, and to Robert Baynard, armigeri, John
     Ludlowe and John Hampton, the heirs and assigns of the said
     Thomas Tropnell; text of the said charter, dated 8 September
     1476, witnesses: Roger Tocotes and Raginald Stourton, kts.,
     William Ludlowe, Nicholas Halle, Richard Erle, and Robert Lygh,
     armigeri, Walter Mervyn, Thomas Southe, and many others; (Fo. 34)
     and institution of the said Christopher Notte to the said parish
     ch. Composition for fruits and revenues during vacancy (no
     details). 16 January 1491.

292 Institution of M. William Lane to Steeple Ashton vicarage, vac.
     by res. of M. Thomas Waget; patron, Walter Hungerford, kt., for

this turn by reason of a grant by the abbess and conv. of Romsey.
Pension to the resigned v., on petition by his proctor,
M. Antony Styleman, gent.: £10 p.a. for life. Ramsbury, 18
January 1491.

293 Institution of M. Laurence Cokkys DCnL to Fisherton Anger ch.,
vac. by death of John Martyn; patron, Roger Tocotes, kt., for
this turn by reason of a grant from Margery Hampden, widow, and
in widowhood heir and lady of Fisherton. Ramsbury, 18 January
1491. (Marginal: Nihil)

294 Institution of M. William Poole BCnL to Winterbourne Bassett ch.,
vac. by res. of M. Laurence Cokkys; patrons, prior and conv. of
Lewes. 18 January 1491.

295 (Fo. 34v) Institution of M. Richard Langcastre, cl., to
Blandford Forum vicarage, vac. by death of M. William Crampley;
patrons, prior and conv. of Christchurch, Twynham. Ramsbury,
22 January 1491.

296 Institution of John Huchenson, chapl., to Biddestone ch., vac.
by res. of Christopher Notte; patrons, prior and conv. of Monkton
Farleigh. 22 January 1491.

297 Institution of M. Henry Gile BCL to Godmanston chantry in
St Thomas's ch., Salisbury, vac. by death of Richard Beton;
patrons, dean and chapter of Salisbury. Ind.: dean and chapter
of Salisbury. 9 February 1491.

HIC EODEM DIE MUTATUR ANNUS TRANSLACIONIS DOMINI SEXTUS IN ANNUM
TRANSCLACIONIS SUE SEPTIMUM.

298 Institution of Richard Hancok, chapl., to Winterborne Farringdon
ch., vac. by death of John Thornicrofte; patron, William Martyn,
armiger. Sherborne castle, 17 March 1491.

299 Institution of M. Robert Shirborn, cl., in the person of James
(blank), literate, his proctor, to Childrey ch., vac. by death
of M. Thomas Chaundeler; patron, Henry Asshborn of the city of
London, for this turn by reason of a grant to him by Thomas
Kyngeston, armiger. Sherborne castle, 24 March 1491.

HIC MUTATUR ANNUS DOMINI MILLESIMUS CCCCus NONAGESIMUS IN ANNUM DOMINI

300 (Fo. 35) Collation to M. Richard Newport BCL of Mildenhall ch., vac. by res. of M. Henry Mompesson, on acceptance of another benefice with cure in Bath and Wells dioc., and falling to the bp.'s collation this turn by lapse. Composition for fruits (no details). Ramsbury, 7 April 1491. (Marginal: Nihil and Notatur)

301 Institution of William Brydde, chapl., in the person of Nicholas Longe, his proctor, to Bradford-on-Avon vicarage, vac. by res. of M. John Bostoke; patrons, abbess and conv. of Shaftesbury. Ind.: archd. of (Wiltshire). Ramsbury, 16 April 1491.

302 Institution of M. David Knollis BCnL to Melksham vicarage, vac. by death of John Curtays; patrons, dean and chapter of Salisbury. 20 April 1491.

303 Institution of M. Christopher Chatres MA, in the person of M. William Russell DCnL, to Bishops Cannings vicarage, vac. by death of M. Richard Baldry; patrons, dean and chapter of Salisbury. Ramsbury, 17 May 1491.

304 (Fo. 35v) Collation to M. William Jonys BCnL of St Peter's ch., Marlborough, vac. by death of M. Richard Toppe. Ind.: M. William Bower BCL. And because the said ch., was vacant from 25 March, composition for the fruits of that ch., for the following year for the sum (blank). Ramsbury, 17 May 1491.

305 Institution of Claudius Panavilioni, chapl., to Tarrant Rushton ch., vac. by res. of M. John Michaell; patrons, John Cheyne, kt., and Margaret his wife, lady of Rushton. Ramsbury, 24 May 1491.

306 Institution of Richard Swanne, chapl., to Chippenham chantry, vac. by death of William Estmonde, last chapl., or cantarist; patrons, prior and conv. of Monkton Farleigh. 24 May 1491.

307 Institution of Philip David, chapl., to St Sampson's vicarage, Cricklade, vac. by res. of M. William Jonys; patrons, dean and chapter of Salisbury. 26 May 1491.

308 Institution of Henry Skidmer, chapl., to Grittleton ch., vac. by death of William Gille; patrons, abbot and conv. of Glastonbury. 2 June 1491.

309 Institution of M. William Elyot, cl., in the person of William Lynton, his proctor, to the free chapel of St Stephen, Little Mayne, vac. by death of William Newburgh, last keeper; patron, John Newburgh, armiger. 7 June 1491.

310 (Fo. 36) Institution of Elisha (Elizeus) Dewhirst, chapl., to Basildon vicarage, vac. by res. of John Bawdwyn; patron, John Bayly, warden or keeper of Shottesbrooke Coll. London, 24 June 1491.

311 Institution of M. William Brewe, cl., to St Nicholas's ch., Abingdon, vac. by death of M. Richard Toppe; patrons, abbot and conv. of Abingdon. London, 29 June 1491.

312 Institution of William Brounsop, chapl., to Durweston ch., vac. by death of William Dounton; patrons, William Huddesfeld, kt., Thomas Husee senior, Thomas Neuborough, and Humfry Pokeswell, gents., for this turn by reason of a grant of one acre of land called 'Orchardeshurne' in Durweston with the advowson of the ch. there by Eleanor Ponyngys, countess of Northumberland. London, 6 July 1491.

313 Institution of M. Thomas Michell MA to Heddington ch., vac. by death of Walter Newman; patrons, prior and conv. of Monkton Farleigh. 20 July 1491.

314 Collation to Robert Gloos, a regular canon, dispensed by the Holy See to hold a benefice with cure, of Tidmarsh ch., vac. and falling to the bp.'s collation this turn by lapse. Shaftesbury, 25 August 1491.

315 (Fo. 36v) Institution of John Lynde, chapl., to Stapleford vicarage, vac. by res. of William Marshall; patrons, prior and conv. of Easton. Pension to resigned v.: £3 p.a. for life. Sherborne, 30 August 1491.

316 Institution of John Walter, chapl., to Compton Abbas ch., vac. by death of Philip Brevynt; patrons, abbess and conv. of Shaftesbury. And because the aforesaid ch., was vacant from 16 March last past until the day of institution, composition for the fruits and income in the meantime for the sum of 66s. 8d. Sherborne, 31 August 1491.

317 Institution of M. Edmund Hamden DTh, in the person of Richard

Holte, his proctor, to Sutton Courtenay ch., vac. by res. of
M. John Arundell; patrons, dean and canons and chapter of the
royal free chapel of St George in the castle, Windsor, as is clear
from an inquisition. Composition for fruits &c. during vacancy,
£20. Sherborne, 2 September 1491.

318 Institution of M. Adrian de Bardys BCL to Wroughton ch., vac. by
death of M. David Husband; patron, Peter (Courtenay), bp. of
Winchester. Sherborne, 5 September 1491.

319 (Fo. 37) Institution of William Yprus, chapl., to Iverne
Minster, vac. by res. of John Corbett; patrons, dean and canons
of the royal free chapel of St George in the castle, Windsor, on
nomination by the abbess and conv. of Shaftesbury. 28 September
1491.

320 Institution of M. Robert Burton MA to Sherston vicarage, vac. by
res. of Thomas Strobull; patrons, abbot and conv. of Tewkesbury.
Pension to resigned v.: £3. 19s. 8d. p.a. for life.

321 Collation to M. John Coldale DTh of Upwey ch., vac. by res. of
M. Richard Newporte. 5 October 1491.

322 (Fo. 37v) Institution of Lewis Davy, chapl., to Coleshill
vicarage, vac. by res. of John Bentley; patrons, r. and conv. of
Edington. Pension to resigned v.: £4 p.a. for life. Ramsbury,
6 October 1491.

323 Institution of M. William Lane BCnL to Buckland vicarage, vac. by
res. of M. John Coldale, with all rights which M. Adam Moreland,
sometime v., had therein; patrons, r. and conv. of Edington.
Ramsbury, 10 October 1491.

324 Collation to Brother William Hulle, r. of Edington, who has an
apostolic dispensation to retain in commendam with his said
rectory whatsoever ecclesiastical benefice, even having cure of
souls, as is customarily governed by secular clerks, of Poulshot
ch., vac. by res. of M. William Lane. Ind.: archd. of
(Salisbury). 12 October 1491.

325 Institution of Thomas Childe, chapl., to Milborne St Andrew
vicarage, vac. by res. of Richard Moore; patrons, Henry Sutton MD,
master or warden, and fellows of Vaux Coll., Salisbury. (Fo. 38)
Pension to said Richard More: £3. 6s. 8d. p.a. for life. London,

18 October 1491.

326 Institution of M. John Reynold BCL, in the person of M. Ralph
Hethcote BCnL, his proctor, to Beeford ch., York dioc., by
commission from Thomas (Rotherham), archbp. of York, on an
exchange of benefices with Edward Newland; patron for this turn,
Robert Eglesfeld, brother of the priory or Hospital of St John
of Jerusalem in England and in remotis agente commissary and
locumtenens of the prior of the Hospital of St John of Jerusalem;
and the institution of Edward Newland, in the person of M. George
Evers, notary public, his proctor, to Stour Provost ch., on an
exchange as above; patrons, provost and scholars of King's
Coll. Cambridge.   20 October 1491.

327 Institution of Richard Lloyde, chapl., to Steventon vicarage, vac.
by res. of William Milys; patrons, prior (sic) and conv. of
Westminster. London, 29 October 1491.

328 (Fo. 38v) Institution of M. Thomas Pope, canon of Salisbury, in
the person of William Mathewe, literate, his proctor, to Hawkchurch ch., vac. by death of M. John Lymbry; patrons, abbot and
conv. of Cerne. Sonning, 12 November 1491.

329 Institution of John de la Herne, chapl., to Woodaford ch., vac.
by res. of Thomas Chylde; patrons, abbot and conv. of Cerne.
Sonning, 24 November 1491.

330 Institution of Robert Richardson, chapl., to Milton Lilbourne
vicarage, vac. by death of John Chamber; patrons, abbot and conv.
of Cirencester. Ramsbury, 3 December 1491.

331 Institution of M. John Atwell MA (proxy clause erased) to
Blandford St Mary ch., vac. by res. of M. Thomas Dokelby;
patrons, prioress and conv. of Clerkenwell. Pension to resigned
r., at petition of the said (sic) M. John Wely, notary public,
his proctor: 6 marks p.a. for life. 11 December 1491.

332 (Fo. 39) Institution of John Smyth, chapl., to Compton vicarage,
vac. by death of John Smyth (sic); patrons, abbess and conv. of
Wherwell. 15 January 1492.

333 Collation to Ralph Langton, cl., of a canonry and the prebend of
Bitton in Salisbury cath., vac. by death of M. David Hopton.
23 January 1492.

334 Collation to M. William Russell DCnL of a canonry and the prebend
of Bedminster and Redclyffe in Salisbury cath., vac. by death of
M. William Chekke. 28 January 1492.

335 Collation to M. Richard Newporte BCL of a canonry and the prebend
of Wilsford and Woodford in Salisbury cath., vac. (Undated.)

336 Institution of Roger Pole, chapl., to Frilsham ch., vac. by death
of Thomas Gay; patron, William Nores, kt. Ramsbury, 31 January
1492.

337 (Fo.39v) Collation to M. William Cousyn, cl., of a canonry and
the prebend of Major pars altaris in Salisbury cath., vac. by
res. of M. Richard Newporte. London, 1 February 1491.

338 Institution of M. William Combe BCL to Puddletown vicarage, vac.
by death of John Turner; patrons, prior and conv. of Christchurch,
Twynham. London, 11 February 1492.

HIC MUTATUR ANNUS TRANSLACIONIS DOMINI SEPTIMUS IN ANNUM OCTAVUM.

339 Collation to M. James Stanley, cl., of a canonry and the prebend
of Yetminster Prima in Salisbury cath., vac. by res. of M. William
Smyth. London, 3 March 1492.

340 Institution of William Lyllyngton, chapl., to Studland ch., vac.
by res. of John Thrope; patrons, Thomas Husee senior and Elizabeth
his wife. 11 March 1492.

341 Institution of M. William Ketilton MA to St Peter's ch.,
Shaftesbury, vac. by res. of M. John Raynold; patrons, abbess
and conv. of Shaftesbury. Ramsbury, 13 March 1492.

342 (Fo. 40) Institution of M. John Barnard MA to Ashton Keynes
vicarage, vac. by death of Richard Cove; patrons, abbot and conv.
of Tewkesbury. Ramsbury, 15 March 1492.

343 Institution of John Kendale, chapl., to Berwick St Leonard ch.,
vac. by death of William Plubell; patrons, abbess and conv. of
Shaftesbury. Ramsbury, 19 March 1492.

344 Institution of William Carver, chapl., to St Mary's vicarage, Reading, vac. by death of William Budde; patrons, abbot and conv. of Reading. 19 March 1492.

345 Collation to Matthew Fox, chapl., of Wroughton vicarage, vac. by death of John Benger and falling to the bp.'s collation this turn by laspse. Ramsbury, 25 March 1492.

HIC MUTATUR ANNUS DOMINI DE ANNO Mo CCCCmo NONAGESIMO PRIMO IN ANNUM DOMINI MILLESIMUM CCCCmum NONAGESIMUM SECUNDUM.

346 (Fo. 40v) Institution of M. Nicholas Rowes BCnL to St Martin's ch., Wareham, vac. by res. of M. Henry Shane; patrons, prior and conv. of Sheen. Ramsbury, 27 March 1492.

347 Institution of George Twynyho, cl., to custody of the hospital of St John the Baptist, Shaftesbury, vac. by res. of M. William Ketilton, last keeper; patrons of that chapel (sic), abbess and conv. of Shaftesbury. Ramsbury, 11 April 1492.

(Marginal 'B' next to 347 and 'A' next to 348 corrects faulty chrono-logical order.)

348 Institution of M. Christopher Tennande MA to East Garston vicarage, vac. by death of M. Henry Sibbe; patrons, prioress and conv. of Amesbury. Ramsbury, 4 April 1492.

349 Institution of Thomas Walkar, chapl., to Wargrave vicarage, vac. by death of John Buste; patrons, abbot and conv. of Reading. Ramsbury, 26 April 1492.

350 Copy of a dispensation of Pope Innocent (VIII) to William Aylward, cl., Winchester dioc., who is below his twentieth year, (Fo. 41) that when he reaches his twentieth year he may receive and retain any benefice with cure or otherwise incom-patible even if a parish church &c. or a major or principal dignity &c., and to resign or exchange it &c., notwithstanding the defect of age. Rome, 17 November 1491. (Marginal, in later, probably 19th-century, hand: Dispensatio)

351 Institution of William Aylward, cl., to Puddletown vicarage, vac. by res. of M. William Combe; patrons, prior and conv. of Christ-church, Twynham; Aylward being twenty years and more, dispensed as above (350). Ramsbury, 28 April 1492.

352 (Fo. 41v) Institution of Richard Elsiner, chapl., to Woolhampton ch., vac. by death of John Newporte; patron, Brother John Kendale, prior of the Hospital of St John of Jerusalem in England. Wilton, 2 May 1491.

353 Institution of M. William Thorneburgh BCL to Cholderton ch., vac. by death of (blank); patron, Thomas Lovell, kt., lord of the manor or lordship of Cholderton. 17 May 1492.

354 Collation to John Ladde, chapl., of Sutton Benger vicarage, vac. by death of William Barry. Bradenstoke, 23 May 1492.

355 Institution of M. Robert Pevesey MA, in the person of John Weston, literate, his proctor, to Preshute vicarage, vac. by res. of Thomas Pykyn; patron, William Gyan, warden of the choristers in Salisbury cath., on nomination by the bp. Ind.: official of the peculiar of Marlborough. Ramsbury, 8 June 1492.

356 Institution of M. William Brewe MD to Milton ch., vac. by res. of M. John Stoykys; patrons, abbot and conv. of Abingdon. 14 June 1492.

357 (Fo. 42) Institution of David Jeffrey, chapl., to St Nicholas ch., Abingdon, vac. by res. of M. William Brewe; patrons abbot and conv. of Abingdon. 14 June 1492.

358 Institution of M. John Thour DCL to Trowbridge ch., vac. by res. of M. John Stokys; patron, King Henry, by reason of his duchy of Lancaster. 17 June 1492.

359 Institution of M. Thomas Martyn DCnL to North Moreton vicarage, vac. by res. of William Lever; patron, M. Oliver Kyng, by reason of his archdeaconry of Berkshire. 20 June 1492.

360 Institution of John Everard, chapl., to Clewer chantry, vac. by death of William Smyth; patron, William Brocas, armiger. London, 27 June 1492.

361 Institution of William Walle, chapl., to Rowde vicarage, vac. by res. of William Higgys; patrons, abbot and conv. of Stanley.

41

London, 30 June 1492.

362 (Fo. 42v) Collation to M. Andrew Patrikke MA of Easton Grey ch.,
vac. and falling to the bp.'s collation this turn by lapse.
2 August 1492.

363 Institution of Thomas Rydley, chapl., in the person of Geoffrey
Botell, his proctor, to Cholsey vicarage, vac. by death of
M. William Henster; patrons, abbot and conv. of Reading.
Sonning, 9 September 1492.

364 Institution of Thomas Harsenape, chapl., to Binfield ch., vac.
by death of William Moreland; patron, Lady Margaret, countess of
Richmond and Derby, for this turn by a grant from abbot and conv.
of Cirencester. (blank) September 1492.

365 Collation to M. John Gunthorp, cl., dean of Wells cath., of a
canonry and the prebend of Bitton in Salisbury cath., vac. by
death of M. Ralph Langton. Mand. for induction into his prebend:
bp. of Worcester. 4 October 1492.

366 Institution of Nicholas Staysett, chapl., to a moiety of
Godmanston chantry in St Thomas' ch., Salisbury, at the altar of
St Bartholomew the Apostle in the south part of the ch., vac. by
death of Henry Gyle; patrons, dean and chapter of Salisbury. Ind.:
dean and chapter of Salisbury. 10 October 1492.

367 (Fo. 43) Institution of William Dade, chapl., to Owermoigne ch.,
vac. by res. of M. Robert Brereton; patron, John Brereton,
armiger, by right and title of Katherine, lady of Owermoigne,
his consort. Salisbury, 11 October 1492.

368 Institution of Geoffrey Fremott, chapl., to Fifehead Neville ch.,
vac. by res. of John Belayne; patron, Thomas Leyett, gent. 24
October 1492.

369 Institution of William Vowell, chapl., to Langton Matravers ch.,
vac. by res. of M. John Thwaites; patron, Thomas (fitz Alan),
earl of Arundel. 30 November 1492.

370 Institution of William Horsley, chapl., to Alton ch., vac. by
res. of M. Robert Brereton; patrons, William Stourton, Lord
Stourton, kt. 2 December 1492.

42

371 Institution of Stephen Frythay to (name of benefice omitted in text but supplied in margin) the chantry of St Michael de Mowndes, Bridport, vac. by death of Richard Harty; patron, William Wykys, r. of Bridport. 11 December 1492.

372 (Fo. 43v) Institution of William Parkar BCnL, in the person of M. Thomas Hare, his proctor, to Appleton ch., vac. by death of M. John Richard Pulley; patron, John Denton of Fyfield, _armiger_. 21 December 1492.

373 Collation to M. Ralph Hethcote BCnL of a canonry and the prebend of Hurstbourne and Burbage in Salisbury cath., vac. by death of M. John Tailour. Mand. for induction in his prebend: keeper of spiritualities of bishopric of Winchester _sede vacante_. Eltham, 30 December 1492.

374 Collation to M. Richard Newporte BCL of a canonry and the prebend of Faringdon in Salisbury cath., vac. 31 December 1492.

375 Collation to M. Richard Lichfeld DC & CnL of a canonry and the prebend of Wilsford and Woodford, late M. Richard Newporte's. 1 January 1493.

376 Institution of Nicholas Fox, chapl., to Sopworth ch., vac. by res. of Thomas Pacye _alias_ Strobull; patrons, prior and conv. of Monkton Farleigh. 11 January 1493.

377 (Fo. 44) Institution of M. John Lychefeld DCL, in the person of John West, literate, his proctor, to Brinkworth ch., vac. by death of M. Richard Machon; patrons, abbot and conv. of Malmesbury. London, 12 January 1493.

378 Collation to M. Stephen Bereworth MD of the archdeaconry of Berkshire, vac. by res. of M. Oliver Kyng. Mand. for installation to dean and chapter of Salisbury. 15 January 1493.

379 Collation to David Jonys, chapl., of Sutton Benger vicarage, vac. 26 January 1493.

380 Institution of M. Edward ap David to East Hagbourne vicarage, vac. by death of John Pendeley; patrons, abbot and conv. of Cirencester. Ind.: archd. of Dorset (_rectius_ Berkshire). 28 January 1493.

381 Institution of Roger Bekynsale, chapl., to Bower Chalke vicarage, vac. by death of Robert Barker; patrons, provost and scholars of King's Coll., Cambridge. 6 February 1493.

HIC MUTATUR ANNUS TRANSLACIONIS DOMINI OCTAVUS IN ANNUM TRANSLACIONIS SUE NONUM NONO DIE VIDELICET MENSIS FEBRUARII PREDICTAE.

382 (Fo. 44v) Collation to M. James Stanlegh, cl., in the person of M. John Crosse, his proctor, of a canonry and the prebend of Beminster Prima in Salisbury cath., vac. 14 February 1493.

383 Collation to Richard Bray, cl., of a canonry and the prebend of Yetminster Prima in Salisbury cath., vac. by res. of M. James Stanley. 15 February 1493.

384 Institution of Richard Waryn, chapl., to All Cannings ch., vac. by death of Richard Henstoke; patrons, abbess and conv. of Nunnaminster, Winchester. London, 16 February 1493.

385 Institution of Robert Gawler, chap., to Winterborne Zelston ch., vac. by res. of M. John Doget; patron, Nicholas Grenehall, armiger, by reason of the title and jointure to Joan, his wife, by John Beamount, sometime her husband, for the term of her life. 21 February 1493.

386 Institution of Henry Garbrandi, chap., to Norton vicarage, vac. by res. of Thomas Okey; patrons, abbot and conv. of Malmesbury. 23 February 1493.

387 (Fo. 45) Institution of Richard Harris, chapl., to West Knighton ch., vac. by death of Thomas Arundell; patrons, Brother John Kendall, prior of the Hospital of St John of Jerusalem in England. 27 February 1493.

388 Collation to M. Edward Hawtre of a canonry and the prebend of Preston in Salisbury cath., vac. by res. of Thomas Key, proctor for Simon Harcourt, cl. Mand. adm.: dean and his locumtenens and chapter of Salisbury. 1 March 1493.

389 Institution of Thomas Orums, chapl., to Cranborne vicarage, vac. by death of Thomas Shirwode; patrons, abbot and conv. of Tewkesbury. 2 March 1493.

390 Institution of John Crokeshank, chapl., to Alvediston vicarage, vac. by res. of Roger Bekensale; patrons, provost and scholars of King's Coll., Cambridge. Ramsbury, 6 March 1493.

391 Institution of M. John Husee MA to Corscombe ch., vac. by death of William Cassy; patrons, abbot and conv. of Sherborne. Ind. of M. John or his proctor. Ramsbury, 7 March 1493.

392 (Fo. 45v) Institution of M. Thomas Hede BCL to Colerne vicarage, vac. by death of M. John Frynde; patron, Geoffrey Simeon, r. of Colerne. Ramsbury, 7 March 1493.

393 Institution of M. Robert Lathes MA to Sparsholt vicarage, vac. by death of Thomas Smythson; patrons, provost and scholars of the Queen's Hall, Oxford. Ramsbury, 20 March 1493.

HIC VIDELICET VICESIMO QUINTO DIE MENSIS MARCII MUTATUR ANNUS DOMINI MILLESIMUS CCCC NONAGESIMUS SECUNDUS IN ANNUM DOMINI MILLESIMUM CCCCmum NONAGESIMUM TERCIUM.

394 Institution of M. Brian Esthorp MA to South Newton vicarage, vac. by res. of Robert Wulff; patrons, abbess and conv. of Wilton. 25 March 1493.

395 Institution of Christopher Harryngton, chapl., to Manston ch., vac. by res. of M. Robert Farmer BCnL; patron, John Welle, armiger, of Manston. Ramsbury, 26 March 1493.

396 (Fo. 46) Collation to Henry Wynfeld, chapl., of St Andrew's ch., Wilton, vac. and falling to the bp.'s collation this turn by lapse. Ramsbury, 27 March 1493.

397 Collation to Robert Husee (full name underlined in ms.), cl., in the person of M. John Huse, his proctor, of a canonry and the prebend of Lyme and Halstock in Salisbury cath., vac. by death of M. Richard Hawarde. Ramsbury, 27 March 1493.

398 Institution of Vincent Veers, chapl., to Hazelbury Bryan ch., vac. by death of M. Richard Heyward; patron, Robert Spencer, kt., by reason of the jointure of lady (blank), sometime countess of Wiltshire, his consort, to her made by (blank) her husband. Ramsbury, 3 April 1493.

(Eleanor, countess of Wiltshire, widow of James Butler, earl of

Ormond and of Wiltshire, who was executed c. 1 May 1461, married apparently in or before 1470 Sir Robert Spencer of Spencercombe, Devon (Complete Peerage, rev. edn., Vol. X (1945), p.129) The manor of Hazelbury Bryan inter alia with advowsons &c. was the subject of many royal grants after the earl's forfeiture: to William Neville, earl of Kent (C.P.R., 1461-7, p.225), and after his death without heirs to George, duke of Clarence (ibid., pp.226-7, 454-5; C.P.R., 1467-77, pp.457-8, 557; cf. pp.517-8). After the death of Clarence, the countess of Wiltshire was successful in recovering many of the manors and other properties which had constituted her jointure, e.g., Toller Porcorum and Punckowle in 1478 (C.P.R., 1476-85, p.106), and Woodsford in 1482 (ibid., p.306), but she does not seem to have recovered Hazelbury Bryan until 1489 (Calendar of Inquisitions Post Mortem, Second Series, Vol. II, no. 524, pp.327-8; Calendar of Close Rolls, 1485-1500, pp.111-2; cf. 114-6.)

399 Institution of Thomas Gielles, chapl., to Winterborn Monkton ch., vac. by death of John Huwit; patron, Eleanor Twynnyho, widow. Ramsbury, 11 April 1493.

400 Collation to M. Ralph Hethcote BCnL of Wroughton ch., vac. by res. of M. Adrian de Bardys and in the bp.'s collation by reason of his custody of the temporalities of the bishopric of Winchester granted to him sede vacante by (Fo. 46v) King Henry. Ramsbury, 17 April 1493.

401 (Added at the foot of fo. 46, intruding upon 400) Collation to Ralph Bull, cl., of Whelpley free chapel, vac. and falling to the bp.'s collation this turn by lapse. 1 April 1493.

402 Collation to M. Ralph Hethcote BCnL of a canonry and the prebend of Ramsbury in Salisbury cath., vac. by res. of M. Adrian de Bardys. Ramsbury, 17 April 1493.

403 Collation to M. Adrian de Bardys BCL of a canonry and the prebend of Hurstbourne and Burbage in Salisbury cath., vac. by res. of M. Ralph Hethcote. 17 April 1493.

404 (This entry in a different hand.) Collation to David Jonys, cl., BA, of the priory or hospital of St John the Baptist, Cricklade, vac. by res. of Thomas Gogh. Ramsbury, 27 April 1493.

405 (Fo. 47) Institution of M. James Dixen MA to Denchworth vicarage, vac. by res. of Thomas Clerk; patrons, abbot and conv.

of Bruern.   28 April 1493.

406 Collation to M. Henry Carnebull, cl., of a canonry and the prebend
of Yatesbury in Salisbury cath., vac. by death of M. Leonard Say.
Ramsbury, 29 April 1493.

407 Institution of William Cotton, chapl., to Asserton free chapel,
vac. by death of M. Richard Burlech, last keeper or chapl.;
patron, Robert Willoughby, lord of Brook, for this turn by
reason of a grant by Hugh Beaumont, _armiger_.   9 May 1493.

408 Institution of Alexander Hody BA to Great Wishford ch., vac. by
death of M. Richard Burlegh; patron, Robert Brent, _armiger_.
11 May 1493.

409 (Fo. 47v)   Institution of M. John Roper BTh ('professor' in
brackets and 'bachelor' written after in ms.) to Ashbury vicarage,
vac. by death of William Godhyn; patrons, president and scholars
of Magdalen Coll., Oxford.   30 May 1493.

410 Collation to William Hulvyrdale, chapl., of Winterborne St
Martin vicarage, vac. by death of Denis Welley.   11 June 1493.

411 (Fos. 47v-48v)   Index to the above institutions, alphabetical by
place.

(The second part of the register has its own foliation, which will be
followed here, with the foliation of the first forty-eight folios —
had it been continued — indicated after.)

412 (fo. 1/49) Account of the election, by royal licence, of a
successor to Alice Comaland, abbess of Wilton, who died 3
September 1485. After the nuns were warned the previous day to
be present, on 24 September 1485, when the mass of the Holy
Spirit had been sung at the high altar, and immediately after the
ringing of the great bell as is customary at the hour of the
chapter, (there assembled) Elizabeth Elwell, prioress, Alice
Hayne, Margaret Hyll, Joan Yonge, Joan Trent, Elizabeth White,
Margaret Newman, Joan Bolney, Elizabeth Hawsok, Cristin
Grattelyng, Agnes Pewsay, Joan Pole, Isabel Trent, Cecily
Wiloughby, professed nuns, Elizabeth Husay, Isabel Jurdan,
Alice Godelonde, Joan Gilbert, Anastasia Holme, Joan Trovy,
Alice Husey, Alice Rumsay, Joan Bothe, Margaret Barowe, Agnes
Grymelby, Elizabeth Pewsay, Elizabeth Sarnyngton, Eleanor
Rumsay, Isabel Wymondeswolde, Joan Strode, fellow nuns and
sisters awaiting profession (commoneales et consorores tacite
professe) and having a voice in the election according to the
custom of the monastery; no one was absent. The word of God was
preached and the Veni Creator Spiritus sung. All those who had
no say in the election withdrew from the chapter house, except
M. Laurence Cokkys DCnL, the bishop's chancellor, director of
the election, M. Bartholomew Underwod BCL, notary public,
recorder (actorum scriba) and registrar, Nicholas Gotfrith BC &
CnL, and Alexander Cater BC & CnL, witnesses without votes in the
election. (Fo. 1v/49v) The royal licence was exhibited; then
M. Laurence described the form and manner of the election to the
electors who proceeded to choose Cecily Wiloughby, nun, to be
abbess of Wilton. Then they sang the Te Deum Laudamus as they
progressed to the choir, all the bells were rung, and Cecily was
placed before the high altar. When the hymn was finished and the
prayers for the elect poured out, the election was published to
the clergy and people in the vulgar tongue by M. Laurence Cokkys.
The nuns, having returned to the chapter house, constituted
Margaret Hill, Joan Yonge, and Joan Trent their proctors to
require the assent of the abbess-elect to her election, which she
gave. (F. 2/50) Then the election decree was drawn up and
sealed and presented by Stephan Semar, one of their proctors, to
the bp. who was then at Bisham. He commissioned M. Laurence
Cokkys DCnL, who first publicly read his commission in the
parish church of St Mary in 'Bridstret', Wilton, and, when the
election decree was presented by M. Alexander Cator, proctor of
the prioress and convent of Wilton, confirmed the election of
Cecily Willoughby, nun, to be abbess of St Mary and St Edith,
Wilton. (Fo. 2v/50v) Subsequently the elect received her
blessing from William, (Westkarre), bp. of Sidon (1), acting on

1   HBC, p.268. This entry adds new information about his career.

a commission from the bp., at the high altar in that church; and
she made her profession of obedience. (1)

413 Petition for the restitution of the temporalities of Wilton Abbey
to Cecily W(illoughby) (Fo. 3/51) whose election has been
confirmed. (Undated) (2)

414 Mandate for installation (of Cecily Willoughby) to the archdeacon of Salisbury or his official. (Undated)

415 Mandate for obedience directed to the prioress and convent of
Wilton. (Fo. 3v/51v) (Undated)

416 Mandate to M. Laurence Cokkys DCnL, canon and prebendary of
Salisbury, to examine the election by way of the holy spirit (per
viam spiritus sancti) of Cecily W(illoughby), nun of St Mary and
St Edith, Wilton, as abbess of that place, and to confirm the
election, if lawful. 6 Oct. 1485.

417 Commission to W(illiam Westkarre), bp. of Sidon (Cidonensi) to
confer episcopal blessing, as above. (Undated)

418 Commission to M. William Nessingwike, canon residentiary of
Salisbury, M. Richard Kelsay, subdean of Salisbury, and
M. Nicholas Gotfryth BCnL, bp.'s commissary in the archdeaconries
of Salisbury and Dorset, to deliver criminous clerks from secular
prisons (Fo. 4/52) in the city of Salisbury and elsewhere in
Wiltshire. (Undated)

419 (Confession and abjuration by Philip Browne of Hinton Waldrist of
consorting with one George Carpenter of Woodstock and learning
his heresies, and of teaching the same to a woman Jone Farlingham
and also to John Sterengare, both of Hinton Waldrist; namely that
the body and blood of Christ is not present in the sacrament of
the altar, an opinion he has held for forty years; twelve years
ago when hired to reap corn speaking the same heresy and teaching

1 Signification of the election, to the crown, 26 September 1485,
P.R.O., C82/2/1. Royal assent, 1 October 1485, C82/3/3, delated
4 October, C.P.R. 1485-94, p.12.

2 Original, 10 October 1485, P.R.O., C82/2/92. Restitution of
temporalities, 16 October, C82/3/93, delated 17 October, C.P.R.
1485-94, p.19.

the Ten Commandments before divers persons; from which heresy by
the exhortation of his curate and of M. Richard Birde, parson of
Northmoor, and most specially by the sermon of John, abbot of
Abingdon, he refrained for one half-year before resorting
thereto. English.)

In the name of the holy trinite fader son and holygoste his
blissid moder & all the holy compeny of hevyn. I Phillip Browne
of Hynton in the diocise of Sar' gretly notid defamyd detect
and to you reverend fader in god thomas by goddis sufferance
bisshoppe of Sar' my jugge and ordinary denowncid for an untrewe
belevyng man, And also that I shulde holde afferme teche and
defende oppynli & prively heresis errors singler oppinions and
false doctrines contrary to the commyn doctrine of oure moder
holichurch and with subtilites evil soundyng & deceyveable to the
eres of trewe simpyll understonding cristen pepyll wiche be to me
nowe by your auctorite proceding of office promotid judicially
objectid.

Firste that I have wetingly and wilfulli drawen familierly &
acompenyde me with one callid george Carpenter of Wodestok the
which hathe holden & affermyd heresies errors opinyons & doctrinys
forbedyn & contrary to the commyn doctrine of holy scripture and
determynacion of holy church, And that I have harde of hym
leevyd and belevyd the same heresies errors oppinyons and false
doctrines, And in like wise taughte & affermyd the same not only
to a woman callid Jone Farlingham of hinton but also to John
Sterengare of the same.

Item that in the sacramente of the auter in forme of brede is not
very god cristis flesshe & his blode but is only corruptible
brede, for he is in (Fo. 4v/52v) hevyn sitting on the right said
of his fader And may not at onys be there in hevyn & here in
erthe in the sacrament of the auter but there above abiding to
the day of dome, in the wiche error and dampnabill opinyon I have
contynued the space xl yere, And xij yere gone I was hirid to repe
Corne and there I seid afore diverse persones I cowde shew the
way in to hevyn & declarid the x commaundementys and aftir that
seid thes wordis: what make thes false prestis that sey them to
make the bodi of criste the which is not in there power seying
that it is as good and as profitable to ete brede of rye at
estir as that that is mynisterd to poure pepull and consecrate by
prestys.

Also where as by the exhortacion of diverse men as wele by my
curate of hinton as by master Richarde Birde parson of more and
most specially by the predicacion of the worshipfull fader John
the Abbot of Abendon in the churche of Stanlake of Lincoln dioc'
prevyng by diverse argumentys & resons myn oppynions to be false
& contrary to the faythe, I was for the tyme of half yere next
folouyng that sermon made in good beleve of the sacrament of the
Auter, but that halfe yere paste I resortid & returnyd to myn olde

errors and heresies ageyne belevyng as I did before.

Thes articles and every of thayme afore rehersid and to me by you
judicially objecte I opinly knowledge my selfe and confesse of my
free wyll to have helde lernyd & belevyd and so have taughte and
affermyd to oder wiche all and every of theyme I understonde and
beleve heresies and contrary to the commyn doctrine and determynacion' of the universal churche of criste and confesse me here
to have be an heretike lerner & techer of heresies errors
oppinions and false doctrines contrary to the cristen fayth; And
for as myche as it be so that the lawes of the churche of criste
and holy canons of Sayntys bene grounded in mercy and god will
not the dethe of a synner but that he be convertid & lyfe, And
also the churche closith not her lappe to hym that will retorne,
I therefore willing to be partener of this forsaide mercy forsake
and renownce all thes articles afore rehersid and confesse theym
to be heresies errors & prohibit doctrine, And now contrite &
fully repentyng theyme all and everich' of theyme (Fo. 5/53)
Judicially and solemly them forsake abjure & wilfully renownce
for ever more, and not onely theyme but all other heresies
errors and dampnable doctrines contrary to the determynacion' of
the universall churche of criste. Also that shall never here
after be to any siche persones or person favorer' counceler
mauntener' or of any siche prevely or openly but if I knowe any
siche here after I shall denownce and disclose theyme to you
Reverende fader in god youre successors or officers of the same
or else to siche persones of the churche as hathe jurisdiccion on
the persones so fawty so helpe god and thes holy evangelis, sub-
mittyng me openly not coacte but of my free will to the payne
vigour and sharpeness of the lawe that a man relapsid owght to
suffre in sich case, if I ever do or holde contrary to this my
present abjuracion in parte or the hole parte of, In wittenesse
whereof I subscribe with myne one hande makyng a crosse, And
require all cristen men in general here present to recorde and
wittenesse ayenste me and this my presente confession and
abjuracion' if I from this day forward offende or do contrary to
the same and ye masters here present.

420 Mandate to the vicars of St Helen Abingdon and Hinton Waldrist,
and to the rector of Newbury, or in their absence their curates,
to receive Philip Brown of Hinton Waldrist for penance, viz. on
one day when the public market is held in those places, that the
greater part of the people may be present, the penitent, bare-
headed and for the rest naked except for a shirt and drawers, with
a bundle of faggots on his back and a stick held upright in
either hand, with an apparitor going before him and the curate of
the place wearing a surplice and carrying a rod to point to the
penitent following after, immediately after a circuit of the
market, and in any public place there, having first read his
abjuration, a copy of which was enclosed, was to be disciplined.
And on one (Fo. 5v/53v) Sunday in Lent, after such penance as
could be performed in a public place, he was to walk penitently
in the procession in those same places before the cross, and

after the procession he was to declare his abjuration in the usual way, so that by this example the other subjects of the dioc. might abhor the crime and fear terribly lest they offend in the same way. Execution of the penance was to be certified to the bp. 27 February 1485.

421 (Fos. 5v/53v-6v/54v) Mandate to the arch. of Dorset or his official for a visitation of his archdeaconry. 23 November 1485.

422 Memorandum of similar mandated to the archds. of Salisbury, Wiltshire and Berkshire; the bp. visited all monasteries in person save Kington St Michael and Broomhall, which afterwards were visited by his commissary; and he visited the deaneries of the archdeaconries for the most part by his commissary by the authority of his commission, the tenor of which follows:

423 (Fos. 6v/54v-7/55) Commission to M. Laurence Cokkys DCnL, canon and prebendary of Salisbury, of full powers of visitation. (Undated)

424 Commission to M. Nicholas Gotfrith BC & CnL, to punish offenders of both sexes detected to the bp. during his recent visitation of the archdeaconries of Salisbury and Dorset, and to levy fines ('multas') imposed by him on contumacious clerks, and to compel non-resident clergy to reside. (Undated)

425 Memorandum of a like commission to M. William Jonis BCnL, commissary-general and sequestrator in the archdeaconries of Wiltshire and Berkshire, for those archdeaconries.

426 (Fos. 7v/55v) Letter for charitable subsidy in favour of John Mortemer of 'Harlyng', who had taken the cross. Salisbury, the palace, 19 April (1486?).

427 (Account of the election of M. Edward Cheyne as Dean of Salisbury.) Since the deanery of Salisbury was vacant by the death of M. John Davyson, who died on 12 October 1485, we, John Doget, chancellor of Salisbury cathedral and president of the chapter, and the chapter, viz. Richard Whitby, treasurer, prebendary of Calne, W(illiam) Nessingwik, prebendary of Faringdon, W. (sic) Gyan, prebendary of Torleton, John Bostoke, prebendary of Minor pars altaris, and Henry Sutton, prebendary of Ratfyn, canons residentiary, met in the chapter house on 19 January 1486, to fix (Fo. 8/56) Monday, 3 April 1486, for the election of a new

dean, for the holding of which election all the absent canons and
prebendaries who had a right and voice in the election were to be
cited according to their prebendal stalls by William Stokfissh and
John Belch, vicars choral of Salisbury. On that day, when the
mass of the Holy Spirit had been solemnly celebrated at the high
altar in the choir of Salisbury cath., immediately after the
ringing of the great bell as is customary for holding a chapter,
we, John Doget, president of the chapter, Richard Whitby,
treasurer, William Ness(ingwik) Gian, John Bostoke, and
Henry Sutton, canons residentiary, David Hopton, prebendary of
Beminster Prima, Peter Rampsham, abbot and prebendary of Sherborne
who appeared by the grace of the chapter and by no other means,
Laurence Cokkys, prebendary of Netheravon, Ralph Hethecottys,
prebendary of Bitton, Richard Salter, prebendary of Netherbury in
Terra, and Robert Day, prebendary of Axford, canons in priest's
orders, were present. When the word of God had been propounded
by M. Henry Sutton MD, and the hymn Veni Creator Spiritus sung,
(Fo. 8v/56v) and the grace of the same Spirit invoked, then the
constitution of the general council Quia propter was read by
M. Laurence Cokkys, and the forms contained in that constitution
were set forth to us by him. Immediately next William Stokfisshe
and John Belche, who had been charged to cite each of our absent
brethren, certified to us that they had cited everyone. Then
everyone who had no voice in the election withdrew from the
chapter house; M. Laurence Cokkys was chosen to direct the
election, and M. Bartholomew Underwod BCL, notary public, chosen
as recorder (actorum scriba) and registrar, and M. William
Branch, subdean of Salisbury, and M. Nicholas Gotfrith BC & CnL,
as witnesses with no right or voice in the election. Then, the
servant of the doorkeeper of the close of Salisbury, our apparitor,
having summoned all the absent canons who had a right or voice in
the election, by right or custom, the following proxies were
recorded: Thomas, bp. of Salisbury and prebendary of Potterne and
Lavyngton, William Bolton of Major pars alteris, and John Taylour
of Hurstbourne and Burbage, by proctor M. Laurence Cokkys; Robert
Morton of Horton and Thomas Davy of Blewbury by Henry Sutton of
Ratfyn; Robert Bothe of Charminster and Bere by John Doget,
chancellor of Salisbury; John Vernham of Grantham Australis and
Nicholas Goldewell of Shipton by William Gyan of Torleton; John
Pese of Grimston, Henry Sharpe of Woodford, Malcolm Cosyn of
Netherbury in Ecclesia, John Gunthorpe of Alton Borealis, John
Seymor of Yatesbury, and John Arundell of Durnford, by William
Nessingwik of Farringdon; Leonard Say of Yattemyster (sic,
rectius Yatesbury), Edward Chayne of Beminster Secunda, Richard
Haywarde of Lyme and Halstock, Stephan Bereworthe of Highworth,
Adrian de Bardys of Ramsbury, Richard Fox of Grantham Borialis,
Edmund Chadderton (Fo. 9/57) of Stratton, Geoffrey Elys of Coombe
and Harnham, and William Smyth of Yetminster Prima, by Richard
Whitby, treasurer of Salisbury, prebendary of Calne; John
Corringdon of Alton Borealis, William Eliott of Bishopstone, and
Christopher Hursewik of Bedwyn, by M. Ralph Hethecottys of Bitton;
George Dawne of Ruscombe Southbury by John Bostoke of Minor pars

altaris; all of which proxies were examined and certified by a
delegation consisting of M. Laurence Cokkys DCnL, M. Richard
Salter DCnL, and M. William Ness(ingwik) BCnL. The following
canons and prebendaries neither appeared nor were represented
by proxy: Richard Burlay of Warminster, Thomas Austell of
Teinton Regis, Maurice ap Davyd of Stratford, Thomas Hoton of
Slape, Christopher Baynebrig of Chardstock, and George Harecowrte
of Preston, whom we had publicly called at the door of our
chapter house by the servant of the doorkeeper of the close of
Salisbury, and, they still not appearing, were declared
contumacious; wherefore M. Henry Sutton, on behalf of and with
the express mandate of the whole chapter, drew up a monition or
protestation. (Fo. 9v/57v) When only the electors were present
(save only the notary & witnesses), we discussed diligently among
ourselves the manner for proceeding in the election, and it
pleased us to proceed by ballot; then, after a further discussion
about how the ballot ought to be taken, we appointed as
scrutineers M. John Doget DCnL, M. Laurence Cokkys DCnL, and
M. William Nessingwik BCnL, in priest's orders. When the votes
had been cast, M. John Doget announced the result: "In the name
of God, Amen. The brothers and canons, thirty-nine canons and
prebendaries, of the cath. church of Salisbury, personally and
by proxies, on the 3 April 1486, gathered in the chapter house
for the purpose of electing a new dean, cast thirty-eight votes
for M. Edward Cheyne, our brother, wherefore he ought to be
elected"; and (on the motion of) first Thomas, bp. of Salisbury
and prebendary, by his proctor, and divers others, viz. the
archdeacon of Exeter (sic), canon and prebendary, and others,
doctors (Fo. 10/58) of decrees, he was elected; wherefore M.
John, on behalf of and in the name of the chapter, drew up the
following declaration: "In the name of God, Amen. (&c.,
rehearsing the account of the election.) (Fo. 10v/58v) And
then singing the psalm (sic) Te Deum Laudamus in a joyful voice
with the whole choir, the electors processed to the high altar.
After the 'psalm' was finished, the election was published, as is
customary, to a great multitude of clergy and people by M.
Laurence Cokkys DCnL. We then returned to the chapter house and
appointed M. Henry Sutton to be the chapter's special proctor to
signify the election result to the elect and to obtain his
consent thereto. which he did on 6 April 1486 in the Carmelite
convent in Fleet Street near the city of London, in the presence
of M. Nicholas Trappe, clerk of the diocese of Bath and Wells,
notary public, and other witnesses, (Fo. 11/59) at about 4.00
p.m.; and after deliberating overnight the elect gave his consent
about 11.00 (a.m.) the next day (7 April 1486), in the form that
follows: "In the name of the Holy and Undivided Trinity, Father,
Son and Most High Spirit, I Edward Cheyne &c".

428 Commission to William Godeyere, sworn apparitor, to cite before
the bp. or his commissary or commissaries in Salisbury cath., on
Thursday, 20 April (1486) all who wish to object in any way to

the above election before it is confirmed, and to certify to the bp. what he has done on the same date. 17 April (1486).

429 On that day, 20 April (1486), there appeared before the bp. in his consistory in Salisbury cath., in the presence of the masters, the chancellor, treasurer, and other canons residentiary named in the aforesaid decree, M. Laurence Cokkys DCnL, the bp.'s chancellor, proctor for the chapter of Salisbury, who presented to the bp. the decree of Cheyne's election and begged confirmation thereof; the bp. fully examined the election decree, and, there being no opposition, confirmed Cheyne, in the person of Richard Whitby, his proctor, (Fo. 12/60) in the form following:

430 Confirmation of the above election of Cheyne. Note of the oath of canonical obedience to the bp. taken by the dean's proctor Richard Whitby; and mandate for installation to the <u>locumtenens</u> and chapter of Salisbury. (Undated)
(See also, <u>Statuta et Consuetudines Ecclesiae Cathedralis Beatae Mariae Virginis Sarisberiensis</u>, ed., C. Wordsworth and D. Macleane (London, 1915), esp. p.5.)

431 (Fo. 12v/60v) To the bp. or his commissary or commissaries from John London, subprior, and the conv. of Reading abbey. The abbacy of Reading became vacant by the death of John Thorne, the last abbot, on 2 July 1486, and licence to elect (1) has been obtained from the king. We, John Thorne (<u>sic</u>), prior of Reading, John Bristowe, Thomas Winchilsay, John London, John Leomyster, Thomas Hendelay, Richard Wokingham, John Blebury, John Hacborn', Nicholas Shinfelde, William Felde, Thomas Hill, William Wargrave, Roger Herford, Richard Leomister, Henry Rading, John Hyde, John Sunnyng, (Fo. 13/61) and John Benet, priests, John Glastenbury, John Clyfton, brothers, all professed monks, met in the chapter house on the Monday next before the feast of St Margaret, viz. 17 July 1486, and fixed as the day for the election of a new abbot the Friday next after the feast of St Margaret, viz. 21 July 1486, each and every monk to be present, save Thomas Hendelay, keeper or subprior of Leominster who by the grace of the chapter and none other lives with us; no one was to be absent except John Grace, our brother, who because of infirmity as well as age and bodily debility could not be present, whom we had notified of this matter in the infirmary by John Stokton, third prior. On that day, 21 July 1486, when the mass of the Holy Spirit had been sung in the choir at the high altar, and immediately after the ringing of the bell as is usual at the hour of the chapter, we, John Thorne, prior, Robert Rading, William Salisbury, William Gloucestre, Clement Bray, John Stokton, John Chivelay, Thomas Appulby, Edmund Rading, John Bristow, Thomas Winchilsay, John Leomister, Henry Reding, Thomas Hendelay, Richard Wokyngham, John Blebury, John Hakeborne, Nicholas

1   10 July 1486; see P.R.O., C82/12/21, and <u>C.P.R.</u>, 1485–1494, p.117.

Shinfeld, William Feld, Thomas Hill, William Wargrave, Roger
Harforde, Richard Leomister, John Hyde, John Sunnyng, John
Benet, John Glastonbury, John Rading, and John Clifton,
professed monks (Fo. 13v/61v) who had a right and voice in the
election, entered the said chapter house; only John Grace was
absent. After the word of God was propounded with the hymn
Veni Creator Spiritus sung and that God's Grace invoked, and
after everyone with no right or voice in the election had
withdrawn, M. Laurence Cokkys DCnL, bp.'s chancellor, as
director of the election, Bartholomew Underwod BCL, notary
public, as recorder (actorum scriba) and registrar, and M. Ralph
Hethcottys BC & CnL, and M. Richard Kelsay BC & CnL, as
witnesses - with no voting rights - were received, selected,
and deputised. First there was exhibited among us the certificate
or decree under our common seal for the fixing of the day of the
election, and then there was exhibited the king's licence, and
this was publicly read by M. Laurence. There were called out the
names of all those who had a right and voice in this election;
they were all present in the chapter house save the exempt John
Grace. John Thorne, prior, on behalf of, and with the special
mandate of, the whole monastery, pronounced that any brothers
summoned but not appearing were contumacious, and the monition
and protestation was drawn up in the common way by John Thorne.
Then there was read the constitution of the general council Quia
propter by M. Laurence Cokkys, our director, and the form of the
election in this constitution explained by him. We discussed
among ourselves by what way we intended to proceed (Fo. 14/62).
Immediately each and every monk, as if inspired by the grace of
the Holy Spirit as we believe, no one contradicting, save John
Thorne, prior, without instigation and as if with one vote and
assent as if with one spirit and one voice, elected John Thorne,
our prior, to be abbot. Immediately, so that all doubt might be
removed, there was drawn up by Robert Rading, monk, deputed
commissary or proctor for this purpose by the convent, the
election decree in the following words: In the name of God, Amen.
(&c. account of the election.) And singing the psalm (sic) Te
Deum Laudamus we left the chapter house and hastened to the choir,
the bell was rung, and we carried the abbot-elect John Thorne to
the high altar, placing him there, as is customary. When the
'psalm' was finished, (Fo. 14v/62v) and the customary prayers
offered for the elect, the election was published in the vulgar
tongue to the clergy and people then gathered in the monastery,
by M. Laurence Cokkys, our director, with the express mandate of
the whole conv., or chapter. And then we, the subprior and conv.,
except the elect, returned to the chapter house and ordained as
proctors and special nuncios Clement Bray, John Stokton, and John
Leomyster and Thomas Henlay, to obtain the assent of the elect to
his election. The proctors went to him on the same day after
dinner when he was in a certain high room in his house, and
straightway they asked for his consent; and he asked for a delay;
they returned the same day a little after five o'clock, finding
him in the hall of his house, and for the second time required

his consent; and he delayed them until the next day at eight in the morning, at which time, after some further deliberation, he gave his assent in the form following: In the name of the Holy and Undivided Trinity, Father and Son and most high Spirit. I, John Thorne (&c.). (Fo. 15/63) Wherefore we unanimously beg you to confirm this election, to bestow episcopal blessing, and to do what is necessary. (Undated)

432 Petition[1] by the subprior and conv. of Reading for the royal assent to the above election. (Undated) (Fo. 15v/63v) Bearers: John Bray and John Leomister, monks.

433 Signification to the bp. of the royal assent to this petition. Westminster, 24 July 1486. Attested by Skypton. (See also P.R.O., C82/12/55, 68, and C.P.R., 1485-1495, p.119.)

434 Request for the restitution of the temporalities of Reading abbey to John Thorne, whose election as abbot, in place of John Thorne, has been confirmed. (Fo. 16/64) (Undated)

(Space is left here, probably for the enrolment of mandates to the arch-deacon for induction and to the convent for obedience.)

435 Clause of a privilege granted to the aforesaid brothers. ET QUIA eiusdem ordinis Fratres de loco ad loco ipsius ordinis sepius transmittuntur propter quod stabilem et perpetuam in certis et determinatis eiusdem ordinis domibus non faciunt mansionem quia eciam bonos et ydoneos et Approbatos a vobis fratres faciatis ad ordines promoveri liceat vobis ordinandos fratres eiusdem ordinis quibuscumque malueritis catholicis pontificibus communionem & graciam Apostolice sedis habentibus presentare Ipsisque pontificibus presentatos a vobis fratres sine qualibet examinacione per eosdem pontifices facienda et absque omni permissione vel obligacione ipsorum ordinandorum fratrum ad ordines promovere. (2)

1   Original, P.R.O., C82/12/54, dated 22 July 1486, and naming Thomas Henlay as bearer with John Leomister (Lemystre).

2   This entry is in a different hand. See also K. Eubel, ed., Bularii Franciscani Epitome, Supplementum, XXXV, pp.263-267. (Fos. 16v/64v - 17v/65v blank)

436 (Fos. 18/66 - 19/67) Royal mandate ordering the collection of a clerical tenth. 13 April 1487.
(See Calendar of Fine Rolls 1485-1509, pp.61-5.)

437 Appointment, in pursuance of the above writ, on 26 April 1487, of the abbot and conv. of Sherborne (Shirborn) as the bp.'s deputies to collect the clerical tenth in the archdeaconry of Dorset. Woodford (Wodeford) by Salisbury, 23 May 1487.

438 (Fo. 19v/67v) Memorandum that on the same day similar letters were directed to the abbot and conv. of Stanley for the collection of the clerical tenth in the archdeaconries of Salisbury and Wiltshire, and to the prior and conv., of Hurley for the archdeaconry of Berks.

439 Certification to the treasurer and barons of the exchequer of the names (as above) of the bp.'s deputies for the collection of the clerical tenth, appointed pursuant to the royal mandate received 27 April 1487; exempt from the clerical tenth: (1) the goods, benefices, and ecclesiastical possessions of the poor religious of the monastery of Bindon, and the nuns of Tarrant OCist., in the archdeaconry of Dorset; the nuns of Lacock, the nuns of Kington St Michael, and the priory of Easton, in the archdeaconry of Wiltshire; the priory of Poughley, the priory of Sandleford, the nuns of Broomhall, and the collegers of Shottesbrooke, in the archdeaconry of Berkshire; (2) the goods &c. of the colleges in the universities of Oxford and Cambridge, and of the college of St Mary, Winchester, of the foundation of William Wykeham, formerly bp. of Winchester; (3) the goods &c. of cures whose value was 12 marks p.a. or less, in which the rectors or vicars or curates were resident or, if absent, were properly licensed to study in either English university, as scheduled below. Woodford, 16 May 1487.

440 The names of all the cures customarily assessed for the clerical tenth, not appropriated, of a modern value of 12 marks p.a. or less, exempt from the said tenth, (Fo. 20/68) in which benefices the rectors or vicars personally reside, or if absent are licensed to study:

ARCHDEACONRY OF BERKSHIRE
Abingdon deanery: Sparsholt vicarage; Letcombe Bassett ch.; Compton Beauchamp ch.; Kingston Bagpuize ch.; East Hendred chapel alias portion of the chancellor of Salisbury in East Hendred ch. Newbury deanery: Inkpen ch.; Frilsham ch.; Brightwalton ch.; Avington ch.; Enborne ch.; Hamstead Marshall ch.; Kintbury vicarage.

Reading deanery: Padworth ch.; Sulham ch.; Woolhampton ch.;
Purley ch.; Aldermaston vicarage; Sulhamstead Abbots ch.;
Arborfield chapel; Reading, St Giles's vicarage.
Wallingford deanery: Wallingford, St Peter's ch.; Wallingford, St
Mary Major ch.; Wallingford, St Leonard's ch.; Streatley vicarage.

ARCHDEACONRY OF SALISBURY
Chalke deanery: Tollard Royal ch., one part; Tollard Royal ch.,
another part; Bishopstone alias Ebbesborne Episcopi ch.
Potterne deanery: East Coulston ch.; Monkton Farleigh ch.
Amesbury deanery: Landford ch.; Idmiston vicarage; Boscombe ch.;
Alton ch. or chapel.
Wyly deanery: Rollestone ch.; Sherrington alias Sherston ch.;
Winterbourne Stoke vicarage.

ARCHDEACONRY OF WILTSHIRE
Cricklade deanery: Latton vicarage; Somerford Keynes vicarage;
Hannington vicarage; Eysey vicarage.
Marlborough deanery: Manningford Abbots ch.; Manningford Bruce
ch.; Huish ch.; Wootton Rivers ch.; Chisledon vicarage; Preshute
ch. alias Preshute ch. with chapel.
Malmesbury deanery: Yatton Keynell ch.; Leigh Delamere ch.;
Malmesbury, St Mary Westport vicarage; Poole Keynes ch.;
Hullavington vicarage; Long Newnton ch.
Avebury deanery: Beechingstoke ch.; Woodborough ch.; Alton Barnes
ch.; Avebury vicarage; Corton ch.

(Fo. 20v/68v) ARCHDEACONRY OF DORSET
Pimperne deanery: Ashmore ch.; Pentridge ch.; Stanbridge ch.;
Chettle ch.; Chalbury ch.; Wimborne All Hallows ch.; Wimborne St
Giles chapel.
Dorchester deanery: Frome Belett ch.; West Stafford ch.; Upwey
ch.; Frome Vauchurch ch.; Kimmeridge ch.; Bettiscombe ch.
Shaftesbury deanery: Melbury Osmond ch.; Shaftesbury, St Rumbold's
ch.; Shaftesbury, St James' ch.
Whitchurch deanery: Wareham, St Martin's ch.; Winterborne
Stickland ch.; Winterborne Zelston ch.
Bridport deanery: Puncknowle ch.; West Bexington ch.; Compton
Abbas ch.; Wraxall ch.

441 Names of benefices exempt from the above clerical tenth because
of their impoverishment:

ARCHDEACONRY OF BERKSHIRE: Speen vicarage in Newbury deanery;
Chieveley vicarage in Newbury deanery; Ufton Nervet ch. in
Reading deanery.

ARCHDEACONRY OF SALISBURY: Alderbury vicarage in Amesbury deanery.

ARCHDEACONRY OF DORSET: Durweston ch. in Whitchurch deanery; Turners Puddle ch. or chapel in Whitchurch deanery; Thornford ch. or chapel in Shaftesbury deanery; Burton vicarage in Shaftesbury deanery; Crofton chapel in Bridport deanery.

ARCHDEACONRY OF WILTSHIRE: West Overton in Avebury deanery.

442 Names of benefices not assessed the true annual value of which in the common estimation exceeds 12 marks, as is clear below, out of which the tenth should be paid:

ARCHDEACONRY OF BERKSHIRE: New Windsor ch.; in Reading deanery, estimated at £20; Bisham ch. in Reading deanery, estimated at £10.

ARCHDEACONRY OF DORSET: Winterborne Clenston ch. in Whitchurch deanery, not assessed but estimated at £8.6s.8d.; Winterborne Came ch. in Dorchester deanery, estimated at 13 marks; Bincombe ch. in Dorchester deanery, estimated at £8.6s.8d.; Imber chapel in Potterne deanery, estimated at 8 marks (sic).

(Fo. 21/69) ARCHDEACONRY OF WILTSHIRE: Knighton vicarage in Malmesbury deanery, not assessed but estimated at 13 marks; Broad Hinton in Avebury deanery, estimated at 20 marks; Liddington vicarage in Cricklade deanery, estimated at 13 marks.

443 Dispensation by Pope Sixtus (IV) to William Marshall, prior of Easton, Trin., to accept and to retain in commendam with the priory, and to exchange, any benefice, with or without cure, customarily held by secular clerks, even if a parish church, provided that the cure be served. Rome, St Peter's, 25 March 1483.
(Printed, Calendar of Papal Registers, Papal Letters, 1471–1484, p.837.)

444 (Fos. 21v/69v – 22/70) Mandate from Thomas (Kempe), bp. of London, rehearsing a mandate from John (Morton), archbp. of Canterbury, dated Mortlake, 5 March 1487, for the collection of a charitable subsidy (1) granted by the convocation of the

1   F.R.H. du Boulay, 'Charitable subsidies granted to the Archbishop of Canterbury, 1300–1489', Bulletin of the Institute of Historical Research 23 (1950), pp.147–164, especially p.157.

province of Canterbury meeting in St Paul's cathedral (London) from 13 to 26 February (1) 1487. Fulham, 2 April 1487.

445 (Fo. 22v/70v) Mandate to M. Nicholas Gotfrith BC & CnL, of Odstock, to be collector and receiver of the above subsidy in the archdeaconries of Salisbury and Dorset. (Undated)

446 Memorandum of like letters directed to M. William Jonis BCnL, to be commissary-general in the archdeaconries of Wiltshire and Berkshire for collection of the above subsidy. (Undated)

447 Certification to John (Morton), archbp. of Canterbury, or his commissary or commissaries, of the appointment of the above deputies for the collection of the above subsidy. (Undated)

448 (Fo. 23/71) Mandate from Thomas (Kempe), bp. of London, re-hearsing a decree of John (Morton), archbp. of Canterbury, dated Lambeth, 19 March 1487, ordaining that the feast of the Transfiguration should be kept throughout the province of Canterbury on the seventh day of August. (Fo. 23v/71v) Fulham, 2 April 1487.
(See R.W Pfaff, New Liturgical Feasts in Later Medieval England (Oxford, 1970), chap. 2.)

449 Dispensation of Pope Innocent (VIII) for John, abbot of Bindon, to accept, retain, or exchange, any benefice with or without cure, even if a parish ch., provided the cure be served. Rome, St Peter's, 20 February 1486.

450 (Fo. 24/72) Letter testimonial certifying that on 23 September 1487, before the bp. in the chapel of St Mary the Virgin in Ramsbury, Geoffrey Middelton vowed himself to the hermit's life. (Undated)
(See no. 464)

451 Exchequer certiorari whether or not the president and scholars of St Mary Magdalen College outside Oxford have and hold, and since when, to their use, the college or chantry of Wanborough in the archdeaconry of Wiltshire, and what sum they customarily render to the king for a tenth. Teste William Hody kt., Westminster, 20 February 1487. Fitzherbert.
(See no. 507)

1   This adds precision to the dates given in HBC, p.563.

452 Return of the above writ, received 20 September (<u>sic</u>) 1487; a
search of the bp.'s register and those of his predecessors has
shown that the president and scholars of St Mary Magdalen
College in the university of Oxford have held the chantry of
Wanborough from 10 October 1483; but what they customarily
render he cannot say. London, 28 November 1487.

453 Licence to Thomas Rogers and Margaret his wife for the celebration
of masses and other divine offices in the chapel or oratory in
their manor, or wherever else in the diocese of Salisbury they
may wish, by a fit chaplain of their choosing. (Fo. 24v/72v)
(Undated)

454 Indulgence of forty days granted for repair of the parish ch., of
St Mary le Strand (de Stronde) outside New Temple Bar, London, in
a great part — and specially on the south side — ruined, and
by thieves despoiled of all its books and ornaments; the bearer,
William Hues, constituted collector. London, <u>in domo mansionis
nostre</u>. (Undated)

455 Signification to the king of the contumacy of Edward Bisshop' of
the vill (ville) of Duntich within the parish of Buckland Newton,
Dorset, excommunicate. Ramsbury, 18 January 1488.

456 Letters to all clergy in the archdeaconries of Wiltshire and
Berkshire to admit Thomas Smyth as true proctor or nuncio for the
house or hospital of St Mary of Bethlehem without Bishopsgate,
London, until next 28 September 1488. Salisbury, 20 December
1487.

457 Commission to Richard Lymyn', v. of Sherborne, John Cole, and
William Taylour', chapls., to deliver criminous clerks and
other ecclesiastical men and literates from secular prisons in
the town (ville) of Sherborne or elsewhere in the county of
Dorset. 2 June 1487.

458 Sentence in a dispute between M. Henry Sutton MD, canon and
prebendary of Chisenbury and Cute, Salisbury cath., and M. John
Westley BCnL, v. (Fo. 25v/73v) of Enford, over the tithes of
lambs and wool &c. in Chisenbury. Ramsbury, 23 January 1488.

(Schedule in later hand, perhaps 19th-century, sewn to the top of
Fo. 25/73 of matters related to the above tithes.)

459 (Confession and abjuration by Joan Vorde _alias_ Forde of Steeple Ashton   of heresies touching the continuing virginity of the B.V.M., the worthiness of priests in deadly sin, and the Lord's Prayer.   English.)

In the name of the fader Son and holy goste iii persones and one godde in the trinite that blyssede mayden and virgyne marie moder of god and all the holy company of heven.   Jone Vorde other wise Forde of the Towne of Stepull Assheton within the diocyse of Sar' growsly diffamed notede and detecte to the Reverende Fader in god Thomas bisshop of Sar' my Juge and ordynarie and to hym denowncide for an untrewe and a mysbelevyng Woman that I shulde holde afferme and defende both privately and openly heresis errours false doctrines and opynyons contrary to the feith and doctrine of our moder holy Churche.

Firste that I shulde say that our lorde Jesu cryste was never conceyvede of and born of our blyssede Lady mary she remaynyng in her virginite (blank - ? words erased for half a line).   Item a preste beyng in dedely synne may not consecrate the body of our lorde Jesu cryste, And when he lyftis that holy sacramente and body of criste over his hede there is not the body of Criste he stille beyng in dedely Synne.   Item the holy prayer of the Pater noster is the (Fo. 26/74) prayer of the devyll and not of god. Item I hadde as leve the water of the lake to be sprynkelde uppon me as the holy water made by the preste beyng in dedely synne. Whiche articles oppynnyons and false doctrines and every of theim by his auctorite to me afore rehercede and Judicially objecte by you master Cokkys my Juge and ordinarie by the auctorite of my seide fader and lorde depute and ordeyned I openly here knowlege my selfe and of my free harte and wille confesse to have holde theym affermed theim belevede theim and tawght theim, The which all and every of theim I nowe understondyng and verely belevyng to be heresis erroris erronyos oppynions and contrary to the feith and techyng of our moder holy Churche Confesse me here and open knowlege make that thei be heresies and that I have be an Erytike lerner techer susteyner and holder of heresies errors erronyous oppynnyons and false doctrines contrary to cristen feith, And for as moch as I nowe understonde by you that the lawes of holy chirche of criste be grownded in mercy I therfor illyng by goddys grace to be partener of the same her openly forsake renownce and forswere thes articles afor rehersede and by me afor holden and all oder Confesse theim all and every of theym to be heresies errors and forbeden doctrine and nowe contrite and fully repentyng my selfe them all and everyche of theim I Judicially and solemply afore you my Juge and ordinarie afore rehersede and all thes company her gaderde and assemblide abjure forsake refuse and wilfully renownce for ever more with all other errors heresies and dampnable doctrines and oppynnyons contrary to the lawes of godd and techyng of all holy churche, And over this promitte and promyse make from this day her after that I will not be to eny suche person or persones favorer counceler mayntener prively ne openly but if I knowe eny such I shall denounce and disclose theim to my ordynarie or 'theis', Submytting me her openly of myn own fre wille and not compellede to the lawe and grevous paynes of the same that eny man or woman relapsid or falling ageyne to the same heresies or any oder dampnabill oppynnyons owthe to suffre if I here after do or holde contrarye to this my present abjuracion, In wittenesse wher of I with mine owne hande and this penne make her a crosse And hartly desire praye and require all trewe cristen pepill both men and wemen her gaderd at this tyme to ber wittenesse and recorde agayne me, And this my confession and abjuracion if I from this day folowyng ever offende or do contrarie to this same.

460 This abjuration was made and read in the consistory, Salisbury, before M. Laurence Cokkys DCnL, official of the consistory, by the above Joan Forde on 14 February 1488, in the presence of Masters Nicholas Gotfrith, president of the said consistory, & William Yate MA, Alexander Cator BC & CnL, Thomas Baker BC & CnL, James Vaughan BC & CnL, and Bartholomew Underwode, recorder (actorum scriba) and registrar of that consistory, and many others.

461 (Fo. 26v/74v) Names of the benefices in·the collation of the bishop of Salisbury:

ARCHDEACONRY OF DORSET:
Winfrith Newburgh ch., £20 (1); Bishop's Caundle ch., 25 marks; Upwey ch., £20; Broad Windsor vicarage, 20 marks; Burstock vicarage, 13 marks; Hilton vicarage, 18 marks; Osmington vicarage, 20 marks; Turnworth vicarage, 12 marks; Winterborne Whitechurch vicarage, 13 marks; Winterborne Farringdon vicarage; (added:) Winterborne St Martin vicarage, £10.

ARCHDEACONRY OF BERKSHIRE:
(Added:) West Ilsley, at the collation of the prior of Sandleford and now of the bp.'s collation because there is no prior there; East Hendred ch.; Pusey ch.; Great Coxwell vicarage; Streatley vicarage; Speen vicarage; (added:) chantry in Sandleford ch.

CITY OF SALISBURY:
Subdeanery of Salisbury cath.; bp.'s vicar in Salisbury cath.; Provostship of St Edmund's, Salisbury, with the priests; royal chantry of North Tidworth; royal chantry of Robert de Borbach in West Dean ch. if vacant for two months; (added:) succentorship

1   All valuations were added in a later hand.

of Salisbury cath.; (added:) chantry of Richard Beauchamp, bp. of Salisbury, in Salisbury cath.; (added:) chantry (Sancti struck out) in St Edmund's ch., Salisbury; (added:) Provostship of St Nicholas', Salisbury.

ARCHDEACONRY OF WILTSHIRE:
(Added:) free chapel of Membury in Ramsbury parish; Preshute ch., 12 marks; West Kington ch., £10 clear; Compton (added: Bassett by Calne) ch., £10 clear; Marlborough, St Peter's ch., £10 clear; Bremhill vicarage; Aldbourne vicarage; Littleton Drew vicarage, 12 m.; Preshute vicarage at the bp.'s nomination (added: and at the presentation of the master sic of the choristers); Stratton St Margaret vicarage at the bp.'s nomination (added: and the presentation of Merton Coll., Oxford); Sutton Benger by Christian Malford in Malmesbury deanery, vicarage; Inglesham vicarage; chantry of the Holy Trinity in Hungerford ch. (rectius archdeaconry of Berkshire; marginal note illegible); Sandleford priory near Newbury, now appropriated to the coll. of Windsor (viz. St George's; rectius archdeaconry of Berkshire); Preshute ch. appropriated to the choristers of Salisbury cath.; (added:) Cricklade, hosp. of St John the Baptist; (added:) chantry of St Katherine in St Peter's ch., Marlborough (superadded: if vacant for two months).

ARCHDEACONRY OF SALISBURY:
Poulshot ch. (1); Boscombe ch; Potterne vicarage; West Lavington vicarage; Idmiston vicarage; Brixton Deverill ch.; Laverstock vicarage; Chitterne All Saints vicarage; Bulbridge vicarage; Shrewton vicarage; Warminster vicarage; chantry of John Alwyn in Broad Chalke ch. if vacant for a month.

462 Memorandum of a composition between the prior of Clatford, then alien, and the r. of Preshute for tithes of lands, etc. (Undated)

463 (Fo. 27/75) Royal inspeximus of records of the fourth year of his reign, viz. among the records of Michaelmas Term, Roll 21, of an inquisition taken at Salisbury on Thursday the Vigil of St James the Apostle, viz. 24 July 3 Henry VII (2) before Henry Longe, John Mompesson, John Wroughton, armigeri, and John Hampton, gent., by letters patent under the exchequer seal, appointed for making

1   The valuations for the archdeaconry of Salisbury are bound in.

2   It seems likely that the dates in this entry follow the practice of the exchequer year.

inquisition into, among other things, all and sundry escapes of whatsoever felonious and convict clerks. Under oath, twelve jurors, whose names were appended to the inquisition (but not recorded in Langton's register) said that 1) William Whipham late of Reading, 'coteler', was indicted of certain felonies before Thomas Wodde, Robert Metford, and Thomas Vyncent, then justices of Richard III the late _de facto_ but not _de jure_ king of England, assigned to deliver the king's gaol at Wallingford, on the Thursday next after the feast of St Barnabas the Apostle in the second year of the late king, at Reading. Convicted of those felonies, he was, therefore, as a criminous clerk – according to the law and custom of the kindom of England – delivered from prison by Lionel (Woodville), late bp. of Salisbury, predecessor of the present bp. Afterwards, on the Wednesday next after the feast of the Epiphany in the second year of the present king, William Whipham escaped from the bp.'s prison and custody. 2) Richard Adam, late of Salisbury, goldsmith, was indicted and convicted before John Catesby and William Daldre, justices of the late king assigned to deliver his gaol at Salisbury castle, at Salisbury on the Wednesday next before the feast of St Mathias the Apostle in the third year of King Richard. Wherefore as a criminous clerk he was delivered from prison by Lionel (Woodville), late bp. of Salisbury, predecessor of Thomas the present bp., and afterwards, on the same day (as William Whipham) he too escaped from the same prison. 3) John Purcer, late of Salisbury, taylor, was indicted and convicted before Henry Louis and John Mompesson and their colleagues, justices of Thomas (Langton), bp. of Salisbury, for the liberties of the city of Salisbury according to the force of letters patent granted by the king to Bp. Thomas, assigned to hear divers transgressions, felonies, and other misdeeds in the city of Salisbury, at Salisbury on the Friday next after the feast of St Lucy the Virgin in the second year of the king (Henry VII). As a criminous clerk he was delivered from prison by Thomas, bp. of Salisbury but afterwards he escaped from the bp.'s prison on the same day as Whipham and Adam. (Fo. 27v/75v). Afterwards, a (writ of) _scire faciatis_ was served on the bp. by the sheriffs of London. On the appointed day, Saturday, 22 November (1488), the sheriffs, Ralph Tylney and William Isaac, returned the writ endorsed thus: the writ was delivered to him at his great house called 'Sirer' in the parish of St Bride Fleet Street, London, in Farringdon ward, through John Forster and Richard Clerk the lawmen of the ward. On the day and place named in the writ Bp. Thomas appeared in the person of Edmund Wylly his attorney, and exhibited a charter of 11 November 2 Henry VII (1486) which confirmed the liberties which King Henry III granted to God, to the church of Salisbury and to Bp. Richard (Poore) and his successors, to be quit of all escapes etc.; this charter was enrolled among the _recorda_ on the roll of the Easter Term, 17 Richard II, and he exhibited also letters from the present king under the great seal to the treasurer and barons of the exchequer, dated Westminster, 22 November 4 Henry

VII reaffirming that confirmation. The court adjourned until the quindene of St Hilary, on which day the bp. appeared in the person of the same proctor. The king's attorney, James Hobart, said that the aforesaid plea by the bp. was quite sufficient in law so that, by the law of the land, he was not bound to respond; whence he petitioned the court that the bp. should make separate fine with the king for these escapes. The bp. replied that he ought to owe nothing to the king for these escapes because James Hobart could not respond sufficiently in law to the bp.'s superior plea, and that the case should (Fo. 28/76) be dismissed by the court. The barons, after mature deliberation, decided that the bp. should be quit of making separate fines for the separate escapes on the pretext of the aforesaid charter and letter of the king, which, together with the details of the rest of the case, was exemplified under the exchequer seal. Witness, William Hody, kt. Westminster, 6 February 4 Henry VII. By the barons. Fitzherbert.

464   Letter testimonial that on 23 September 1487 before the bp. in the chapel of St Mary the Virgin in his manor of Ramsbury, Geoffrey Middelton vowed himself to the hermit's life. Dated as above.
(See no. 450)

465   Letter to the archdeacon of Dorset and his official and all other clergy in the archdeaconry, commending John Petegrewe, literate, as true proctor or nuncio for the hospital of St Thomas of Acon, London, during one year from the present date.
(Undated)

466   (Fo. 28v/76v) Letter testimonial that Thomas Baker, prior of St John, Wilton, is the legitimate administrator of the goods of a certain John Hall of Fisherton Anger, whence litigation and controversies have arisen, and that the bp. caused his registers to be searched on behalf of the same. London, 18 January 1489.

467   Royal licence for the appropriation of the parish ch. of Sutton Courtenay in the archdeaconry of Berkshire, by John Devoreux, James Baskervile, John Lyngen', Richard Corbet, Thomas Cornwayle, kts., Thomas Monyngton', armiger, and William Wykes, gent., feoffees of Walter Devoreux de Ferrers, kt., and with his consent, to the dean and canons of the free chapel of St George in Windsor Castle. (Fo. 29/77) Westminster, 19 February 1481. Irheler.
(Cf. C.P.R., 1476-1485, p.242.)

468   Grant by the feoffees, with the additional name of John ap Richard clerk, deceased, to the college. (See above.) 22 February 1481.

469 Appointment by the dean and canons of Windsor of James Birkhede, chapl., and vicar of the said chapel (see 467), to be their proctor for receiving the grant. (Fo. 29v/77v) Windsor, 23 February 1481.

470 Union of the parish ch. of Ringstead with the vicarage of Osmington; they are insufficient for the support of a priest and unlikely to be sufficient in future, wherefore they have been without any chapls., at divers times. The distance between the two was no impediment, as appeared by inquisition. The consent of M. Robert Langton, archd. of Dorset was obtained. The parish ch. of Ringstead was in the patronage of the abbot of Milton, whose rights were to be protected. One mass was to be celebrated on the feast of dedication in the parish ch. of Ringstead each year, in the chancel, whose upkeep was to remain the responsibility of the abbot and conv. of Milton. Pensions for indemnification for the loss of institution at Ringstead were to be paid by the vicar of Osmington. (Fo. 30/78) To the bp. of Salisbury 3s. 4d., to the cathedral of Salisbury 8d., and to the archd. 12d., for procurations. Ramsbury, 6 November 1488.

471 Letter from Richard (Hill), bp. of London, rehearsing a letter from John (Morton), archbp. of Canterbury, touching Pope Innocent VIII's bull, annexed in the vulgar tongue, concerning the marriage of Henry VII and Elizabeth of York, (Fo. 30v/78v) Lambeth, 20 February 1490, with a mandate to publish it in every parish ch. in the vulgar tongue during Lent. Certification was to be made to that effect to the archbp. by 1 July following. Lingfield, 25 February 1490.

472 (Fos. 30/78v-31/79) Schedule annexed to the above setting forth in the vulgar tongue Pope Innocent VIII's bull concerning the marriage of Henry VII and Elizabeth of York. (Undated) (Printed, The Camden Miscellany, vol. I, 1847 (Camden Society, Old Series, vol. 39.)

473 Appointment of John Wodde, king's sergeant at law, to be seneschal of Sonning, Berkshire, and of the lordship of Eye, Oxfordshire. Ramsbury, 1 January (Fo. 31v/79v) 1491.

474 Appointment of Richard Beauchamp, kt., to be seneschal of the city of Salisbury and of all lands and tenements pertaining to the bishopric in the counties of Wiltshire and Hampshire, and of the lordship of Winterbourne and of the rectory of Speen, Berkshire, parcel of the said bishopric. Ramsbury, 1 January 1491.

475 Mandate to John, abbot of St Mary, Abingdon, to restore Miles Salley, once a monk of that monastery, hitherto imprisoned for the crime of lèse-majesté, on supplication by the king (1) in letters enclosed (but not recorded in the register), to his place in the monastery. Ramsbury, 22 January 1491.

476 (Fo. 32/80) Monition to the curates of Newbury, Speen, Shaw, and Thatcham, for the denunciation of known heretics and traitors in those parishes. R(amsbury). (Undated)

477 Bull (Marginal: ficta) of Pope Innocent VIII to the abbot of Glastonbury, granting to Alice Laurence, the prioress, and the conv. of St Mary, Kington St Michael, exemption from visitation by the bp. of Salisbury as ordinary, and to be visited by any regular prelate. (Fo. 32v/80v) Rome, St Peter's, 28 June 1490.

(Fo. 33/81): the top two-thirds of this folio are blank.)

478 Innocent VIII's mandate to procure the originals of the above privilege and to send them to him. Rome, St Peter's, 27 July 1491.

479 (Fo. 33v/81v) Return to the above, enclosing the false bulls and reporting that an Irish friar, OFM, appeared to have produced them, but whether in Ireland or in England was not known; the bp. would write again if he obtained more information or captured the friar. London, 10 November 1491.

480 (Fo. 34/82) Provision of Katherine Moleyns, nun of Shaftsbury, to the priory of Kington St Michael in the place of Alice Laurens who had resigned. 9 April 1492.

481 Mandate to the arch. of Wiltshire or his official to install Katherine Moleyns as prioress. Ramsbury. (Undated)

482 Decree, to the subprioress and convent of Kington St Michael priory, OSB, by whom the right of election etc., was unanimously given to the bp., announcing the election or provision of Katherine Moleyns to be prioress in the place of Alice Laurens, the last prioress, who resigned, and mandate for obedience. (Undated)

483 (Fo. 34v/82v) Decree in the dispute between Anthony Zouche the prior, and the conv. of Wallingford, with M. Thomas Hopkyns, v.

1   See P.R.O., C82/91/15 and C.P.R. 1485-1494, p.381.

69

of West Hendred, over the v.'s portion in that parish ch. held
by the prior and convent to their use. Ramsbury, 16 July 1491.

484 (Fo. 35/83) (Confession and abjuration by Thomas Tailour of
Newbury, fuller, of heresies touching pilgrimages and images,
the priesthood, the sacraments of baptism and penance, the pope,
and the possession of a lollard book. English.)

In the name of the holy trinite fader son and holy goste His
blessed moder And all the Compeny of Hevynn. I Thomas Tailour of
Newbery, Fuller (in the usual form of confession to Bp. Langton)
First that I have seid and affermed theim Folis which goith to
Seynt Jamys in pilgremage or to eny odir places whereto pilgremys
be wonte and usid to go and visitte And that it shulde be more
meryte to geve a peny to a poreman than to visitte hym (<u>sic</u>,
<u>rectius</u> theym) or eny such places Ferthermor shewyng and therto
adding that seynt Jamys had no fote to com ayenst theim no hand
to welcom theym nether tonge to spek to theym, so reprevyng the
wurshipping of ymages and all odir holy peregrinacions.

Item I have taught seid and affermed ayenst the power and doctrine
of prysthod in this wise: that all men be disseyved by theim for
thei shuld shew the lanterne of the right wey And thei shewith
and techeth all contrarie to the same.

Item I have feeled seyd and affermyd both ayenst the sacrament of
Baptym And penaunce oft tymes aunsweryng when I have ben questioned
with: What were a man at his first begynnyng and his latter
endyng withoute the helpe of a priste, wherin I have hold that it
skelith not atte begynnyng if he be borne of a Cristen man and a
cristen woman, and as for the latter endyng he is in as goode
case that dieth sodenly in the way as he that dieth shrevyn and
houseld, so he aske god mercy.

Item I have hold erroniously and byfore dyvers men shewid and
declared that when a man or woman dieth in body then also dieth
in soule, for as the light of a candell is don owte by Castyng a
way or odir weys queynchid by blowyng or projection, so the soule
is queynchid by the deth of the body.

Item I have seid and openly affermed before grete multitude of
people in despite of seint Petir goddis vicar contempnyng hym and
his power callyng hym a panyer maker.

Item I have feeled seyd and manifestly shewid before divers in
despite of pristhode that the order of pristhode was never
ordeyned ne made by god but only matrimony.

Item I have kepte and holde by the space of ii yere one suspecte
boke of commaundementis wreten in the same that no man shuld
wurship eny thing graven or made with mannys (hand) wherby aftir

that doctrine I have beleved that no man aught to wurship ymages
or odir pilgremages.

485   This abjuration was read before Langton in the chapel in the manor
of Ramsbury by Thomas Tailour on 22 January 1491 in the presence
of Masters Laurence Cokkys DCnL, bp.'s chancellor, John Day DTh,
John Wroughton, armiger, William Birley, Brian (blank) MA, Thomas
Clerk BCL, and John Wely, scribe and registrar of the said bp.,
and many others. On that day the bp. imposed the following part
penance: that Thomas Tailour to be brought bare-legged, bare-
footed, and bare-headed, wearing a shirt and breeches, with a
bundle of faggots on his back and bearing one stick in his hand,
on the following days and to the following places, viz. in the
parish ch., of Newbury and in the market there, in the monastery
of Reading and the parish ch. there, in the town of Reading
aforesaid and in the market there, and in the market of Wokingham,
and in the parish churches of Ramsbury and Sonning, before the
processions around the churches, monastery, and markets aforesaid,
in the usual humble manner, and to expound to all the people
present his abjuration; after which the bp. was certified by the
curates of the aforesaid churches that the penance was done; and
in his manor of Sonning on 18 April 1491 he imposed this further
penance: on every day of his life he (Tailour) is to genuflect
before the crucifix saying five times the pater noster and five
times the Ave maria and one Credo (sic), and on the vigil of St
James and on Good Friday every year for the rest of his life he
is to fast on bread and water.

486   (Confession and abjuration of various heresies by Augustine Sterne
of Speen, Henry Benet of Speen, William Brigger of Thatcham,
Richard Hignell of Newbury, William Priour of Newbury, and
Richard Goddard of Newbury. English.)

In the name of the Holy trinite Fader son and Holy goste his
blessed modir and al the holy compeny of hevyn. We Austyn Stere
of (blank), Henry Benette of Spene, William Brigger of Thacham,
Richard Hignell, William Priour, and Richard Goddard of Newbery
(&c. in the usual form of confession to Bp. Langton).

(Fo. 36/84) Fyrste that I Augustyn Stere (marginal: de Spene)
have hold affermed and seyd that the Church of Criste is butt a
Sinagoge and a hous of marchaundise and that pristis be but
scribis and Pharisais not profyting the Cristen people but
disseyvyng theim.

Item I have hold affermed taught and Beleved that in the sacramente
of the Auter is not the very body of Criste ferthermor shewing
and seyng that pristis may bie XXXti suche goddis for one peny
And woll not selle on of theim but for two penys.

Item I have misbeleved and to dyvers manyfestly shewid that
ymagis of Seyntis be not to be wurshipped aftir the doctrine
of a Boke of Commaundementis which I have had in my keping
wherin is wreten that no man shall worship eny thing made or
graven with mannys hand, attending the wordis of the same
litterally And not inclynyng to the cense of the same.

Item I have spoken and diverse tymes shewid that pristis be
the Enmyes of Criste.

Item I have belevyd seid and taught that seynt Petir was never
priste but a litell before his dethe, Ferthermor shewing that
Symeon Magos geve hym his tonsure of prysthode And in Spyte of
hym goddis vicar contempnyng hys power called hym A panyer
Maker.

Fyrst that I Herry Benet (marginal: de Spene) have hold and
kept this opinion that pilgremagis be not to be made moeved for
this cause for only god is to be wursshiped And so not the
immagis of sayntis in so moch that I wold never goo a pilgremage
but onys And I have oftyn tymes repreved such as wold spend
their money in pilgremage doyng seing thei myght better spend
hit at home.

Item I have not belevyd stedfastly in the sacrament of thauter
seing of hit this wise: that if ther wer thre hostys in one
pikkis one of theim consecrate and the odir not consecrate A
mowse woll aswell ete that hoste consecrate as the odir tweyn
unconsecrate the which he myght not if ther were the very body
of Criste, for if ther wer the fadir son and holy goste he myght
not Ete theym.

Fyrste that I William Brigger (marginal: de Thacham) have erred
and mysbeleved in the sacramente of the Auter seyng And hobyng
that ther shuld not be the very body of Criste so taught and
enformed in this same grete errour and heresie by one Richard
Sawyer late of Newbery.

Item I have spoke and hold a yenst the sacrament of penance seing
in this wise: if I have take a mannis goode or stole his cowe And
be sory in harte I may as well be saved as though I were shreven
therof, for it is inowe to be shryve to god.

Item I have feeled And seyde ayenst the doctrine of Prystys
Affermyng of theim that all prystes techeth a false and a blynde
way to bryng us all in to the myer ferthermor addyng herte and
seyng howe may it be that Blynde William Harper may lede Anodir
blynd man to Newbery but both fall yn to the dyche so dothe all
thes pristis to Bryng us alle to Dampnacion.

(Fo. 36v/84v) Fyrste that I Richard Hignell (marginal: de
Newbery) have hold and mysbeleved of long tyme in the Sacramente

of the Auter seyng that Criste offerd to Simeon is the very
sacramente of thauter so meanyng and belevyng in myn opinion that
the sacramente in forme of Brede shuld not be very godde but only
Criste hymselffe in hevyn is the sacramente and none odir And so
I have mysbelevyd and continewed in this errour and heresie unto
this tyme of examnacion.

Item I have be adherente and associat with heretikis abjured by
whos doctrine I have erred as I have afore spoken.

Fyrste that I William Priour (marginal: de Newbery) have seid and
hold ayenst the auctorite and power of prystis Callyng theim
scribis Pharisies And thenmyes of Criste not teching but disseyving
the Cristen people.

Item I have belevyd and divers tymes shewid that Ymagis of
seyntis be not to be wurshipped nether oblacions to be made unto
theim seyng and holding no such thing to be wurshipped that is graven
or made with mannys hande.

I Richard Goddard (marginal: de Newbery) in long tyme here
before have had grete dought howe god myght be in the fourme of
Brede in thauter a moste syn the yeres of discrecion And nowe in
fewe yeres thought and utterly beleved that in asmoch as god is
in hevyn he shuld not be in the sacramente of thauter (sic) And
so in this errour have continewed unto the tyme of this my
presente abjuracion.
(Account concludes on Fo. 37/85 top.)

487 This abjuration was read and made before the bp. in the parish
ch. of St John, New Windsor, by the aforesaid on 28 January
1491 in the presence of Masters Laurence Cokkys, Edmund Martyn,
John Mayhowe all DCnL, (Robert) Daye DTh, Ralph Hethcote, canon
of Salisbury cathedral, William Thurlowe, vicar of New Windsor,
Brian and William Birley MAs, Thomas Clerk BCL, and John Wely,
scribe and registrar of the aforesaid bishop, and many others.
On that day the bp. imposed the following part penance: Augustine
Stere to be brought bare-legged, bare-footed, and bare-headed,
wearing a shirt and breeches, with a bundle of faggots on his
back and bearing a brand in his hand, on Saturday, 29 January
1491, around the market of the town (ville) of New Windsor where
and when the greatest number of people are present, on the
following Sunday, viz. 30 January ('die dominica extunc sequente
viz. ultimo die mensis eiusdem'), around the parish church of St
Mary, Reading, on Saturday, 5 February, around the market of
Newbury, and on the following Sunday (6 February) around the
parish church there, on the first Sunday in Lent (20 February
1491) in Salisbury cathedral, and on the Tuesday following (22
February 1491) around the market there, and on divers other days
through the monasteries of Cerne, Milton, Abbotsbury, Bindon, and
Sherborne, and around the market there, before the processions

around the churches, monasteries, and places, in the usual humble manner, and when the processions have ended, and Augustine has read and declared his heresies and abjuration in English, any of the curates of the churches aforesaid shall go into the pulpit and preach on them. Afterwards the bp. was certified by the curates of the aforesaid churches, that the penance was done (Fo. 37v/85v) and at the time of the certification, he imposed this further penance: on every day of his life Stere is to genuflect reverently before the crucifix saying five times the lord's prayer and five times the angelic salutation and once the Apostles' Creed, and, on Good Friday and the vigils of the B.V.M. for the whole year following, to fast on bread and water; and during the period he is not to travel more than seven miles from the town of Newbury unless he has first obtained license from the bp.

On the same day, 28 January (1491), the bp. imposed the following part penance on Richard Hignell: he was to be brought bare-legged, bare-footed, and bare-headed, wearing a shirt and breeches, with a bundle of faggots on his back and bearing a brand in his hand, on Saturday, 29 January, around the market of the town of New Windsor where and when the greatest number of people were present, on the following Sunday, viz. 30 January, around the parish ch. of St Mary, Reading, on Saturday, 5 February, around the market of Newbury, and on the following Sunday (6 February) around the parish ch. there, and on the third Sunday in Lent (6 March) around the chapel of 'Pole', on Passion Sunday (20 March) in the parish ch. of St Helen, Abingdon, on the following Wednesday (23 March) in the market at Highworth, on Friday, the Annunciation (25 March) in the parish or prebendal ch. of Farringdon, on the Sunday next following (27 March) in the parish ch. of Wantage, before the processions around the churches and places, in the usual humble manner, and when the processions have ended, the aforesaid Richard's heresies and abjuration are to be read from the pulpit by any of the curates of the aforesaid churches and then preached on. Afterwards the bp. was certified by the curates of those churches that the penance was done, and on 6 April 1491 at Ramsbury he imposed this further penance: each day of his life Hignell was to genuflect reverently before the crucifix saying five times the lord's prayer and five times the angelic salutation and once the Apostles' Creed, and each year for the rest of his life to fast on bread and water on the vigil of the Purification of the B.V.M. and on Good Friday, and during the next 17 days he was not to travel more than two miles from Newbury unless he had first obtained licence from the bp.

(Fo. 38/86) On the same day, 28 January (1491) the bp. imposed the following part penance on Henry Benet of Speen: in the aforesaid manner and form on divers dates in divers places. Afterwards the bp. was certified that the penance was done by the curates of those places, and he imposed this further penance: each day of his life Benet was to genuflect reverently before the crucifix saying five times the lord's prayer and five times the

angelic salutation and once the Apostles' Creed, and each year
for the rest of his life to fast on bread and water on the vigil
of the Annunciation of B.V.M. and on Good Friday.

On the same day (28 January 1491) the bp. imposed the following
part penance in the form of Richard Hignell above on William
Brygger of Thatcham: before the processions around the churches
and places, in the usual humble manner, and the processions being
ended, the aforesaid William's heresies and abjuration to be read
from the pulpit by any of the curates of the aforesaid churches
and then preached on; after which the bp. was certified by the
curates of the said churches that the penance was done; then he
imposed this further penance: each day of his life Brigger was
to genuflect reverently before the crucifix saying five times the
lord's prayer and five times the angelic salutation and once the
Apostles' Creed, and each year for the rest of his life to fast
on bread and water on the vigil of the Assumption of the B.V.M.
and on Good Friday, and he was not to travel more than three
miles from Thatcham until the feast of St Michael the Archangel
(29 September) unless he had first obtained licence from the bp.

Penance was imposed on William Priour of Newbury identical in
form to that of Brygger except that Priour was not to travel more
than three miles from Newbury for two months unless he had first
obtained license from the bp.

Penance was imposed on Richard Goddard of Newbury identical in
form to that of Brygger except Goddard was not to travel more
than two miles from Newbury for (blank) unless he had first
obtained license from the bp.

488 (Fo. 38v/86v) (Confession by Richard Hyllyng of Newbury of
heresies touching the priesthood, the sacraments, the power of
the Pope and other prelates, and the possession of a Lollard book.
English.)

ARTICULI ABJURACIONIS ISTORUM TRIUM SEQUENCIUM VIZ. RICARDI
HILLING JOHANNIS EDWARD' AND ROBERTI ELTON

First that I Richard Hyllyng of Newbery have hold and affermed in
the presence of diverse and many manifestly that pristis the
mynysters of god deceyve the people and that thei be blynde and
lodismen of blyndemen. Also that the Sacramentis of the Church
profite no man. Also pardons graunted of holy popes or of odir
prelatis as of Bisshopps profiteth not to the helth of mannys
soule.

Item that all pristis be the discipuls of the Antecriste as it
shell openly appere in the commyng of Ennok And Ely. Also I
have dyverse tymes shewid that pristis in mynystrynge aboute the
Sepulture of Cristen men say in this wise: As thowe hast do So
fonge therto wher in troughthe no such wordis be spoke but as
holy prayers as may be thought.

Item I have seyd that within X yere space ther shalbe one folde
and one sheppard meanyng herby that all heretikis and lollardis
the which have receyved grace shall preche openly and no man shall
dare say agayn theim. Item I have kept a suspecte boke conteynyng
Errours and heresies wherby I lernyd such errours and heresis as
afore is spoken of the which I have callid And named a preciouse
boke and of grete valewe.

489   On which day (4 February 1491) the bp. imposed the following part
penance on Richard Hyllyng: he was to be brought bare-legged and
bare-headed, wearing a shirt and breeches, with a bundle of
faggots on his back and bearing a brand in his hand, on Saturday,
5 February (1491), around the market of the town of Newbury, where
and when the greatest number of people were present, on the
following Sunday (6 February) around the parish ch. of Newbury,
on the Second Sunday in Lent (27 February) in Salisbury cath.,
on the Third Sunday in Lent (6 March) in the parish ch. of St
Laurence, Shaftsbury, on the Fourth Sunday in Lent (13 March) in
the ch. or chapel of 'Pole', on Friday, the Feast of St Edward,
King and Martyr (18 March) in the parish ch. of Corfe Castle, on
Passion Sunday (20 March) in the parish ch. of St Peter, Dorchester, and on the Feast of the Annunciation (25 March) in the
parish ch. of Bridport, before the processions around the said
churches or chapels, or in those churches or chapels as the
weather permits, in the usual humble manner. When processions
were ended, and when his heresies and abjuration have been read
out from the pulpit in English by any of the curates of those
churches, with Richard repeating them, the curate was to preach
in a loud and clear voice. Afterwards, the curates of those
churches certified to the bp. that the penance was done. In
Sherborne Castle on 28 March 1491, the bp. imposed this further
penance: on every day of his life Richard was to genuflect
reverently before the crucifix saying five times the lord's
prayer and five times the angelic salutation and once the
Apostles' Creed, and on the vigils of Christmas and the
Assumption of B.V.M. and Good Friday each year for the rest of
his life he was to fast on bread and water.

490   (Fo. 39/87) (Confession by John Edward of the town of Newbury of
heresies touching the sacrament of the altar, the continuing
virginity of Our Lady, &c. English.)

Firste I John Edward of the Town of Newbery have grevously erryd
as an untrewe cristen man holdyng and affermyng that in the
sacramente of the Auter is not the very body of Criste but a
thing confecte in commemoracion of the same and a signe of a
better thinge.

Item I have beleved taught and manyfestly shewid that our
blessid lady conceyved and bore aftir the Ascencion of Criste
another Son. Also I have shewid and dyvers tymes seid ayenst
praying in the Church saynge that men shuld no rather pray in the

76

Churche than in the felde Adding that the place saintifieth not a man.

491 On which day (4 February 1491) the bp. imposed the following part penance on John Edward: He was to be brought bare-legged, bare-foot, and bare-headed, wearing a shirt and breeches, with a bundle of faggots on his back and bearing a brand in his hand, around the market of Newbury, where and when the greatest number of people were present on next Saturday (5 February), and on the following Sunday (6 February) around the parish ch. there, before the processions &c., and on Sunday, 1 April (sic), in the parish ch. of Newbury, on Saturday, 7 April, around the market at Salisbury, on the following Sunday (8 April) in the cathedral there, on Thursday, 12 April, in the market at Devizes, on the following Sunday (15 April) in the parish ch. of St Helen, Abingdon, on the Monday following (16 April) in the market there; a further penance was imposed as below: (added at bottom of Fo. 39/87 after no. 494:) he was to fast on bread and water on the vigil of the Annunciation and (the vigil of) the Purification and on Good Friday each year for the rest of his life, and on every day of his life John was to genuflect reverently before the crucifix saying five times the lord's prayer and five times the angelic salutation and once the Apostles' Creed.

492 (Confession by Robert Elton of Newbury of heresies touching the sacraments of the altar and penance, and of infecting Richard Whithed of Newbury with heresy. English.)
Fyrste that I Robert Elton of Newbury have been a proctour to perverte Cristenmen And to induce theim to Errours and heresies, And in speciall on Richard Whithed of Newbery informyng hym that for as moch as god made the priste or pristis therfor pristis may not make godde, And so I have not belevyd in the sacramente of the Auter willing hym to do the same.

Item I have dyvers tymes shewid ayenst the sacramente of penaunce sayng and affermyng that confession made to a priste availeth not.

493 On the same day (4 February 1491) the bp. imposed the following penance on Robert Elton: that in the manner of a penitent in the form of the aforesaid John Edward (he was to be led) through the market and church of Newbury; and on the Sunday after the procession was finished, M. Laurence Cokkys, bp.'s chancellor, cited Robert to the city of Salisbury where on Friday, 11 February (1491), he was to have heard and received further penance; but on that day he did not appear but took flight to a place outside the diocese, and did not return. (Marginal: relapsed)

494 The abjurations above were read and made by the aforesaid Richard Hilling, John Edward, and Robert Elton before the bp. in the parish ch. of Newbury on 4 February 1491; witnesses: William

Nores, kt., Laurence Cokkys, bp.'s chancellor DCnL, John Day DTh, Roger Cheyne, _armiger_, John Esterfeld, rector of Newbury, John Howell BCnL, and John Wely, scribe and registrar, and others.

495 (Fo. 39v/87v) (Confession and abjuration by Alice Hignell of Newbury of heresies touching images of the saints. English.)

In the name of godde, Amen. I Alis Hignell of Newbery of the dioc' of Salesbery byfore you Thomas by the grace of godde bysshopp of Saresbury and my ordinarie knowlich opynly And with my fre wille make confession that I have before this tyme belevid erroneosly And also openly have seid before divers that ymagys of seintis be not to be wurshiped and for the Impugnacion of wurshipping of theim have mysseyd as moch as in me was for the most despite of theim as her aftir folowith: First that when devot Cristen people of their devocion be wonte to offre their candels bernyng to the Image of seint leonard I have for their devocion callid theim folis, Ferthermor shewing in this wise when sent leonard woll ete a candell and blowe owte anodir than I woll offir hym a Candell els I wol not. Also when I have seen copwebbis hangyng before the face of the Image of our lady I have seid And reputed theim folis that offerith to that Image but if she couthe blowe away the same copwebbis from her face. Also I have missaid ayenst the Image of seint Martyn in this wise seyng seint Martyn is but a foole: if he wer wise he wold not stonde so longe in that high place colde in the church but com down and sit by som poreman fier Over this when devote Cristen people be offering their candels to the ymage of seint Erasme I have wold I had an hachet in my hand And wer behynde theim to knoke theim on the heddis, And for the mor despite of the seid Imagis have seid and ben in full mynd willing and wysshing all tho Imagys that stondith in void placis of the church wer in my yarde at home havyng an axe in my hand to hewe theim to sethe my mete and to make my potte to boyle. Thes poyntes Artucules and opinions (&c. abjuration in the usual form).

496 This abjuration was read before the bp. at Newbury by Alice Hignell on 5 February 1491 in the presence of Masters Laurence Cokkys DCn1, bp.'s chancellor, John Day DTh, Robert Day, canon of Salisbury cathedral, John Esterfeld, Rector of Newbury, and John Howell BCL, with others. On that day he imposed the following part penance on Alice: She was to be led bare-legged and bare-headed, with a bundle of faggots on her back and bearing a brand in her hand, through divers places, before the processions in the humble manner of a penitent, her abjuration being declared after the sermon of the curates of the aforesaid places; after which the bp. was certified by the curates of those places that the penance was done. Then the bp. imposed this further penance: that each day for the rest of her life she was to genuflect before the images of the Crucifix and Blessed Mary the Virgin saying five times the lord's prayer and five times the angelic salutation and once the Apostles' Creed, and each year for the

rest of her life she was to fast on bread and water on the vigils
of the Assumption of Blessed Mary the Virgin and St Leonard and
on Good Friday; and she was not to stray more than two miles from
the town of Newbury after Easter next, without first having
obtained license from the bp.

497 (Fo. 40/88) (Confession and abjuration by William Carpenter
alias Harford _alias_ Daniell of Newbury of heresies touching the
sacrament of penance, images, the priesthood, &c. English.)

In the name of the holy trinite fadir son and holy goste his
blessid modir and all all (sic) the Compeny of hevyn I William
Carpenter otherwise called William Harford otherwise called
William Daniell of Newbery of the dioc' of Sar' byfore you
Thomas Bisshop of Sar' by goddis sufferaunce and myn ordinarie
knowlich openly and with my fre wille make confession that I
have before this tyme beleved erroniously, And also openly have
seid before divers that Confession verball is not necessarily to
be made to pristis for that confession so made is not to the
helthe of Cristenman soule, Ferthermor seing that it were as goode
for eny cristen man to be shrive of his felowe as of a priste.
Also I have belevyd and seid divers tymes that ymagis of seintis
be not to be wurshippid adding to the same that no man aught to
wurship eny thing that is made or graven with mannys hand,
ferthermor shewing that it were better to geve a poreman a peny
than to go a pilgremage to eny such or to do or make eny offeringis
to theim adding therto that offeryngis be made but only for the
availe and lucre of the pristis And not for soule helthe. Also I
many seasons have seid ayenst the power & doctrine of pristis
seing this wise that prelates of the Churche and pristis be but
scribes and phariseis disseyving Cristen people in their doctrine
and nothing profiting theim, Ferthermor seying in despite of
theim that when thei be reveste to masse thei be as Angelis and
when thei be unreveste thei be as blak brondis of hell and ther
be none odir of theim but all in like so meaning and belevyng by
that same that ther shuld be no very sacramente of the auter
nether eny othir sacramente of holy church that eny priste had
power or auctorite to mynystre. Also that thei nether none odir
can tell or shewe whether thes sayntys whom we calle seyntis be
in hevyn or in hell. Item I have taught and belevyd that if the
feith of lollardis wer not the world shuld be sone destroyed And
in shortyme that Feith whos have it shuld be unto the uttermoste
makyng and advaunsemente so he kepe that feith in counseill
prively. Thes pointis articules and opinions (&c. abjuration in
the usual form).

498 This abjuration was read before the bp. in the chapel in the manor
of Ramsbury on 10 February 1491, in the presence of Robert Day,
canon and prebendary of Salisbury cathedral, M. William Birley MA,
M. Briand (blank) MA, M. Thomas Clerk BCL, William Horseman,
chaplain, and John Wely, notary public, the bp.'s scribe and
registrar, with others. On that day the bp. imposed on that

William the following part penance: he was to be led bare-legged,
bare-footed, and bare-headed, wearing a shirt and breeches,
around the places and markets and churches on divers days, before
the processions in the manner of a penitent, his abjuration being
made publicly in the manner of the aforesaid Richard Hilling;
after which the bp. was certified by the curates of those places
that the penance was done. Then he imposed this further final
penance: that each day for the rest of his life William was to
genuflect before the image of the Crucifix (Fo. 40v/88v) reverently
saying five times the lord's prayer and five times the angelic
salutation and once the Apostles' Creed, and each year for the
rest of his life he was to fast on bread and water on the vigils
of Christmas and the Assumption of the B.V.M. and on Good Friday;
and he was not to stray more than two miles from Newbury for
forty days after Easter next without first having obtained
license from the bp.

499 (Confession and abjuration by Richard Lyllyngston of Castle Combe
of various heresies. English.)

In the Name of the holy trinite Fadir son and holy goste thre
persons and one god his blessed modir And all the holy Compeny
of hevyn I Ricard lyllyngston of Castelcombe in the dioc' of
Sar' gretly noted and diffamed and to my Reverend Fadir in god
Thomas by his grace bisshop of Sar' my Juge and ordinarie
detected and to hym denounced for a false belevyng man and that
I shuld hold afferme preche teche and defende pryvely and openly
at the alehouse and odir places heresies errours singuler
opinions and false doctrines contrarie to the commen doctrine and
faith of our modir holy church with subtilites evill soundyng and
deceyveable to the heryng of true understondyng cristen people
the which hath be to me by his auctorite Judicially objected.

Firste that I have wysshed that all the Churches within all
Cristendome wer in the myddys of helle And all tho that holdith
of theim And also all tho persons that belevyth uppon theim, And
wher as I have be Axyd And examyned by dyvers persones specially
by one called Richard Nores of Bildesdon whedir I seid eny such
wordis or nay I seyd I wold byde ther bye.

Item whan so ever was eny prechyng or techyng of the word of god
in the pulpyte I wold contrary hit atte alehouse, and I wold aske
the prechour whedir he wold byde by the wordys that he seid in
the pulpite or no, and so I caused such as wer the saiers of the
word of allmyghty god to be lothe to com in to the seid pulpite
agayn, and thus I did not only I tyme but this used thorough
owte the yer dispising and settyng at nowght the prechyng of the
word of god. Also wher as I have and was examined why I wold
talke and meddyll of the word of holy scriptur I beyng no Clerke
ne cowde tell what was to say Domine labia mea aparies I
aunswerd and said it was no mor to say but a sparowe bredith in
a Ivebushe to the derision and settyng at nought the prechyng of
the word of god and such holy wordis of divine service.
(Abjuration in the usual form, finishing F.41/89.)

500 This abjuration was read and made by the said Richard Lyllyngston in the episcopal Consistory at Salisbury on the Thursday next after the Feast of SS. Tiburtius and Valerian, viz. 21 April 1491, before M. Laurence Cokkys DCnL, bp.'s chancellor and president of the consistory, in the presence of (blank). On which day the following penance was imposed on the said Richard by Cokkys: he was to be led, in the manner of one of the abjured, wearing shirt and breeches, with a bundle of faggots on his back and bearing a stick in his right hand, in the processions in the churches and other places below, abjuring in the said places in the customary manner, viz. Saturday, the Feast of St Gregory (<u>rectius</u> St George: 23 April 1491) at Salisbury in the market place, on the following Sunday (24 April) in the cathedral ch., of Salisbury, on 30 April at Cricklade in the market place, and on the following Sunday, 1 May, in the parish ch. there, on the following Saturday, 7 May, at Malmesbury in the market place, and on the following Sunday (8 May) in the ch. of St Paul there, and on the following Monday (9 May) at Castle Combe in the market place, and on the following Sunday (15 May) in the parish ch. there, and on the following Saturday, 21 May, at Chippenham in the market place, and on the following Sunday (22 May) in the parish ch. there.

501 (Confession and abjuration by John Tanner of Steventon of heresies touching the sacraments of the altar and baptism, and images. English.)

In the Name of the holy trinite fadir son and holy gost his blessed modir and all the Compeny of hevyn I John Tanner of Stevynton of the dioc' of Sar' before you my Reverende Fadir in god Thomas Bisshop of Sar' my Juge and ordinarie knowelege openly and with my fre wille make confession that I have before this tyme beleved erroniously and also openly have seyd befor diverse ayenst the sacramente of the Auter on this wise: that the sacramente is undir this forme As almty god was offerd on the Auter to the hand of Simeon that is the sacramente of the Auter for that that is nowe used is but a signe of his pashion, ferthermor seyng howe may he be made that was withoute eny begynnyng and shalbe withoute eny endyng, And howe may priste make god insomoch as god made hym and all thingis of nought. Item I have seid and preched ayenst the sacramente of Baptym shewing that it availeth not to be wasshid in watir as thes pristis use nowe for it is but for the singuler advaile of the Crisom to theim, For it is Inowe to be baptised in fire and in the holy gost that is in perfyte love and Charite and in perfite beleve to god for seint John seid when Criste com to be baptised he seid lord it behoveth to be baptised of the that is to sey in that word seint John was baptised by his beleve, And so is every man that stedfastly beleveth in god though he be never wasshid in watir. Also ayenst (F. 41v/89v) <u>wurshipping of ymagis seing that we shall wurship no stokkis ne stonys ne nothing made or graven with mannys hand of no lykenesse of thingis in heven ne erth.</u> Thes poyntis articules And opinions and all odir that be <u>ayenst</u>

of all holy church (&c. abjuration in
the usual form).

502 This abjuration was read and made befor the bp. in the chapel of
St Mary in Abingdon abbey on 15 July 1491, in the presence of John,
abbot of Abingdon, Laurence Cokkys DCnL, bp.'s chancellor, Thomas
Say, armiger, James Hyde MA, Roger Hulse MA, Brian Esthorp MA,
Thomas Holes BCL, and John Wely, notary public, and many others.
(Space was left for a record of the penance imposed.)

503 (Confession and abjuration by Isabel Dorte of East Hendred of
heresies touching images, pilgrimages, and the sacrament of the
altar. English.)
In the Name of the holy trinite Fadir son and Holy gost his
Bledded modir and all the compeny of hevyn I Isabell Dorte of
Esthenred in the dioc' of Sar' before you my Reverend Fadir in
god Thomas bisshop of Sar' my Juge and ordinar' knowledge
openly and with my Fre wille make confession that I have before
this tyme beleved erroniously And also openly have seid befor
dyverse ayenst wurshipping of Ymagis of seyntis and pilgramage
doyng shewyng that no man shuld wurship no stokkis ne stonys ne
nothing made or graven with mannys hand understondyng and felyng
in my mynd that it wer better to geve a poor blynd or lame man a
peny than to bestowe their mony in pilgre goyngys And wurshippyng
the inmagys of seyntys, for man is the very ymage of godde which
ought all only to be wurshipped and no stokky ne stonys. Item I
have seid ayenst the sacramente of the Auter in this wise and hath
hold opinion that sith it is so that god was withoute begynnyng
and is and shalbe withoute endyng no prist hath power to make hym
ne to consecrate the body of criste, And have said that it is not
possible that that whete or corn that growith in the Feld this
day shuld be god or the body of Criste to morowe, for and it were
very godde a mowce or a Ratte hath no power to Ete hit.

504 This abjuration was read and made on 19 July 1491 in the chapel
of St Mary in Ramsbury manor before the bp. by the said Isabel,
in the presence of Thomas, prior of Bradenstok, John Day DTh,
William Ewike MA, Thomas Clerk BCL, William Horsman, chapl., and
John Wely, notary public, scribe, and others. On which day the
bp. imposed on Isabel the following penance: she was to be led,
dressed in the manner of one abjured, with a bundle of faggots
over her left shoulder and bearing a stick in her hand, in the
processions in the churches and other places below, viz. on
Sunday, 7 August (1491) in Sherborne parish ch., on the Assumption
of the B.V.M. (15 August) in East Hendred parish ch., before the
procession there with a taper in her hand. When this penance had
been done the bp. imposed this further penance: that every day
for the rest of her life she was to genuflect before the image of
the B.V.M. reverently saying five times the Lord's prayer, five
times the angelic salutation, and once the Apostles' Creed, and
each year for the rest of her life she was to fast on bread and
water on the vigil of the Assumption of the B.V.M., and during

the next year if she lived in East Henred was to go on pilgrimage
in the manner of a penitent to St Mary of Cokethorpe, or if she
lived in another village was to make a pilgrimage to the nearest
shrine of St Mary.

505 (Account of the election of Richard Page as prior of Ivychurch.)
(Fo. 42v/90v) The subprior and convent of Ivychurch (Ederose),
OSA notified the bp. and his commissaries or vicegerents that the
priory had become vacant by the death of Edward Thacham, the
last prior, who died on 21 February 1493 and was buried on 23
February, and that licence to elect a successor had been obtained from the king. James Keverig the subprior, and the
convent - Simon Bartlot cellarer, John Thacham and Richard Page
priests, canons and brothers - decided on Monday 4 March 1493,
in the chapter house that they would hold the election on
Tuesday 5 March. On that day those canons, after celebrating the
mass of the Holy Spirit, about 10 a.m., met in the chapter house.
All those entitled to be electors were present save William
Marchaunt, canon, who had been imprisoned for divers felonies,
and first they sang the hymn Veni Creator Spiritus and then read
the royal licence to elect. (Fo. 43/91) The only non-electors
present were Masters Laurence Cokkys DCnL, counsellor and director
of the election, Richard Neuporte BCL, scribe, Thomas Holes BCL,
and John Esterby priest, of the dioceses of Salisbury and York, as
witnesses, and Henry Mersh acolyte, professed. Cokkys read the
constitution Quia Propter and explained it in the vulgar tongue.
Then, by the way of inspiration, the canons elected Brother
Richard Page. The subprior drew up the election in the
conventual church (Fo. 43v/91v) in the vulgar tongue to the clergy
and people assembled there. Brother Simon Barlot was deputed to
obtain the elect's consent to this election, and the prior-elect
was carried to the high altar of the priory church while the hymn
Te deum Laudamus was sung. M. Laurence Cokkys then published the
election in the church. On Tuesday, 5 March between 1 and 2 p.m.
Simon Barlot found the prior-elect in the south aisle of the
conventual church and asked his consent to his election. But he
replied that he wished to deliberate on this. Again between 2
and 3 p.m. the proctor approached him in the same place and
obtained his consent. The subprior and convent then sought
episcopal confirmation of Richard Page's election. 5 March 1493.
(See also, P.R.O., C82/104/5 and C.P.R., 1485-1494, pp.410, 419.)

506 (Fo. 44/92) Confirmation of the election. (Undated)
(See also, P.R.O., C82/104/17 and C.P.R., 1485-1494, p.426.)

(Fos. 45/93 and 46/94 are wanting.)

507 (Fo. 47/95) (Appropriation of the church or chapel of St Katherine,
Wanborough to St Mary Magdalen College, Oxford, temp. Lionel
(Woodville) bp. of Salisbury.)

John, abbot of Hyde, Winchester dioc., commissary of the bp. of

Salisbury reported as follows (in the matter of the appropriation). He held an enquiry in the parish ch. of St Peter ad Vincula, Bishop's Waltham, Winchester dioc., by licence of William (Waynflete), bp. of Winchester, on 10 October 1483, at which M. Richard Colnet, notary public, acted as recorder. M. David Person appeared as proctor for the president – M. Richard Mayhewe DTh – and scholars of Magdalen College; M. David Husband as Proctor for the dean and chapter of Salisbury cath. and for the bp. of Winchester, patron of the college of chapel of St Katherine, Wanborough; M. Michael Clyve as proctor for M. Hugh Pavy archd. of Wiltshire in whose jurisdiction the college lay. William Gifford MTh, and Richard Brone MA, were sworn in as witnesses. The various commissions, licences, and proctorial letters were then examined, as follows:

1) Commission of Lionel (Woodville), bp. of Salisbury (Fo. 47v/ 95v) to the abbot of Hyde, OSB, and Masters John Baker DTh, Richard Salter DCnL, Richard Hayward DCL, and Walter Hodgys BC & CnL to act in the matter of the appropriation. Thornbury, Worcester dioc., 22 September 1483.

2) Commission of William (Waynflete), bp. of Winchester to John, abbot of Hyde, for the same matter. Waltham, 7 October 1483.

3) (Fo. 48/96) Appointment by the president and scholars of Magdalen College, Oxford, of M. David Persons BC & CnL, to act as their proctor. Oxford, 30 September 1483.

4) Appointment by John Davyson, the dean and the chapter of Salisbury cath. (Fo. 48v/96v) of David Husband DCnL, to act as their proctor. Salisbury, the chapter house, 8 October 1483.

5) Appointment by Hugh Pavy, archd. of Wiltshire in Salisbury cath., of M. Michael Clyve DCnL, and M. David Persons BC & CnL, or either of them, to act as his proctors. (Fo. 49/97). Salisbury, 7 October 1483.

6) Appointment by William (Waynflete), bp. of Winchester, patron of the chapel of St Katherine, Wanborough, of M. David Husbande and M. Michael Clyve DCnLs, or either of them, to act as his proctors. St Mary Magdalen College, of the bp.'s foundation and in his jurisdiction. (Undated)

7) (Fo. 49v/97v) Mandate of Pope Calixtus III, in connection with the proposed dissolution of the hospital of St John the Baptist, Oxford, OSA, and its conversion into a secular academic college, to the bps. of Lincoln, Worcester, and Hereford, to receive the resignation of Richard Wyse the present master or warden; also to grant Richard Wyse who held the rectory of 'Farlegh' in Winchester dioc. in plurality with the hospital, licence to hold any other benefice with his rectory even if incompatible; to grant dispensation to any of the four brothers of the hospital, viz. John Selam, John Vobe, Walter Rede and Robert Heyes, priests, to hold any benefice even if with cure of souls; and to dispense all five to resign or to exchange their benefices, as often as they please. Rome, St Peter's, 14 May 1457.
(Printed, Calendar of Papal Registers: Papal Letters XI, 1455-1464 pp.69-70, where the date is identified differently. See also, C.P.R., 1452-1461, p.343.)

8) Grant by Francis, Viscount Lovell, patron of the college or
free chapel of St Katherine the Virgin, Wanborough, of the
advowson of the same to William (Waynflete), bp. of Winchester,
and William Catesby, esquire of the body of the king, and to his
heirs and assigns; and guarantee by Francis and his heirs of the
said advowson to the said bp. and William Catesby and his heirs
against John, abbot of Westminster, and his successors. 16
August 1483.
(Fo. 51/99) John Colyngborn, abbot of Hyde, fixed
13 October 1483 for a final decree in this matter. On that day
there appeared M. David Person, proctor of the president and
scholars of Magdalen College, Oxford, and in the presence of the
other proctors he demanded a final decree, which was granted to
him. (Fo. 51v/99v) On the same day M. Michael Clyve DCL, master
or keeper of that college or chapel of St Katherine (Fo. 52/100)
resigned. St Peter ad Vincula, Bishop's Waltham. Witnesses:
Masters Walter Hodgys and Nicholas Belle BC & CnLs, Winchester dioc.
Given under the seal of the abbot and convent of Hyde, and, for
the greater faith of all and singular, also under the seal of
M. Richard Hayward DCL, official of the consistory of the bp. of
Winchester, who was present. The notarial instrument recording
the business was drawn up by Richard Colnet BCL, notary public,
clerk of the diocese of Canterbury.

508 Grant by the president and scholars of the college of St Mary
Magdalen, Oxford University, to Thomas (Langton), bp. of Salisbury,
and his successors, of a pension of 5s p.a. to indemnify him for
the above appropriation. (Fo. 52v/100v) Oxford, Magdalen College,
5 November 1487.

509 (Fo. 52v/100v) (Appropriation of the vicarage of Buckland to the
rector and convent of Edington OSA (sic, rectius Bonshommes),
saving the portion of M. Ralph Hethcote the vicar; he and his
successors are to receive £12 p.a. (Fo. 53v/101v) Ramsbury, 28
April 1488.
(This entry was struck through and a marginal note added: 'void
because the bp. reduced the vicarage to its pristine state'.)

510 (Fos. 53v/101v-24/102) Commission to the archd. of Dorset or his
official to visit the clergy and people of his archdeaconry.
Ramsbury, 12 March 1489.

511 Memorandum that similar commissions were issued to the archds. of
Salisbury, Wiltshire and Berkshire.

512 (Fo. 54v/102v) Notification to the abbot of Sherborne that the
bp. intends to visit the monastery in person or by commission or
commissaries, with mandate to warn all who are bound to attend,
and to certify to the bp. that he has done so. Ramsbury, 26
March 1489.

513 Certification by the abbot of Sherborne that he has cited everyone who ought to be visited to appear as in the notification above. (undated)

514 Memorandum that similar notices were sent to the abbots of Abingdon, and Reading, and to the priors of Poughley, and Bisham in the archdeaconry of Berkshire; to the prior of Bradenstoke, and the abbess of Lacock, and the prioress of Kington St Michael, in the archdeaconry of Wiltshire; to the rector of Edington, and the abbess of Wilton, and priors of Maiden Bradley, and Ivychurch (Edenrose), in the archdeaconry of Salisbury; and to the abbots of Cerne, Milton, and Abbtotsbury, and to the abbess of Shaftesbury, in the archdeaconry of Dorset. (Undated)

515 (Fo. 55/103) Mandate to attend a meeting of convocation. Royal request to the archbp. of Canterbury for a meeting of convocation. Westminster, 19 November 1488. Archiepiscopal summons to a meeting of convocation to be held in St Paul's cath., London, on 14 January 1489. Lambeth, 21 November 1488. Letter forwarded to the bp. of Salisbury by Thomas (Kempe), bp. of London. (Fo. 55v/103v) London, 25 November 1488.

516 Langton received the above letter on 27 November 1488, and consequently addressed a mandate to the archd. of Salisbury or his official to convene the clergy of his archdeaconry in Salisbury cath. on 22 December 1488 to choose two proctors for the clergy of the whole dioc. for this convocation. Ramsbury, 1 December 1488.
Memorandum that similar mandates were sent to the other archds.

517 Certification to John, archbp. of Canterbury, primate of all England and apostolic legate, of the above provision (516) for convocation, with the names of the proctors attached (below). No date.
For the chapter of Salisbury cath.: M. Edward Cheyne DCnL, dean of Salisbury.
(Fo. 56/104) For the archdeaconry of Salisbury: M. Edward (sic) Chaderton, archd. of Salisbury; Brother William Hulle, r. of Edington; prior of Monkton Farleigh; prior of Maiden Bradley; prior of Ivychurch.
For the archdeaconry of Wiltshire: M. Christopher Urswik, archd. of Wiltshire; Thomas, abbot of Malmesbury; John, abbot of Stanley; Thomas, prior of Bradenstoke.
For the archdeaconry of Dorset: M. Robert Langton, archd. of Dorset; Roger, abbot of Cerne; Peter, abbot of Sherborne; (erased:) abbot of Milton; Hugh, abbot of Abbotsbury, John, abbot of Bindon.
For the archdeaconry of Berkshire: M. Oliver Kyng, archd. of Berkshire; John, abbot of Abingdon; John, abbot of Reading; Richard, prior of Bisham; John, prior of Hurley; Thomas, prior of

Poughley; John, prior of Wallingford.
For the whole diocese: M. Laurence Cokkys DCnL, canon of Salisbury cath.; M. Ralph Hethcote BCnL, canon of Salisbury cath.

518 Royal writ ordering collection of the clerical subsidy granted by the convocation which met in St Paul's cath. from 14 January to 27 February 1489, and to appoint collectors for the same who will answer to the exchequer; with signification of the names to the exchequer by 15 March 1489 for the first moiety, and by 15 September 1489 for the second. Westminster, 28 February 1489.

519 (Fo. 56v/104v) Certification to the exchequer of the names of the collectors of the first moiety of the above subsidy: archdeaconry of Dorset, the abbot and conv. of Milton; archdeaconry of Berkshire, the abbot and conv. of Reading; archdeaconries of Salisbury and Wiltshire, the abbot and conv. of Malmesbury. London, Fleet Street, 7 March 1489.

520 Commission to the abbot and conv. of Milton for collection of the first moiety of the above subsidy in the archdeaconry of Dorset, with the usual exemption; (Fo. 57v/105v) the goods, benefices and ecclesiastical possessions of any persons listed in the following schedule were not to be taxed except as directed in that schedule. 5 March 1489.

521 Sums to be received by the collectors of the first part of the major subsidy granted to the king from the ecclesiastical persons, goods, benefices, and possessions listed herein in the archdeaconry of Dorset. (The scribe is not always accurate in his distinction of churches and vicarages in the next three entries.)
Shaftesbury deanery: Melbury Osmond ch., 4s. 4d.; Shaftesbury, St Rumbold's ch., 5s.; Shaftesbury, St James's ch., 5s.; Shaftesbury, St Laurence's ch., 9s.
Pimperne deanery: Ashmore ch., 5s.; Pentridge ch., 4s.; Stanbridge ch., 5s.; Chettle ch., 5s. 4d.; Chalbury ch., 5s.; Wimborne All Hallows ch., 5s.; Wimborne St Giles ch., 5s.
Dorchester deanery: Frome Belett ch., 4s. 4d.; West Stafford ch., 4s. 4d.; Upwey ch., 8s.; Frome Vauchurch ch., 4s. 4d.; Kimmeridge ch., 4s. 4d.; Bettiscombe ch., 4s. 4d.
Whitchurch deanery: Warham, St Martin's ch., 4s. 4d.; Winterborne Stickland ch., 4s. 4d.; Winterborne Zelston ch., 5s.
Bridport deanery: Puncknowle ch., 4s. 4d.; West Bexington ch., 5s.; Compton Abbas ch., 4s. 4d.; Wraxall ch., 5s.
(Additional group:) Winterborne Clenston ch. in Whitchurch deanery, 8s. 4d.; Winterborne Came ch. in Dorchester deanery, 10s.; Bincombe ch. in that deanery, 16s. 8d.
(Fo. 58/106) Spiritual and temporal possessions in the archdeaconry of Dorset of the following: Bindon abbey, £6. 8d.; Tarrant monastery, 108s. 10d.; Bradenstoke monastery, 20s. 8d.

522 Sums to be received by the collectors of the first part of the aforesaid major subsidy in the archdeaconry of Berkshire.
Abingdon deanery: Letcombe Bassett ch., 6s. 8d.; Sparsholt ch., nil; Compton Beauchamp ch., 13s. 4d.; Kingston Bagpuize ch., 13s. 4d.; East Hendred chapel <u>alias</u> portion of the chancellor of Salisbury there, nil.
Wallingford deanery: Wallingford, St Peter's ch., 3s. 4d.; Wallingford, St Mary's ch., 3s. 4d.; Wallingford, St Leonard's ch., 3s. 4d.; Streatley vicarage, 3s. 4d.
Newbury deanery: Inkpen ch., 10s.; Frilsham ch., nil; Brightwalton ch., 10s.; Enborne ch., 6s. 8d.; Hamstead Marshall ch., 10s.; Kintbury vicarage, 5s.
Reading deanery: Padworth ch., 3s. 4d.; Sulham ch., 3s. 4d.; Purley ch., 3s. 4d.; Sulhamstead Abbots ch., 5s.; Aldermaston vicarage, 3s. 4d.; Arborfield chapel, 5s.; Reading, St Giles's vicarage, 4s. 4d.
Spiritual and temporal possessions in the archdeaconry of Berkshire of the following: Edington, 46s.; abbot and conv. of Westminster, nil because of exoneration from tax by the prayers and petitions they make for the king and his progenitors; abbess and conv. of St Clare outside the walls of the city of London, 9s. 6d.; Broomhall monastery, nil; prior and conv. of Poughley, 27s. 3d.; Sandleford priory, 15s. 11½.; Shottesbrooke coll., 25s. 4d.
(Additional group:) New Windsor ch. in Reading deanery, estimated at £20:40s.; Bisham ch. in Reading deanery, estimated at £10:20s.

523 (Fo. 58v/106v) Similar schedule for the archdeaconries of Wiltshire and Salisbury.
Chalke deanery: Tollard Royal ch., one part, 4s. 4d.; Tollard Royal ch., another part, 4s. 4d.; Bishopstone vicarage, 4s. 4d.
Wyly deanery: Rollestone ch., 4s. 4d.; Sherrington ch., 6s. 8d.; Winterbourne Stoke ch., 4s. 4d.
Cricklade deanery: Latton vicarage, nil; Somerford Keynes vicarage, 4s. 4d.; Hannington vicarage, 4s. 4d.; Eysey vicarage, 10s.
Malmesbury deanery: Yatton Keynell ch., 16s.; Leigh Delamere ch., nil; Malmesbury, St Mary Westport vicarage, 8s. 8d.; Poole Keynes ch., 6s. 8d.; Hullavington vicarage, 8s. 8d.; Long Newton ch., 8s.
Potterne deanery: East Coulston ch., 5s.; Monkton Farleigh ch., 5s.
Amesbury deanery: Landford ch., nil; Idmiston vicarage, 8s. 8d.; Boscombe ch., 4s. 4d.; Alton chapel, 4s. 4d.
Marlborough deanery: Manningford Abbots ch., nil; Manningford Bruce ch., 10s. 8d.; Huish ch., nil; Wootton Rivers ch., 10s.; Chiseldon ch., 5s.; Preshute ch., nil.
Avebury deanery: Beechingstoke ch., 10s.; Woodborough ch., 6s. 8d.; Alton Barnes ch., 5s.; Avebury vicarage, 4s. 4d.; Corton ch., nil.
Spiritual and temporal possessions in the archdeaconries of Wiltshire and Salisbury of the following: prior and conv. of

Bisham, 20s.; Dartford monastery, 13s. 4d.; Edington, £4. 16s.
8d.; prior of Easton, 21s. 4d.; Lacock monastery, 102s. 3¾d.;
Kington St Michael priory, nil; Bradenstoke priory, 100s.
(Additional group:) Imber chapel in Potterne deanery, 10s. 8d.;
Kington St Michael vicarage in Malmesbury deanery, 17s. 4d.;
Broad Hinton ch. in Avebury deanery, 26s. 7d.; Liddington
vicarage in Cricklade deanery, 17s. 4d.

524 (Fo. 59/107) Certification to the exchequer of the names of
collectors of the first moiety of the same subsidy, with the sums
to be rendered by each: the abbot and conv. of Milton, archdeaconry of Dorset, £277. 14s. 2d.; the abbot and conv. of
Malmesbury, archdeaconries of Salisbury and Wiltshire, £518. 17s.
8d.; the abbot and conv. of Reading, archdeaconry of Berkshire,
£303. 6s. 7d.; they with the £103. 16s. 10d. for the bishopric
total £1,203. 15s. 3d. for the dioc. Ramsbury, 4 April 1489.

525 (Fo. 59v/107v) Commission to John, abbot, and the conv. of
Abingdon to act as collectors of the second moiety of the
subsidy in the archdeaconry of Berkshire, in accordance with the
annexed schedule. (Fo. 60/108) Ramsbury. (Undated)

526 Memorandum that similar mandates were sent to the abbot of Milton,
for the archdeaconry of Dorset, and to the abbot of Malmesbury
for the archdeaconries of Salisbury and Wiltshire.

527 Schedule of certain benefices with the sums to be taken from them
by the collectors of the second half of the above subsidy in the
archdeaconry of Berkshire. (Identical with 522.)

528 (Fo. 60v/108v) The same archdeaconries of Salisbury and Wiltshire.
(Identical with 523, with the following amendments:)
(add:) Compton Chamberlayne ch. in Chalke deanery, nil; Idmiston
vicarage in Amesbury deanery, 4s. 4d. (not 8s. 8d.); Eysey ch. in
Cricklade deanery, 5s. (not 10s.); (add:) Cricklade, St
Sampson's vicarage in Cricklade deanery, nil; Yatton Keynell ch.
in Malmesbury deanery, 8s. (not 16s.); Malmesbury St Mary
Westport vicarage in Malmesbury deanery, 4s. 4d. (not 8s. 8d.);
Poole Keynes ch. in Malmesbury deanery, nil (not 6s. 8d.);
Hullavington vicarage in Malmesbury deanery, 4s. 4d. (not 8s.);
Long Newnton ch. in Malmesbury deanery, 4s. 4d. (not 8s.);
Beechingstoke ch. in Avebury deanery, 6s. 8d. (not 10s.); Dartford
monastery, 26s. 8d. (not 13s. 4d.); Bradenstoke priory, nil (not
100s.); (entries relating to Imber, Kington St Michael vicarage,
Broad Hinton, and Liddington are omitted; bottom quarter of folio
is blank).

529 (Fo. 61/109) The same for the archdeaconry of Dorset.
(Identical with 521, with the following amendments:)
Shaftesbury, St Laurence's ch. in Shaftesbury deanery, 2s. 4d.
(not 9s.); Upwey ch. in Dorchester deanery, 16d. (not 8s.);
Winterborne Zelston ch. in Whitchurch deanery, nil (not 5s.);
Winterborne Clenston ch. in Whitchurch deanery, 3s. 4d. (not
8s. 4d.); Winterborne Came ch. in Dorchester deanery, 3s. 4d.
(not 10s.); Bincombe ch. in Dorchester deanery, 6s. 8d. (not
16s. 8d.).

530 Certification to the exchequer of the names of the collectors of
the second moiety of the same subsidy. (As above, nos. 525-6,
with the sums to be rendered for each archdeaconry as in no. 524.)
(Undated)

531 (Fos. 61v/109v-63/111) Mandate of John (Morton) archbp. of
Canterbury to appoint collectors for the two minor
(charitable) (1) subsidies granted in the convocation which met
in St Paul's cath. from 14 January to 27 February 1489. Lambeth,
1 March 1489. Contained in a letter from Thomas (Kempe), bp. of
London. Fulham, 4 March 1489.

532 Commission to M. John Westlay BCnL, bp.'s commissary in the
archdeaconries of Salisbury and Dorset, to collect the minor
(charitable) subsidy in the archdeaconry of Salisbury. Ramsbury,
14 March 1489.

533 (Fo. 63v/111v) Certification to the archbp. of Canterbury of the
appointment of collectors for the above minor (charitable) subsidy,
viz. M. Richard Newporte, official of the archd. of Dorset, in
the archdeaconry of Dorset; M. John Westley, bp.'s commissary, in
the archdeaconry of Wiltshire; and M. George Wodde, official of
the archd. of Berkshire, in the archdeaconry of Berkshire.
Salisbury, the palace, 26 April 1489.

534 (Fo. 63v/111) Revocation by John (Morton), archbp. of Canterbury,
of the second (charitable) subsidy. Croydon, 12 August 1489.
Contained in a letter of M. Richard Lichefeld DCL, canon
residentiary of St Paul's cath., official and keeper of the
spiritualities of the dioc. of London, sede vacante. (Fo. 64/
112) London, 16 August 1489

1   See F.R.H. du Boulay, 'Charitable subsidies granted to the
Archbishop of Canterbury, 1300-1489', Bulletin of the Institute of
Historical Research 23 (1950), pp.147-164, especially 157, 161-2.

535 Notification to M. John Westlay, commissary-general in the archdeaconries of Salisbury and Dorset, and collector of the subsidy
in the archdeaconry of Salisbury, (Fo. 64v/112v) implementing this
remission. (Undated)

536 Memorandum that similar directives were sent to the other
collectors.

537 Commission to M. William Harward, William Gydding', William Miles,
and William Thurlowe, vicars of the parish churches of St Helen,
Abingdon, Wantage, Steventon, and New Windsor, and to M. Thomas
Raynes and William Pest, vicars-choral of the free chapel of
St George in Windsor castle, M. Owen Morgan, Thomas Gloucetour,
and William Barton, rectors of the parish churches of St Leonard,
St Mary Major, and St Peter, Wallingford, William Lever and
William Budde, vicars of the parish churches of St Mary, Reading,
and Northmorton, for delivering clerks, other churchmen, and
literates from goals at New Windsor, Reading, Abingdon, Wantage,
Wallingford or elsewhere in Berkshire. (Undated)

538 Appointment, by the bp.'s letters patent, of William Twyneho,
armiger, as seneschal of all the bp.'s lands etc., in the county
of Dorset, with payment of £5 p.a. from the income of the manor
of Sherborne. (Fo. 65/113) Ramsbury, 1 February 1491.

539 Royal request for a meeting of convocation. Westminster, 9 May
1491. Mandate from John (Morton), archbp. of Canterbury to
attend convocation in St Paul's cath. on Tuesday, 21 June 1491.
Lambeth, 10 May 1491. Contained in a letter of Richard (Hill),
bp. of London. (Undated)

540 (Fos. 65v/113v-67/115) Royal writ ordering collection of the
tenth granted at the convocation which met from 21 June to 8
November 1491. Westminster, 4 December 1491.
(Cf. no. 548)

541 Commission to the abbot and conv. of Cerne to be collectors of
the tenth in the archdeaconry of Dorset. Ramsbury, 26 December
(Fo. 67v/115v) 1491.

542 Memorandum that on the same day similar mandates were sent to the
prior and conv. of Maiden Bradley as collectors in the archdeaconries of Salisbury and Wiltshire, and to the prior and conv.
of Bisham as collectors in the archdeaconry of Berkshire.

543 Certification to the exchequer of the names of those appointed as collectors of the tenth. Ramsbury, 30 December 1491.

544 (Fo. 68/116) The names of all the cures customarily assessed, not appropriated, of a modern value of 12 marks p.a. or less, exempt from the said tenth, in which benefices the rectors or vicars reside, or if absent are licensed to study (as in no. 440, with the following additions:) Tidpit ch. in Chalke deanery; West Dean ch. in Amesbury deanery; Upavon vicarage in Potterne deanery; Compton Chamberlayne ch. in Wyly (<u>rectius</u> Chalke) deanery; Baverstock ch. in Wyly (<u>rectius</u> Chalke) deanery; Cricklade, St Sampson's vicarage in Cricklade deanery; Inglesham vicarage in Cricklade deanery; (Fo. 68v/116v) Sopworth ch. in Malmesbury deanery; Tarrant Rushton in Pimperne deanery; Woodsford ch. in Dorchester deanery; Buckhorn Weston ch. in Shaftesbury deanery.

545 Names of benefices exempt from the above clerical tenth because of their impoverishment (as in no. 441, with the following amendments:) (additions)Faringdon vicarage in Abingdon deanery; Batcombe ch. in Shaftesbury deanery. (Omissions) Durweston ch. in Whitchurch deanery; Turners Puddle ch. or chapel in Whitchurch deanery.

546 (Fo. 69/117) Names of benefices not assessed the true annual value of which in the common estimation exceeds 12 marks, out of which the tenth should be paid (as in 442, with the following additions:) Durweston ch. in Whitchurch deanery, £10; Shaftesbury, St Laurence's ch. in Shaftesbury deanery, £9.

547 (Fos. 69/117-70v/118v) Mandate of John (Morton), archbp. of Canterbury, to collect a minor (charitable) subsidy granted in the convocation which met from 21 June to 8 November 1491. Lambeth, 9 December 1491. Contained in a letter of Richard (Hill), bp. of London. Fulham, 22 December 1491.

548 (Fos. 70v/118v-72v/120v) Royal writ ordering collection of the tenth granted at the same convocation. Westminster, 24 February 1492.
(Printed, <u>Calendar of Fine Rolls, 1485-1509</u>, pp.169-173.)

549 Commission to the abbot and conv. of Abbotsbury, rehearsing the above writ, received on 23 March 1492, appointing them collectors of the tenth in the archdeaconry of Dorset. (Fo. 73/121) 24 May 1491 (<u>sic. rectius</u>, 1492.)

550 Memorandum that similar mandates were sent to the abbot and conv. of Stanley for the archdeaconries of Salisbury and Wiltshire, and to the prior and conv. of Wallingford for the archdeaconry of Berkshire.

551 Certification to the exchequer of the names of these collectors. (Fo. 73v/121v) Ramsbury, 26 March 1492.

552 The names of all the cures customarily assessed, not appropriated, of a modern value of 12 marks p.a. or less, exempt from the said tenth, in which benefices the rectors or vicars reside, or if absent are licensed to study (as in 544, with the following additions:) Wickham ch. in Newbury deanery, because of the fire in the houses there; West Dean ch. in Amesbury deanery: M. Denby is non resident; (1) Compton Chamberlayne ch. in Wyly deanery: appropriated to St Edmund's coll.; (1) Baverstock ch. in Wyly (_rectius_ Chalke) deanery: W. Horsman in chapel of (the bp. of) Winchester; (1) (Fo. 74/122) Cricklade, St Sampson's ch. in Cricklade deanery: viz. £20, Philip, chapl. of (the bp. of) Winchester: non resident; (1) Manningford Bruce ch. in Marlborough deanery: Thomas Whithley is non resident, he holds the free chantry in Gloucestershire at Chipping Campden; (1) Wooton Rivers ch. in Marlborough deanery: Richard Skot is non resident, moreover (conjectural: he holds) the cure at West Knoyle in the archdeaconry of Salisbury; (1) Yatton Keynell ch. in Malmesbury deanery: 20 marks; (1) Poole Keynes ch. in Malmesbury deanery: non resident, Clifford. (1)

553 Names of benefices exempt from this clerical tenth on account of their impoverishment. (Identical with no. 545.)

554 (Fo. 74v/122v) Names of benefices not assessed, of which the true annual value according to the common estimate is more than twelve marks, and on which a tenth ought to be paid. (Identical with no. 546.)

555 Decree given in a controversy concerning tithes, between John Clyff, rector of Whaddon, and John Clerke, rector of Hilperton. Ramsbury, 3 April 1492.

556 (Fos. 75/123-78v/126v; Fo. 77/125 is lacking) Account of the election of a prior of Bisham, OSA. Following the resignation of

1 Marginalia.

Richard Sewy, the last prior, and the granting of a royal
licence to elect, the electors decided on 5 February 1492 that
they would hold the election the next day at 9 a.m. The
electors were: John Rowland, subprior, William Coston', Robert
Stoner', precentor and novice-master, William Greve, sub-
treasurer and granger ('granatorum dispensator'), William
Barnaby, cellarer, William Kyng, Thomas Hunte, Thomas Evottys,
John Rowland, Richard Smyth, priests, Richard Blakborne and
Thomas Wylde, canons, professed. Also present at the election
were M. Laurence Cokkys DCnL, M. Richard Neuporte, scribe and
notary, M. Thomas Birchold BCnL, r. of Great Marlow, Lincoln dioc.,
and John Easterby, priest of Salisbury dioc., witnesses. The
electors decided that they would proceed by way of a compromise and
chose John Rowland, subprior, William Coston and Robert Stoner to
make the election. These consulted each elector individually
and found that the majority favoured William Greve; so John
Rowland on behalf of the whole chapter elected William Greve.
M. Laurence Cokkys published the result of the election in the
priory church, and William Greve was led to the high altar during
the singing of <u>Te deum Laudamus</u> 'partum per organa partumque per
humanarum vocum modulamina solemniter'. William Coston and Robert
Stoner were deputed by the electors to obtain William Greve's consent.
They first found him in an upper chamber in the infirmary, and he
asked for time to deliberate. They returned to the same place at
about 2 p.m., and he gave his consent. Account of the election
with petition for episcopal confirmation attested by M. Richard
Neuport, notary, and sealed with the priory seal. 6 February 1492.

557 Commission of the subprior and conv. of Bisham to M. Richard
Neuporte, William Coston, and Robert Stoner, priests and canons,
to act as proctors to petition the bp. for confirmation of the
election. (Fo. 79/127) 7 February 1492.

558 Commission to M. Laurence Cokkys DCnL, canon residentiary of
Salisbury cath., and bp.'s chancellor, to confirm the election,
to instruct the archd. of that place to install the prior-elect,
and to assign a pension to Richard Sewy, the former prior.
(Fo. 79v/127v) London, 11 February 1492.

559 Grant to Thomas Barker, <u>familiaris noster</u>, to be parker of
Sonning, Berkshire, and custodian of the woods called 'Berewood
alias Wodward de Bisshoppesbere', Berkshire. Sonning, 20
February 1493.

560 Ratification and confirmation of these letters by the dean
(Edward Cheyne DC & CnL), and chapter of Salisbury cath., saving
always the rights of the cath. Salisbury, the chapter house,
3 June 1493.

561 (Fos. 80/128–80v/128v) Index to the contents of part II of the register.

562 (Fo. 81/129) (Letter of Henry Deane, archbp. of Canterbury, to Edmund Audley, bp. of Salisbury, dated Lambeth, 4 December 1502, concerning the alleged resignation of John Ashe, rector of Sutton Veny, in February 1502. English.)

To my lord of Sarum. My Lord where as it is soe that one sir John Ashe callyng hym self parsone of the paryshe Churche of Fennysutton' within your diocyse of Saresbury as it is seid and to us shewed in the Monyth of February last passyd shuld have resigned the said parish Church before us in the Chamen Rome at Westmynstre and affirmyth that we shulde thanne & there decre his seid resignacion voyde and of no strength nor vertue veryly (1) we remembre not wele that the said Sir John Ashe made any suche resignacion before us ne that we shulde make any suche decre uppon the said resignacion in the place Aforsaid. And yf any suche thyng were doone whyche as nowe we do not remembre after our mynd it myght not stond to any effecte for these condideracions for we had noo Jurisdiccion in that exempt place and peculiar Jurisdiccion of Westmynstre, And also at that tyme the iurisdiccion of Saresbury the see there being voide was hooly by us committyd into the hande of the officiall ther by us deputed according to the composicion made betwene our church of Canterbury and your Church of Saresbury For the which causis we thinke yf any suche processe were then and there by us as is pretendid made it shuld be voide and of no strength. Wherefore we intending not to do anything prejudiciall to your Church of saresbury ne to your iurisdiccion certyfye you by these our letters uppon the premisses to the intent that yf any suche resignacion come byfore you sufficiently that ye may use your iurisdiccion and ordinary power the seid pretensyd decre notwithstonding acording to good Lawe and conscience as unto you shalbe thought most convenient. And thus fare ye wele in our Lord Ihesu. Frome Lamehith the iiijth day of decembre.

Yours Henr' Cant'

---

1   'where remembre' erased.

ORDINATION LISTS

(All ordinations are by Thomas, bishop of Salisbury. All ordinands are of the diocese of Salisbury unless otherwise stated. Abbreviations: dim., having a letter dimissory from the candidate's own bishop; tons., having a first tonsure.)

563 (Fo. 82/130) Ordinations celebrated in Wilton abbey on the first Saturday in Lent, viz. 18 February 1486, the first (<u>rectius</u> second) year of the bp.'s translation.

Acolytes:
William Hall, Lincoln dioc., dim., tons.
John Frye of Martock, Bath and Wells dioc., tons.
Henry Bryan, title of Malmesbury (abbey).
John Chamber, tons.
John Hyde, tons.
Thomas Spicer, tons.
Robert Basset <u>alias</u> Godyer, tons.
Thomas Gardyner, tons.
John Garnet, tons.
Thomas Drover of Salisbury, tons.
John Wynter, tons.
William Howchyns, Worcester dioc., dim.

Subdeacons:
John de la Gowche, Bayeaux dioc., acolyte, dim., title of £20 tournois.
Thomas Thomys of Gloucester, acolyte, dim., title of his choral stall in Salisbury cath.
James Sargeante, Exeter dioc., acolyte, dim., title of Launceston priory.
John Ray BA, acolyte, title of Ivychurch priory.
Nicholas Seerle, Exeter dioc., acolyte, dim., title of Osney (abbey), Lincoln dioc.
Walter Pirrot, acolyte, title of Montacute priory, Bath and Wells dioc.
Henry Fisher, Carlisle dioc., acolyte, dim., title of Sopwell (priory), Lincoln dioc. (<u>sic</u>.)
Thomas Marrall, Coventry and Lichfield dioc., acolyte, dim., title of St John of Haughmond (abbey), same dioc.

Deacons:
William Braye, OFM of Salisbury (Greyfriars).
Lucas de Camera, OFM of Salisbury (Greyfriars).
Walter Bale, Exeter dioc., subdeacon, dim., title of Barnstaple priory, same dioc.
(Fo. 82v/130v) John Mauntell, subdeacon, title of 'Bewforde'.
John Roberdis, Worcester dioc., subdeacon, dim., title of 'Langton', Llandaff dioc. (<u>sic</u>).

John Hawson, Durham dioc., subdeacon, dim., title of his choral
stall in Salisbury cath.
William Mose BA, Bath and Wells dioc., subdeacon, dim., title of
Stavordale priory, same dioc.
Thomas Boteler _alias_ Smyth, subdeacon, title of Witham (priory),
OCarth.
John Brigge, subdeacon, title of St John the Baptist (Minchin
Buckland priory), Bath and Wells dioc.

Priests:
John Drake, Exeter dioc., deacon, BA, dim., title of Weare
Giffard parish ch., Exeter dioc.
William Pere, Bath and Wells dioc., deacon, dim., title of
Taunton priory, same dioc.
Richard Lokar, Exeter dioc., deacon, dim., title of 'Orcharde'
parish ch., same dioc.
Thomas Moreman, Exeter dioc., deacon, dim., title of Frithelstock
priory, same dioc.
John Croppe, Bath and Wells dioc., deacon, dim., title of Taunton
(priory), same dioc.
John Holme, London dioc., deacon, dim., title of his choral stall
in Wells cath.
John Hoper, deacon, title of Cerne (abbey).
Thomas Walcote, deacon, title of Easton priory.
John Smyth, OP.

564   (Fo. 83/131) Ordinations celebrated in Edington conventual ch.
on 11 March 1486, the first (_rectius_ second) year of the bp.'s
translation.

Acolytes:
Richard Nele, tons.
John Harforde, of Maiden Bradley (priory), OSA.
Maurice Huchyns, tons.

Subdeacons:
John Whytyng, Hereford dioc., acolyte, dim., title of Flaxley
(abbey) in the forest of Dean.
John Hyde, acolyte, title of Newenham (abbey), Exeter dioc.
Henry Bryan MA, acolyte title of Malmesbury (abbey).
John Aylberton, monk of Malmesbury (abbey).
John Wynter, acolyte, title of St Margaret's (priory), Marlborough.
John Chamber, acolyte, title of vicarage of Salisbury cath.
Thomas Nores, acolyte, title of his benefice of Castle Combe.
John Frye, Bath and Wells dioc., acolyte, dim., title of Montacute,
same dioc.
John Garnet, acolyte, title of Longleat priory.

Deacons:
James Sargeant, Exeter dioc., subdeacon, dim., title of Launceston
priory.

John de la Gownch, _de sancta matre ecclesia in exempcione de loco sanctorum_, Bayeux dioc., subdeacon, dim., title of £20 tournois.
Thomas Marrall, Coventry and Lichfield dioc., subdeacon, dim., title of Haughmond (abbey).
John Rogborn, monk of Malmesbury (abbey), OSB.
William Upton, monk of Malmesbury (abbey), OSB.
Roger Farley, monk of Malmesbury (abbey), OSB.
Thomas Thomys, Worcester dioc., subdeacon, dim., title of vicarage in Salisbury cath.
Nicholas Serle, Exeter dioc., subdeacon, dim., title of Osney (abbey), Lincoln (dioc.).
Henry Fyssher, Carlisle dioc., dim., title of Sopwell (priory), Lincoln (dioc.) (_sic_).

Priests:
William More, deacon, monk of Malmesbury (abbey), OSB.
Thomas Bremelham, deacon, monk of Malmesbury (abbey), OSB.
John Combe, deacon, monk of Malmesbury (abbey), OSB.
William Wotton, deacon, monk of Malmesbury (abbey), OSB.
Robert Evesham, deacon, monk of Malmesbury (abbey), OSB.
William Hedley, deacon, OFM of Salisbury (Greyfriars).
William Bray, deacon, OFM of Salisbury (Greyfriars).
(Fo. 83v/131v) John Brigge, deacon, title of St John the Baptist (Minchin Buckland priory), Bath and Wells dioc.
Thomas Jule, Exeter dioc., deacon, dim., title of Taunton priory, Bath and Wells dioc.

565 Ordinations celebrated in Edington conventual ch. on Holy Saturday, viz. 25 March 1486, the first (_rectius_ second) year of the bp.'s translation.

Subdeacons:
William Fynymore, Worcester dioc., acolyte, dim., title of Osney (abbey), Lincoln (dioc.).
Thomas Spycer, acolyte, title of Stanley (abbey).
Thomas Diar, Exeter dioc., acolyte, dim., title of Bodmin priory.
John Pynnoke, acolyte, brother of Edington (collegiate ch.).
Richard Erbery, acolyte, brother of Edington (collegiate ch.).

Deacons:
John Garnet, subdeacon, title of Longleat priory.
Henry Bryan, subdeacon, title of Malmesbury (abbey).
Thomas Noreys, subdeacon, title of his benefice of Castle Combe.

566 Ordinations celebrated in the chapel of SS Peter and Paul the Apostles in Cumnor manor on Ember Saturday, the vigil of Trinity, viz. 20 May 1486, the first (_rectius_ second) year of the bp.'s translation.

Acolytes:
John Walger, monk of Abingdon (abbey), OSB.
William Elworton, monk of Abingdon (abbey), OSB.
M. Richard Carpenter, Hereford dioc.
(Fo. 84/132) George Ogyll, Durham dioc.
William Hakkar.
James Willey, York dioc.
Alexander Cromer, Canterbury dioc.
M. Thomas Thornton MA, York dioc.
Edward Strangwysche, York dioc.
John Denham, Durham dioc.
George Lacy, York dioc.
George Norham, York dioc.
Thomas Sysson, York dioc.
Richard Peronyll, York dioc.
John Lyndeley, York dioc.
John Salkylde, York dioc.
Robert Lucas, York dioc.
Richard Sylle, York dioc.
William Marchall, OFM.
Robert Burton, OFM.
William Albryton, OP.
William Versam, OP.
John Hoskyns, OP.
Richard Gregory, OP.
Richard Whitell, OP.
Robert Ferne, OP.
Benedict Tregoes, Exeter dioc.
Pascasius Hopkyns, Exeter dioc.
Robert Barbour, Exeter dioc.
Richard Trot, Exeter dioc.
John Sutton, Exeter dioc.
John Cruce, Exeter dioc.
Maurice Sydenham, Bath and Wells dioc.
John Smyth, Lincoln dioc.
Thomas Dagnall, St David's dioc.
Walter Banbury, 'dominus', Osney (abbey).
Thomas Wolgercote, 'dominus',Osney (abbey).

Subdeacons:
William Knyght, Winchester dioc., acolyte, dim., title of his
fellowship in New College, Oxford.
Thomas Hardyng, Exeter dioc., dim., title of Plympton priory, same
dioc.
Maurice Tyndall, Worcester dioc., dim., title of Malmesbury (abbey).
William Wake, Durham dioc., dim., title of coll. of St Laurence
(Poultney) or Corpus Christi, London.
William Benet, monk of Abingdon (abbey), OSB.
Thomas Bradeley, acolyte, OFM.
Edmund Cayter, canon of Bradenstoke (priory), OSA.

John White, canon of Bradenstoke (priory), OSA.
Robert Wodbrig, canon of (the priory of) St Frideswide, Oxford.
M. John Newman, Canterbury dioc., acolyte, dim., title of All
Souls Coll., Oxford.
(Fo. 84v/132v) John Marchall, canon of Osney (abbey), OSA.
John Oxforde, canon of Osney (abbey), OSA.
Robert Legate, OC.

Deacons:
Roger London, canon of (the priory of) St Frideswide, Oxford.
David Coniwey, canon of (the priory of) St Frideswide, Oxford.
Aylburton (sic), monk of Malmesbury (abbey), OSB.
John Doo, OFM.
John Blakborn, OFM.
Teodericus Wykyn, OP of Oxford (Blackfriars).
William Radclyff, monk of Abingdon (abbey).
John Lechelade, monk of Abingdon (abbey).
Thomas Burges, monk of Abingdon (abbey).
Rutlonde (sic), OC.

Priests:
John Palmer, deacon, Exeter dioc., dim., title of Osney (abbey),
Lincoln (dioc.).
M. Henry Bryan MA, deacon, title of Malmesbury (abbey).
Thomas Ivottys, canon of Bisham (priory), OSA.
Thomas Margrave, York dioc., deacon, dim., title of Monk Bretton
(priory), same dioc.
William Salford, OFM.
Thomas Marrall, Coventry and Lichfield dioc., deacon, dim., title
of Haughmond, same dioc.
Giles Inglyssh, York dioc., deacon, dim., title of 'Tropton',
Lincoln (dioc.).
John Robarde, Worcester dioc., dim., title of 'Langton' priory,
London dioc. (sic). (See 563)
John Stephyn, Exeter dioc., deacon, dim., title of (the priory of)
St Frideswide, Oxford, Lincoln dioc.
Francis Oxforde, canon of (the priory of) St Frideswide, Oxford,
Lincoln dioc., OSA.
John Westbury, monk of Abingdon (abbey), OSB.
Henry Thewe, monk of Durham (priory), OSB.
Thomas Swalwell, monk of Durham (priory), OSB.
Roger Harforde, monk of Reading (abbey), OSB.
Richard Leompstar, monk of Reading (abbey), OSB.
John Hyde, monk of Reading (abbey), OSB.
John Sonnyngys, monk of Reading (abbey), OSB.

567 Ordinations celebrated in the parish or prebendal ch. of Ramsbury
on Ember Saturday, 13 June 1489, the fifth year of the bp.'s
translation.

(Fo. 85/133) Acolytes:
Thomas Mychell.

Christopher Palle.
John Cusse.
Thomas Harrys, canon of Maiden Bradley (priory).
Henry Purdewe, Winchester dioc., dim.
John Tapnaile, Exeter dioc., dim.

Deacons: ('Sub' erased)
William Scrogge, OP of Oxford university.
John Cooke, Lincoln dioc., dim., title of (hospital of) St John
(the Baptist), Wilton.
William Lyllyngton, title of (hospital of) St Nicholas, Salisbury.
John Vyncent, Bath and Wells dioc., dim., title of Stanley (abbey).
John Molle, title of Malmesbury (abbey), dim.
John Johnson, York dioc., dim., title of Swine (priory).
William Jonyngys, canon of Maiden Bradley (priory).

Subdeacons:
John Carvar, acolyte, title of Tarrant (abbey).
Nicholas Derby, title of Milton (abbey).
Robert Mawghthill, title of Osney (abbey), Lincoln dioc.
William Gray, title of Newenham (abbey), Exeter dioc.
John Strong, title of Bradenstoke priory.
Richard Huntley, Worcester dioc., dim., title of Llanthony
(priory).
Thomas Hewys, St Asaph dioc., dim., title of Dorchester (abbey),
Lincoln dioc.
Richard Wilde, OP of Oxford university.

Priests:
M. John Wethers, Bath and Wells dioc., fellow of Magdalen Coll.,
Oxford, dim., title of his fellowship.
M. John Jenyn, Bath and Wells dioc., dim., title of Muchelney
(abbey).
M. John Jolyff, title of Milton (abbey).
Nicholas Tarrand, Carlisle dioc., title of Nocton Park (priory),
Lincoln dioc.
(Fo. 85v/133v) Thomas Williams, Llandaff dioc., dim., title of
Margam (abbey), same dioc.
William Hyghmor, Carlisle dioc., dim., title of (the priory of)
St Frideswide, Oxford.
William Branche, Carlisle dioc., dim., title of Bicester priory,
Lincoln dioc.
Robert Legatt, OC of Oxford university.
William Houchynson, OP of Oxford university.
Edmund Keytyng, canon of Bradenstoke (priory).

568 Ordinations celebrated in the parish or prebendal ch. of Ramsbury
on Ember Saturday, 19 September 1489, the fifth year of the bp.'s
translation.

'Benedicti':
Thomas Grevell, Worcester dioc., dim.
Robert Whyssyng.
William Tailour.
Thomas Cely.

Acolytes:
Robert Whyssyng.
William Tailour.
James Nicholas.
Thomas Cely.
Thomas Grevell, Worcester dioc., dim.
George Hichman, Worcester dioc., dim.
Richard Kam, monk of Malmesbury (abbey).
Pascasius Salesbury, monk of Milton (abbey), OSB.
John Middelton, monk of Milton (abbey), OSB.

Subdeacons:
M. William Lovell, BCL, Durham dioc., dim., title of Osney
(abbey), Lincoln dioc.
William Towers, Lincoln dioc., dim., title of Croxton (abbey).
Robert Marshall, OP of Salisbury (Blackfriars).
Richard Abbot, Lincoln dioc., dim., title of Thornholme priory,
same dioc.
Christopher Palle, title of Newenham (abbey), Exeter dioc.
John Tapnaile, Exeter dioc., dim., title of Monkton Farleigh
(priory).
Thomas Bradford, monk of Abbotsbury (abbey), OSB.
Thomas Patwyn, Norwich dioc., dim., title of Osney (abbey),
Lincoln dioc.
Henry Purdewe, Winchester dioc., dim., title of a choral stall
in Salisbury cath.

(Fo. 86/134) Deacons:
John Kerver, title of Tarrant (abbey).
Philip Perot, monk of Abbotsbury (abbey), OSB.
John Lychet, monk of Abbotsbury (abbey), OSB.
Henry Rading, monk of Reading (abbey), OSB.
John Pynnok, bonhomme of Edington (collegiate ch.).
Richard Erberfelde, bonhomme of Edington (collegiate ch.).
John Stronge, title of Bradenstoke priory.
Robert Mawghthille, title of Osney (abbey), Lincoln dioc.

Priests:
John Venby, OFM of Salisbury (Greyfriars).
Gerard de Coloma, OFM of Salisbury (Greyfriars).
Henry Frome, monk of Sherborne (abbey), OSB.
William Moore, monk of Sherborne (abbey), OSB.
William Upton, monk of Malmesbury (abbey).
John Cokke, Lincoln dioc., dim., title of (hospital of) St John
(the Baptist), Wilton.
John Molle, title of Malmesbury (abbey).

Thomas Newton, London dioc., dim., title of Bisham priory.
Robert Hill, monk of Milton (abbey), OSB.
William Smyth, bonhomme of Edington (collegiate ch.).
John Vyncent, Bath and Wells dioc., dim., title of Stanley
(abbey).
William Lyllyngton, title of hospital of St Nicholas, Salisbury.

569 Ordinations celebrated in the parish or prebendal ch. of Ramsbury
on Ember Saturday, 19 December 1489, the fifth year of the bp.'s
translation.

Acolytes:
Richard Colstane, Carlisle dioc., dim.
Peter Broune, Glasgow dioc., dim.
M. Richard Watson, Carlisle dioc., dim.
Thomas Shereve.

Subdeacons:
Richard Whissyng, title of the priory of St Frideswide, Oxford.
John Oram, Bath and Wells dioc., dim., title of Stavordale
(priory).
George Hichman, Worcester dioc., dim., title of Poulton (priory).

Deacons:
John Abbot, Lincoln dioc., dim., title of Thornholme priory.
William Wursley, OFM of Reading (Greyfriars).
Thomas Paytwyn, Norwich dioc., dim., title of Osney (abbey).
William Rayn, York dioc., dim., title of Rewley (abbey) by
Oxford.
John Taple, Exeter dioc., dim., title of Monkton Farleigh priory.

(Fo. 86v/134v) Priests:
Henry Radyng, monk of Reading (abbey), OSB.
M. William Fowell, Exeter dioc., dim., title of Plympton (priory).
John Whyte, canon of Bradenstoke priory.
John Strong, title of Bradenstoke (priory).

570 Ordinations celebrated in Salisbury cath. on Holy Saturday, 10
April 1490, the sixth year of the bp.'s translation.

'Benedicti':
John Burges, Durham dioc.
Thomas Makkys.
Philip Anger, OP of Salisbury (Blackfriars).
William Maltus, OP of Salisbury (Blackfriars).
William White, OP of Salisbury (Blackfriars).

Acolytes:
John Burges, Durham dioc.

Thomas Makkys.
Philip Anger, OP of Salisbury (Blackfriars).
William Maltus, OP of Salisbury (Blackfriars).
William White, OP of Salisbury (Blackfriars).
John Whithed.
William Pakkar, OP.
John Wheler.

Subdeacons:
Henry Gile, title of Ivychurch priory.
John Cusse, title of Bruern (abbey, Lincoln dioc.).
Thomas Mychell, title of Bradenstoke (priory).
William Whiston, Lincoln dioc., dim., title of St James's
(abbey), Northampton.
Philip Robyns, Lincoln dioc., dim., title of Biddlesden (abbey).
John Lewes, Bath and Wells dioc., dim., title of Milton (abbey).
William Wright, York dioc., dim., title of Felley (priory), same
dioc.
Richard Page, canon of Ivychurch (priory) by Salisbury.

Deacons:
Robert Whissyng, title of (the priory of) St Frideswide, Oxford.
John Sharp, Carlisle dioc., dim., title of Poughley (priory).
Richard Colstane, Carlisle dioc., dim., title of Shap (abbey).
John Beyle, York dioc., dim., title of Llanthony (priory).
George Hichman, Worcester dioc., dim., title of Poulton (priory).
Thomas Flynte, Winchester dioc., dim., title of a choral stall in
Salisbury cath.
Thomas Burnell, Worcester dioc., dim., title of a stall in
Salisbury cath.
Henry Purdewe, Winchester dioc., dim., title of a stall in
Salisbury cath.
Robert Mershall, OP of Salisbury (Blackfriars).

(Fo. 87/135) Priests:
William Asshe BA, title of Amesbury (priory).
M. George Rede BCL, fellow of New College Oxford.
Richard Huntley, Worcester dioc., dim., title of Llanthony
(priory).
Richard Seynt John, London dioc., dim., title of hospital of
St Nicholas, Salisbury.
Thomas Wymborn, canon of Christ Church, Twynham (priory).
Robert Mawghthille, title of Osney (abbey).
William Rondell, Exeter dioc., dim., title of Ivychurch (priory).

571 Ordinations celebrated in the chapel of Sherborne castle on
     Ember Saturday, 5 June 1490, the sixth year of the bp.'s
     translation.

     Acolytes:
     John Gerard, tons.

104

Richard Harris, tons.
John Bisshop.
William Lewis.
Nicholas Penfold.
Thomas Rylyng.
Stephen Wodlond, monk of Sherborne (abbey), OSB.
John Flynte, monk of Sherborne (abbey), OSB.
Roger Piers, monk of Sherborne (abbey), OSB.
Thomas Poucherdon, monk of Sherborne (abbey), OSB.
Henry Abyndon, monk of Cerne (abbey), OSB.
John Cerne, monk of Cerne (abbey), OSB.
William Neulond, monk of Cerne (abbey), OSB.

Subdeacons:
Thomas Makkys, title of Wilton (abbey).
John Whithed, title of Wilton (abbey).
William Taylour, title of Cerne (abbey).
Pascasius Salesbery, monk of Milton (abbey), OSB.
John Mylton, monk of Milton (abbey), OSB.

Deacons:
John Cusse, title of Bruern (abbey), dim.
M. Thomas Mychell MA, title of Bradenstoke (priory).
William Wright, York dioc., dim., title of Felley (priory), same dioc.
Thomas Duke, title of Cerne (abbey).
Philip Robyns, Lincoln dioc., dim., title of Biddlesden (abbey).

(Fo. 87v/135v) Priests:
Robert Whissyng, title of (the priory of) St Frideswide, Oxford.
John Sharp, Carlisle dioc., dim., title of Poughley (priory).
Richard Colstane, Carlisle dioc., dim., title of Shap (abbey).
John Lychet, monk of Abbotsbury (abbey).
John Heskyn, OP of Bristol (Blackfriars).
William Jonyngys, canon of Maiden Bradley (priory).
John Beyle, York dioc., dim., title of Llanthony priory, Worcester dioc.
George Hichman, Worcester dioc., dim., title of Poulton (priory), same dioc.

572 Ordinations celebrated in the parish or prebendal ch. of Ramsbury
on Ember Saturday, 18 September 1490, the sixth year of the bp.'s
translation.

'Benedicti':
Richard Beche, Coventry and Lichfield dioc.
John Forster, Bath and Wells dioc.
John Kyngman.

Acolytes:
John Beche, Coventry and Lichfield dioc., dim.
John Forster, Bath and Wells dioc., dim.
John Kyngman.
William Lane, Lincoln dioc., dim.
John Trenche, Bath and Wells dioc., dim.

Subdeacons:
Thomas Sheryff, title of Malmesbury (abbey).
Richard Cam, monk of Malmesbury (abbey), OSB.

Deacons:
William Whiston, Lincoln dioc., dim., title of St James's
(abbey), Northampton.
William Taylour, title of Cerne (abbey).
Thomas Makkys, title of Wilton (abbey).
Robert Wellis, monk of Hurley (priory), OSB.
Richard Page, canon of Ivychurch (priory), by Salisbury.

Priests:
John Cusse, title of Bruern (abbey, Lincoln dioc.).
William Clerke, Worcester dioc., dim., title of Malmesbury
(abbey).
Richard ap John, St Asaph dioc., dim., title of Strata Marcella
(abbey), same dioc.
John Whittemor, OCist., of Dunkeswell (abbey), Exeter dioc.
William Wright, York dioc., dim., title of Felley (priory).
Philip Robyns, Lincoln dioc., dim., title of Biddlesden (abbey).
John Kerver, title of Tarrant (abbey).
Robert Holyday, Worcester dioc., dim., title of Kingswood
(abbey).
John Rowell, monk of Abingdon (abbey), OSB.
M. Thomas Michell MA, title of Bradenstoke (priory).
John Pynnok, bonhomme of Edington (collegiate ch.).
Richard Yerbery, bonhomme of Edington (collegiate ch.).
John Aylberton, monk of Malmesbury (abbey), OSB.

573 (Fo. 88/136) Ordinations celebrated in the chapel of the B.V.M.
     in the manor of Ramsbury on Ember Saturday, 18 December 1490,
     in the sixth year of the bp.'s translation.

     'Benedicti':
     Thomas Walkar.
     Thomas Smyth.
     John Broune.
     Andrew Story, OC.

     Acolytes:
     William Lancaster, Carlisle dioc., dim.
     John Gold.
     Peter Andrewe, Exeter dioc., dim.

Thomas Smyth.
Henry Petipace.
John Alfforde.
Andrew Story, OC.
Thomas Walkar, Carlisle dioc., dim.
John Broune.

Subdeacons:
M. John Hobyll MA, fellow of New College, Oxford, title of his coll.
M. Thomas Kyng MA, fellow of Merton Coll., Oxford, Worcester dioc., dim., title of his coll.
John Forstere, Bath dioc. (sic), dim., title of Poughley (priory).
Richard Beche, Coventry and Lichfield dioc., dim., title of Burnham (abbey).
Richard Balteswell, title of his pension for life from West Dean ch.
Thomas Mordy, OC.
Robert Willyamson, OC.
Cornelius Lemes, OC.
Alexander Shaftisbroke, monk of Abingdon (abbey), OSB.
Robert Westwod, monk of Abingdon (abbey), OSB.
Thomas Comnore, monk of Abingdon (abbey), OSB.
Thomas Westgate, monk of Abingdon (abbey), OSB.
Robert Morton, monk of Abingdon (abbey), OSB.
Robert Cholsey, monk of Reading (abbey), OSB.
Robert Radyng, monk of Reading (abbey), OSB.
John Harris, title of Easton (priory).

Deacons:
Thomas Sheryff, title of Malmesbury (abbey).
Robert Lancaster, OC.
John Bugge, OFM of Dorchester (friary).
John Clifton, monk of Reading (abbey).
William Leompster, monk of Reading (abbey).

(Fo. 88v/136v) Priests:
Edmund Radclyff, Coventry and Lichfield dioc., dim., title of Osney (abbey).
Thomas Makkys, title of Wilton (abbey).
Robert Wellis, monk of Hurley (priory).
Richard Page, canon of Ivychurch (priory).

574 Ordinations celebrated in the chapel of the manor of Ramsbury on Ember Saturday in the first week of Lent, viz. 26 February 1491, the seventh year of the bp.'s translation.

Acolytes:
Richard Highmore, Carlisle dioc., dim.
John Smyth.
Hugh Prilacy.

John ap David ap Gwyn, St Asaph dioc., dim.
Thomas Skykard, Exeter dioc., dim.
Richard Sedner, Canterbury dioc., dim.
John Adam, Exeter dioc., dim.
John Michell, Exeter dioc., dim.

Subdeacons:
William Smyth, Coventry and Lichfield dioc., dim., title of Vale
Royal (abbey), same dioc.
Marcus Carre, Durham dioc., dim., title of Bullington priory,
Lincoln dioc.
William Denham, Durham dioc., dim., title of Notley (abbey).
Peter Andrewe, Exeter dioc., dim., title of Osney (abbey).
Thomas Smyth, title of Vaux Coll., Salisbury.
Thomas Walkar, Carlisle dioc., dim., title of Shap (abbey).
Richard Harris, title of Cerne (abbey).
William Howell, St David's dioc., dim., title of Osney (abbey).
John Carver, OC, Exeter dioc.
Andrew Story, OC.
John Burgis, vicar-choral of Salisbury cath., title of his stall
there.

Deacons:
M. John Hobill, MA, fellow of the New College, Oxford, title
of his coll.
Richard Balteswell, title of his pension from West Dean ch.
Richard Beche, Coventry and Lichfield dioc., dim., title of
Burnham (abbey).
Robert Williamson, OC of Oxford university.
John Forster, Bath and Wells dioc., dim., title of Poughley
(priory).

Priests:
M. William Cherite, r. of Easton, title of same.
William Whiston, Lincoln dioc., dim., title of St James's (abbey),
Northampton.
Thomas ap John, St Asaph dioc., dim., title of Valle Crucis
(abbey).
Thomas Sheriff, title of Malmesbury (abbey).
(Fo. 89/137) Geoffrey de Meyndek ap Pell, St Asaph dioc., title
of Basingwerk (abbey).
Richard Howell, St Asaph dioc., dim., title of Basingwerk
(abbey).

575 Ordinations celebrated in Sherborne abbey on <u>Sitientes</u> Saturday,
19 March 1491, the seventh year of the bp.'s translation.

Acolytes:
Thomas Maundevile, tons.
David Lloyd, St David's dioc., dim.
Roger Mathewe, monk of Cerne (abbey), OSB.

John Yong.
Richard Avenell, monk of Bindon (abbey), OCist.
John Buklande, monk of Bindon, OCist.

Subdeacons:
Stephen Wodlond, monk of Sherborne (abbey), OSB.
John Flynte, monk of Sherborne (abbey), OSB.
Roger Piers, monk of Sherborne (abbey), OSB.
Thomas Poucherdon, monk of Sherborne (abbey), OSB.
John Michell, Exeter dioc., dim., title of Osney (abbey),
Lincoln dioc.
Thomas William, Exeter dioc., dim., title of Plympton (priory).
Thomas Skykard, Exeter dioc., dim., title of Launceston
(priory).
Henry Abendon, monk of Cerne (abbey), OSB.
John Cerne, monk of Cerne (abbey), OSB.
William Newlond, monk of Cerne (abbey), OSB.

Deacons:
M. Robert Dale, MA, Bath and Wells dioc., dim., title of a
fellowship in Merton Coll., Oxford.
Marcus Carre, Durham dioc., dim., title of Bullington (priory),
OGilb.
Thomas Smyth, title of Vaux Coll., Salisbury.
Richard Harris, title of Cerne (abbey).
John Burges, vicar-choral of Salisbury cath., title of his stall.
William Smyth, Coventry and Lichfield dioc., dim., title of Vale
Royal (abbey).

Priests:
John Forster, Bath and Wells dioc., dim., title of Poughley
(priory).
John Portesham, monk of Abbotsbury (abbey), OSB.
Philip Peret, monk of Abbotsbury (abbey), OSB.

576 Ordinations celebrated in the chapel of the manor of Ramsbury on
Holy Saturday, viz. 2 April 1491, the seventh year of the bp.'s
translation.

Acolytes:
Robert Peryngcorte of Castle Combe.
John Gile alias Smyth.

(Fo. 89v/137v) Subdeacons:
John Trenche, Bath and Wells dioc., dim., title of Ivychurch
(priory).
M. William Portland MA, Norwich dioc., fellow of All Souls Coll.,
Oxford, dim., title of his coll.
John Alfford, title of his benefice of Rolleston.
Walter Vaugham, Llandaff dioc., dim., title of Llantarnam (abbey).

Deacons:
Richard Sednor, Canterbury dioc., dim., title of Leeds (priory),
same dioc.
Thomas Croser, canon of St Margaret's (priory), Marlborough, OGilb.
Thomas Hardegate, York dioc., dim., title of Stavordale (priory).

Priests:
John Burges, vicar-choral of Salisbury (cath.), title of his stall.
William Smyth, Coventry and Lichfield dioc., dim., title of Vale
Royal (abbey), same dioc.
Marcus Carre, Durham dioc., dim., title of Bullington (priory),
Lincoln dioc.
William Denham, Durham dioc., dim., title of Notley (abbey),
Lincoln dioc.
Thomas Flynte, title of his choral stall in Salisbury cath.
M. Edward Repe MA, Winchester dioc., fellow of New College, Oxford,
dim.
Henry Purdewe, vicar-choral of Salisbury cath., title of his stall.

577 Ordinations celebrated in the chapel in the manor of Ramsbury on
Ember Saturday, viz. 28 May 1491, the seventh year of the bp.'s
translation.

Acolytes:
John Towkar alias Favell.
Richard Edmonde.

Subdeacons:
Thomas Ryling, title of his choral stall in Salisbury cath.
William Bele, title of Sherborne (abbey).
John Yong, title of Abbotsbury (abbey).

Deacons:
John Whithede, title of Wilton (abbey).
Richard Cam, monk of Malmesbury (abbey).
John Trench, Bath and Wells dioc., dim., title of Ivychurch
(priory).
Alexander Shottesbroke, monk of Abingdon (abbey).
Robert Westwode, monk of Abingdon (abbey).

Priests:
Thomas Croser, canon of St Margaret's (priory), Marlborough, OGilb.
William Taylour, title of Cerne (abbey).
Thomas Smyth, title of Vaux Coll., Salisbury.

578 (Fo. 90/138) Ordinations celebrated in the chapel in Sherborne
castle on Ember Saturday, viz. 24 December (sic; rectius
September) 1491, the seventh year of the bp.'s translation.

Acolytes:
Henry Cryche.
William Dalaware.
Richard Grobam.

Subdeacons:
John Gile alias Smyth, title of Bradenstoke (priory).
John Buckland, monk of Bindon (abbey), OCist.
Richard Avenell, monk of Bindon (abbey).
John Aleynson, Carlisle dioc., dim., title of Lambley (priory).

Deacons:
John Yong, title of Abbotsbury (abbey).
William Bele, title of Sherborne (abbey).
Henry Abendon, monk of Cerne (abbey), OSB.
John Cerne, monk of Cerne (abbey), OSB.
William Neulond, monk of Cerne (abbey), OSB.
Pascasius Salesbery, monk of Milton (abbey).
John Middelton, monk of Milton (abbey).

Priests:
Thomas Hardgate, York dioc., dim., title of Stavordale (priory).
Richard Harris, title of Cerne (abbey).

579   Ordinations celebrated in the chapel in the manor of Ramsbury on
      Ember Saturday, 17 December 1491, the seventh year of the bp.'s
      translation.

Acolytes:
Robert Dixon, brother of Easton (priory), tons.
Thomas Hopkyns, tons.
Gilbert Rygge, Carlisle dioc., dim., tons.
William Walter.
John Asshe, vicar-choral of Salisbury cath.

Subdeacons:
John Biggys, title of Amesbury (abbey).
Eugenius Dale, Norwich dioc., dim., title of (the hospital of) St
John the Baptist, Wells, Bath and Wells dioc.
William Dalaware, title of Stanley (abbey).
Thomas Johnson, title of Osney (abbey).

Deacons:
John Gile alias Smyth, title of Bradenstoke (priory).
John Aleynson, Carlisle dioc., dim., title of Lambley (priory).
John Harris, title of Easton (priory).

Priests:
(Fo. 90v/138v) Richard Cam, monk of Malmesbury (abbey).
John Trenche, Bath and Wells dioc., dim., title of Ivychurch
(priory).

111

Richard Balteswell, title of his pension from West Dean ch.
Roger Awbrey, Hereford dioc., dim., title of Llanthony (priory).

580 Ordinations celebrated in the parish or prebendal ch. of Ramsbury on Ember Saturday, 17 March 1492, the eighth year of the bp.'s translation.

Acolytes:
John Fynys, tons.
John Newe, tons.
Walter Baker, tons.
John Wente, tons.
Robert Smyth, tons.
Richard Marten, tons.
Richard Whittpoll, Worcester dioc., tons., fellow of the New College, Oxford.
Lewis Richard, Bangor dioc., tons.
William Cok, York dioc., dim., tons.
William Hanont, Exeter dioc., dim., tons.
William Hilton, York dioc., dim., tons.

Subdeacons:
Thomas Broune, Worcester dioc., dim., title of Malmesbury (abbey).
John Asshe _alias_ Knowdeshille, Bath and Wells dioc., dim., title of his choral stall in Salisbury cath.
John Lee, Coventry and Lichfield dioc., dim., title of Poughley (priory).
Oswald Bullok, Durham dioc., dim., title of Osney (abbey).
Richard Harding, Durham dioc., dim., title of the priory of St Frideswide, Oxford.
M. Edmund Willisford, Exeter dioc., MA, fellow of Oriel Coll., Oxford, dim., title of his coll.
Simon Chapman, Norwich dioc., dim., title of Osney (abbey), Lincoln dioc.
Thomas Casson BA, York dioc., dim., title of North Ferriby priory, order of the Temple (1) York (dioc.).
Robert Marshall, Durham dioc., dim., title of hospital of St James the Apostle, Northallerton.
John Barneby, York dioc., dim., title of Selby (abbey).
William Lancastre, Carlisle dioc., dim., title of Reading (abbey).

Deacons:
David Cadigan, St David's dioc., dim., title of Osney (abbey).
Edward Banys, York dioc., dim., title of (hospital of) St John, Cambridge, Ely dioc.

1   This order of the Temple of St John Jerusalem was of canons OSA, See Knowles, David, and Hadcock, Nevill, Medieval Religious Houses, England and Wales, 2nd ed. 1971, p.168.

M. Walter Godyere, fellow of Oriel Coll., Oxford, of London dioc., dim., title of his coll.
(Fo. 91/139) John Biggys, title of Amesbury (abbey).
William Dalaware, title of Stanley (abbey).
Thomas Johnson, title of Osney (abbey), Lincoln dioc.
Thomas Walkar, Carlisle dioc., dim., title of Shap (abbey), same dioc.

Priests:
M. Thomas Mugwurthy BCL, Exeter dioc., dim., title of St Germans priory.
William Gelys, Exeter dioc., title of Buckfast (abbey), same dioc.
John Abendon, canon of (the priory of) St Frideswide, Oxford.
Thomas Redman, Norwich dioc., dim., title of Osney (abbey), Lincoln dioc.
John Aleynson, Carlisle dioc., title of Lambley (priory), Durham dioc.
John Gile _alias_ Smyth, title of Bradenstoke (priory).
John Saunders, Durham dioc., dim., title of Thame (abbey).

581 Ordinations celebrated in the parish or prebendal ch. of Ramsbury on _Sitientes_ Saturday, viz. 7 April 1492, the eighth year of the bp.'s translation.

Acolytes:
Morgan Williams, St David's dioc., dim., tons.
Raginald Philip, St David's dioc., dim.
Thomas Colmore, Exeter dioc., dim., title of Barnstaple priory, OClun.
Roger Shipley, Lincoln dioc., dim., title of Newstead priory.
William Cesson, Lincoln dioc., dim.

Subdeacons:
Thomas Watson, Coventry and Lichfield dioc., dim., title of Osney (abbey).
William Hall, Worcester dioc., dim., title of Bruern (abbey), Lincoln dioc.
William Hamonde, Exeter dioc., dim., title of (the priory of) St Frideswide.
M. William Broke, fellow of All Souls (Coll.), Oxford, BCL, Canterbury dioc., dim.
Gilbert Rygge, Carlisle dioc., dim., title of (the priory of) St Frideswide, Oxford.
John Wente, title of monastery of St Mary, Winchester.
John Birde, Bangor dioc., dim., title of Osney (abbey).
John Lethome, York dioc., dim., title of Selby (abbey), same dioc.
David Tallay, canon of Talley (abbey), St David's dioc.
John Fynde, London dioc., dim., title of Bindon (abbey).

Deacons:
Simon Chapman, Norwich dioc., dim., title of Osney (abbey),

Lincoln dioc.
Thomas Brome, Worcester dioc., dim., title of Malmesbury (abbey).
John Lee, Coventry and Lichfield dioc., dim., title of Poughley
(priory).
John Barnaby, York dioc., dim., title of Selby (abbey).
Oswald Bullok, Durham dioc., dim., title of Osney (abbey).
Thomas Cesson, York dioc., dim., title of North Ferriby priory,
order of Templars, (1) same dioc.
Richard Florence, Norwich dioc., dim., title of hospital of St
Mary Bishopsgate, London.
Richard Hardyng, Durham dioc., dim., title of (the priory of) St
Frideswide.
John Piers, fellow of the New College, Oxford, Chichester dioc.,
dim.
(Fo. 91v/139v) Robert Marshall, Durham dioc., dim., title of
(hospital of) St James, Northallerton.
William Lancastre, Carlisle dioc., dim., title of Reading (abbey).
M. Edmund Wilsford MA, Exeter dioc., dim., title of a fellowship
in Oriel Coll., Oxford.
John Alford, title of his benefice of Rollestone.
Bartholomew Tarton, Coventry and Lichfield dioc., dim., title of
Osney (abbey).

Priests:
David Cadigan, St David's dioc., dim., title of Osney (abbey).
John Biggys, title of Amesbury (abbey).
Thomas Johnson, title of Osney (abbey).
Henry Abendon, monk of Cerne (abbey).
John Cerne, monk of Cerne (abbey).
William Bele, title of Sherborne (abbey).

582 Ordinations celebrated in the oratory in the manor of Ramsbury on
Holy Saturday, viz. 21 April 1492, the eighth year of the bp.'s
translation.

Deacons:
M. William Broke, Canterbury dioc., fellow of All Souls Coll.,
Oxford, dim.
Gilbert Rigg, Carlisle dioc., dim., title of (the priory of) St
Frideswide.

Priests:
Richard Florence, Norwich dioc., dim., title of hospital of St
Mary Bishopsgate, London.
John Lee, Coventry and Lichfield dioc., dim., title of Poughley
(priory).
M. Edmund Wilsforde, MA, Exeter dioc., fellow of Oriel Coll.,

1   See 580, n.1.

114

Oxford, dim.
John Piers, Bath and Wells dioc., fellow of the New College,
Oxford, dim.
Robert Edmunde, title of Bro(illeg.).
Robert Marshall, Durham dioc., dim., title of (hospital of) St
James, Northallerton.
William Lancastre, Carlisle dioc., dim., title of Reading (abbey).

583 Ordinations celebrated in the oratory in the manor of Ramsbury on
Ember Saturday, viz. 16 June 1492, the eighth year of the bp.'s
translation.

(Fo. 92/140) Acolytes:
M. John Estmond, tons.
Philip Jonys, tons.
Richard Pykton, London dioc., dim.
John Clerk, tons.

Subdeacons:
John Clyff, monk of Abingdon (abbey).

Deacons:
Roger Shipley, Lincoln dioc., dim., title of Newstead priory, OSA.
Thomas Comnor, monk of Abingdon (abbey).
Robert Morton, monk of Abingdon (abbey).

Priests:
Oswald Bullok, Durham dioc., dim., title of Osney (abbey).
Gilbert Rigge, Carlisle dioc., dim., title of the priory of St
Frideswide, Oxford.
John Alforde, title of his benefice of Rollestone.

584 Ordinations celebrated in the parish or prebendal ch. of Ramsbury
on Ember Saturday, viz. 2 March 1493, the ninth year of the bp.'s
translation.

Acolytes:
M. Thomas Haukyns, MA, Hereford dioc., fellow of All Souls Coll.,
Oxford, dim., the title of his coll.
Walter Blonte, Hereford dioc., dim., title of Halesowen (abbey).
John Warwikhill, Glasgow dioc., dim.
John Pilton, monk of Malmesbury (abbey).
Robert Walston, monk of Malmesbury (abbey).
Thomas Lacok, monk of Malmesbury (abbey).
Thomas Olveston, monk of Malmesbury (abbey).
Henry Hammond, OP of Salisbury (Blackfriars).
M. Andrew Patrik alias Stephynson, r. of Easton Grey.

Subdeacons:
Richard Marshall, Durham dioc., dim., title of Greatham hospital.
William Belle, Carlisle dioc., dim., title of Osney (abbey).
M. William Mores BCL, Bath and Wells dioc., dim., title of his
benefice of Porlock, same dioc.
John Coole BA, fellow of All Souls Coll., Oxford, title of his
coll.
M. Andrew Scarbot MA, exempt jurisdiction of the abbot of Bury,
dim., title of Magdalen Coll., (Oxford).
M. John Haynes MA, Exeter dioc., fellow of All Souls Coll.,
Oxford, dim.
M. Richard Edmondys, Bath and Wells dioc., dim., title of a
fellowship in Merton Coll., (Oxford).
(Fo. 92v/140v) John Fyttok, Bath and Wells dioc., title of his
choral stall in Salisbury cath.
David Cleiset, St Andrew's dioc., dim., title of Osney (abbey),
Lincoln (dioc.).
Richard Beste, York dioc., dim., title of Gokewell (priory),
Lincoln (dioc.).
Henry Crich, title of Milton (abbey).
Robert Benham, monk of Reading (abbey).
Walter Kyngesland, monk of Reading (abbey).
Thomas Bristowe, monk of Abingdon (abbey).
John Sutton, monk of Abingdon (abbey).
John Cornish, monk of Abingdon (abbey).
Henry Petipace, title of a fellowship in Vaux Coll., Salisbury.
Thomas Barre, Lincoln dioc., title of the priory of St Mary
Overy, Southwark.

(Fo. 92/140) Deacons:
M. John Estmonde MA, title of Poughley priory.
M. Roger Church DCnL, Canterbury dioc., dim., title of his
benefice of Kenardington, same dioc.
M. William Bustard, Lincoln dioc., dim., title of a fellowship in
All Souls Coll., Oxford.
William Sissin, Lincoln dioc., dim., title of Bruern (abbey), same
dioc.
Thomas Ryling, title of his choral stall in Salisbury cath.
Thomas Westgate, monk of Abingdon (abbey).
William Fiffeld, monk of Abingdon (abbey).

Priests:
Robert Westwode, monk of Abingdon (abbey).
John Cliffe, monk of Abingdon (abbey).

585 Ordinations celebrated in the parish or prebendal ch. of Ramsbury
on Sitientes Saturday, viz. 23 March 1493, the ninth year of the
bp.'s translation.

Acolytes:
John Codryngton, monk of Abingdon (abbey), tons.

Henry Davy, Bangor dioc., dim., tons.
Robert Gaskyn.
John Bemonde, monk of Malmesbury (abbey).

Subdeacons:
M. Thomas Haukyns MA, Hereford dioc., dim., title of a fellowship in All Souls Coll., Oxford.
Walter Blonte, Hereford dioc., dim., title of Halesowen (abbey), Worcester dioc.
M. Andrew Patrik alias Stephynson MA, r. of Easton Grey.
Robert Woleston, monk of Malmesbury (abbey).
Thomas Lacok, monk of Malmesbury (abbey).
Philip Jonys, title of Malmesbury (abbey).

Deacons:
John Buckland, monk of Bindon (abbey).
Richard Avenell, monk of Bindon (abbey).
Henry Petipace, title of a fellowship in Vaux Coll., Salisbury.
Thomas Barre, Lincoln dioc., dim., title of the priory of St Mary Overy, Southwark.
M. Richard Edmundys MA, Bath and Wells dioc., dim., title of a fellowship in Merton Coll., Oxford.
M. John Coole, fellow of All Souls Coll., Oxford, dim.
John Sneth, OFM of Reading (Greyfriars).
M. John Haynes MA, Exeter dioc., fellow of All Souls Coll., Oxford, dim.
M. Andrew Skarbot MA, exempt jurisdiction of the abbot of Bury, dim., title of Magdalen Coll., Oxford.
(Fo. 93/141) Richard Marshall, Durham dioc., dim., title of Greatham hospital.
Richard Beste, York dioc., dim., title of Gokewell (priory).
William Belle, Carlisle dioc., dim., title of Osney (abbey).
Thomas Mason, Lincoln dioc., dim., title of Owston (abbey).

Priests:
M. Roger Church DCnL, Canterbury dioc., dim., title of his benefice of Kenardington.
M. Thomas Hede BCL, Worcester dioc., dim., title of Torksey priory.
M. William Bustard, Lincoln dioc., dim., title of a fellowship in All Souls Coll., Oxford.
John Cotteswold, Lincoln dioc., dim., title of Osney (abbey).
William Sisson, Lincoln dioc., title of Bruern (abbey).
John Baill, Coventry and Lichfield dioc., dim., title of Notley (abbey), Lincoln dioc.
William Fiffelde, monk of Abingdon (abbey).
Thomas Westgate, monk of Abingdon (abbey).
John Harris, title of Easton (priory).

586 Ordinations celebrated in the oratory in the manor of Ramsbury on Holy Saturday, viz. 6 April 1493, the ninth year of the bp.'s translation.

Subdeacons:
Robert Gascoyn, title of Milton (abbey).
John Bemond, monk of Malmesbury (abbey).
John Codryngton, monk of Malmesbury (abbey).

Deacons:
M. Rouland Philippes MA, Worcester dioc., dim., title of Oriel
Coll., Oxford.
Walter Blont, Hereford dioc., dim., title of Halesowen (abbey),
Worcester dioc.
Henry Criche, title of Milton (abbey).
M. Thomas Haukyns, Hereford dioc., MA, fellow of All Souls Coll.,
Oxford, dim., title of his coll.
M. Andrew Patrik alias Stephynson, MA, title of his rectory of
Easton Grey.
David Cleiser, St Andrew's dioc., dim., title of Osney (abbey).

Priests:
M. Richard Edmundys MA, Bath and Wells dioc., title of his
fellowship in Merton Coll., Oxford.
Richard Beste, York dioc., dim., title of Gokewell (priory).
William Belle, Carlisle dioc., dim., title of Osney (abbey).
Thomas Smyth, Worcester dioc., dim., title of Malmesbury (abbey).
M. Andrew Scarbot MA, exempt jurisdiction of the abbot and conv.
of Bury, Norwich dioc., title of a fellowship in Magdalen Coll.,
Oxford.
John Sneth, OFM of Reading (Greyfriars).
Richard Marshall, Durham dioc., dim., title of Greatham hospital.
Henry Petipace, fellow of Vaux Coll., Salisbury.

587 (Fo. 93v/141v) Ordinations celebrated at Ramsbury on Ember
Saturday, 1 June 1493, the ninth year of the bp.'s translation.

Acolytes:
Robert Caviller, tons.
M. Richard Rob(erd) MA.
Nicholas Graunt, canon of Bradenstoke (priory).
Thomas Penne, canon of Bradenstoke (priory).
William Jervys, canon of Bradenstoke (priory).
Richard Bedforde, canon of Bradenstoke (priory).

Subdeacon:
Roger Mathewe, monk of Cerne (abbey).

Deacons:
John Gascoyn, title of Milton (abbey).
John Asshe alias Knowdeshill, Bath and Wells dioc., dim., title
of his choral stall in Salisbury cath.
John Bemonde, monk of Malmesbury (abbey).
John Cotryngton, monk of Malmesbury (abbey).

118

Priests:

M. Thomas Haukyns MA, Hereford dioc., fellow of All Souls Coll.,
Oxford, dim.

William Newlond, monk of Cerne (abbey).

Thomas Blaksore, Worcester dioc., dim., title of (the priory of)
St Frideswide, Oxford.

Thomas Barre, Lincoln dioc., dim., title of the priory of St Mary
Overy, Southwark.

M. Andrew Patrik _alias_ Stephynson MA, title of his benefice of
Easton Grey.

M. John Haynes MA, Exeter dioc., fellow of All Souls Coll.,
Oxford, dim.

M. Rouland Philipes MA, Worcester dioc., dim., title of Oriel Coll.,
Oxford.

Walter Blunt, Hereford dioc., dim., title of Halesowen (abbey).

David Cleiser, St Andrew's dioc., dim., title of Osney (abbey).

William Hurne, title of Cerne (abbey).

APPENDIX A

Additional Acta not in Bishop Langton's Salisbury Register

588 Mandate of (Robert) Stillington bp. of Bath and Wells, dated 20 March 1486, to the v. of Writhlington or his vicegerent to put into corporal possession of the prebend of (Fordington and) Writhlington and induct Robert Langton, clerk, collated thereto by Thomas, bp. of Salisbury, as appears by his letter dated 29 September 1485.
(The Registers of Robert Stillington, bishop of Bath and Wells, 1466-1491 and Richard Fox bishop of Bath and Wells, 1492-1494, ed. H.C. Maxwell-Lyte. Somerset Record Society 52 (1937), p.137.)

589 Presentation by King Henry of M. Geoffrey Elys, chaplain, to the parish church of Winterborne Earls, void by the death of the last r. 12 November 1490.
(P.R.O., C.82/74/3; C.P.R., 1485-1494, p.333.)

590 Confirmation of the election of Alice Gybbys as abbess of Shaftesbury in place of Margaret Seynt John, who died on 1 June 1492, and petition for restitution of the temporalities. Ramsbury, 6 September 1492.
(P.R.O., C.82/98/15; see also C.82/95/34, C.82/96/14, C.82/97/4, C.82/98/13,14, C.82/94/18; C.P.R., 1485-1494, pp.386, 405, 409.)

591 Petition to the king for the restitution of temporalities to Richard Page, whose election as prior of Ivychurch in place of Edward Thacham, deceased, he has confirmed. Ramsbury, 22 March 1493.
(P.R.O., C.82/104/17; see also C.82/104/5; C.P.R., 1485-1494, pp.410, 419, 426.)

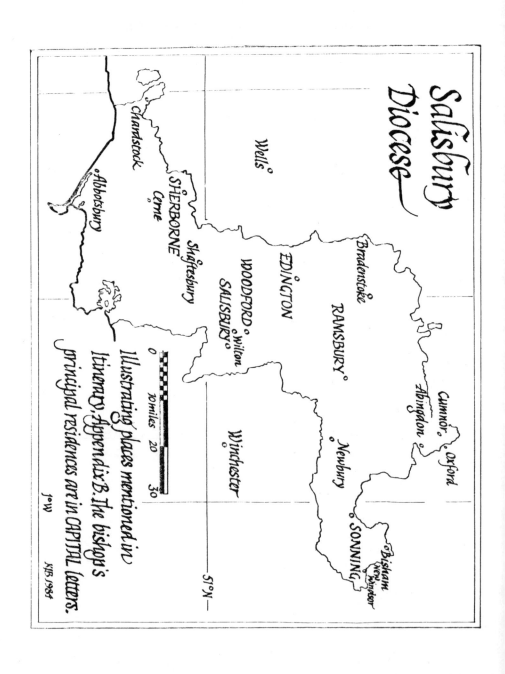

Salisbury Diocese

Illustrating places mentioned in
Itinerary, Appendix B. The bishop's
principal residences are in CAPITAL letters.

J°W   KJB 1984

0   10 miles   20   30

— 51°N —

Chardstock
Abbotsbury
SHERBORNE
Cerne
Shaftesbury
Wells
Bradenstoke
EDINGTON
RAMSBURY
WOODFORD
Wilton
SALISBURY
Winchester
Newbury
Abingdon
Cumnor
Oxford
SONNING
Bisham
New Windsor

APPENDIX B

Itinerary of Thomas Langton, Bishop of Salisbury 1485-93

(All references are to his register as bp. of Salisbury, unless
otherwise stated)

Custody of temporalities, 15 March 1484 (P.R.O., C.81/1530/31; C.P.R.,
1476-85, p.387).   Licence to elect, 3 December 1484 (P.R.O., C.81/902/
808);   delivered 19 December 1484 (C.P.R., 1476-85, p.488.   Translated
from St Davids by pope, 9 February 1485 (Calendar of Papal Letters,
Lateran Registers, Vol. XV, 1484-92, No.90).   Restitution of temporalities, 3 May 1485 (P.R.O. C.81/906/1046), upon receipt of bull of
translation, delivered 4 May (C.P.R., 1476-85, p.521).   Langton was
certainly still in Rome on 18 February 1485 (Knecht thesis, op.cit.,
p.294) and probably on 23 February (Calendar of Papal Letters, Vol.
XIV, 1484-92, pp.8-10, 12-13).

1485

31 May	Shaftesbury	2	
14 June	Sonning	1	
24 Sept. x 6 Oct.	Bisham	412-16	(Parliament met at Westminster, 7 Nov.-10 Dec. 1485 and 23 Jan. -c.4 March 1486)

1486

7-8 Feb.	Edington	39-40, 43
10 Feb.	Edington	42
18 Feb.	Wilton	563
5 March	Edington	44
10-11 March	Edington	45, 564
25 March	Edington	565
27 March	Edington	47
11 April	Woodford	51
19-20 April	Salisbury	426, 429
24 April	Salisbury	61-3
12 May	Sonning	60
20 May	Cumnor	566
22 May	Sonning	64
3 June	Sonning	66
25 June	Sonning	68
11 July	Sonning	71

20 July	Sonning	72
5 Aug.	Sonning	78
27 Aug.	Sonning	79
1 Sept.	Sonning	80
12 Sept.	Salisbury	81
29 Sept.	Ramsbury	91
12 Oct.	London	85
18 Oct.	London	87
11 Dec.	Woodford	95

1487   (Convocation met at
St Paul's, 13–26 Feb.)

11 April	Woodford	105
24 April	Woodford	103
16 May	Woodford	439
23 May	Woodford	437
29 June	Ramsbury	113
12 July	Ramsbury	114
8 Aug.	Ramsbury	117–8
24–25 Aug.	Ramsbury	121, 123
23 Sept.	Ramsbury	450, 464
6 Oct.	Ramsbury	129
11 Oct.	Ramsbury	130
28 Oct.	Ramsbury	132–3
30 Oct.	Sonning	134
28 Nov.	London	452
20 Dec.	Salisbury	456

(Parliament met at
Westminster, 9 Nov.–
c.18 Dec.)

1488

2 Jan.	Woodford	138
5 Jan.	Woodford	139
18 Jan.	Ramsbury	455
23 Jan.	Ramsbury	458
26 Jan.	Ramsbury	140
15 Feb.	Ramsbury	146
5 April	Salisbury	156 (Holy Saturday)
18 April	Ramsbury	157
28 April	Ramsbury	509
12 May	Ramsbury	159
23 July	Ramsbury	167
4 Aug.	Ramsbury	173
1 Sept.	Ramsbury	177
29 Sept.	Ramsbury	180
6 Nov.	Ramsbury	470
10 Nov.	London	186
1 Dec.	Ramsbury	516

			(Parliament met at Westminster, 13
14 Jan.	London	199	Jan.-13 Feb.-
18 Jan.	London	466	further sessions
7 March	London	519	below; Convocation
12 March	Ramsbury	510	met at St Paul's,
14 March	Ramsbury	532	14 Jan.-27 Feb.)
22 March	Ramsbury	203	
26 March	Ramsbury	512	
1 April	Ramsbury	208	
4 April	Ramsbury	524	
17 April	Salisbury	210	
26 April	Salisbury	533	
7 May	Cerne	214	
10 May	Abbotsbury	216	
12 May	Sherborne	512	
1 June	Ramsbury	218	
13 June	Ramsbury	567	
21 June	Bisham	224	
25 July	Ramsbury	225	
11 Aug.	Ramsbury	228	
19 Sept.	Ramsbury	568	
29 Sept.	Ramsbury	234	(Second session of
20 Oct.	London	240	Parliament, 14 Oct.-
25 Oct.	London	241	4 Dec.)
14 Nov.	London	242	(? Second session of
27 Nov.	London	244	Convocation, 23 Oct.)
19 Dec.	Ramsbury	569	

8 Jan.	Ramsbury	249	
11 Jan.	Ramsbury	250	(Third session of
21 Feb.	London	253	Parliament, 25 Jan.-
23 March	London	259	27 Feb.)
6 April	Ramsbury	263	
10 April	Salisbury	570	(Holy Saturday)
19 April	Salisbury		Statutes and Customs of . . .
27 April	Salisbury	264	Salisbury, ed.
28-29 April	Sherborne	265-7	Christopher Wordsworth
2 May	Sherborne	268	& Douglas Macleane
4-5 May	Sherborne	269-70	(1915), p.344.
11 May	Sherborne	271	
17 May	Sherborne	272	
5 June	Sherborne	571	
10 June	Sherborne	273	
27 June	Sherborne	274	
2 July	Sherborne	275	
29 July	Sherborne	276	
14 Aug.	Sherborne	277	
20 Aug.	Chardstock	278	

15 Sept.	Ramsbury	281	
18 Sept.	Ramsbury	282, 572	
30 Sept.	Ramsbury	284	
4 Oct.	Ramsbury	285	
13 Oct.	Ramsbury	286	
8 Nov.	Ramsbury	287	
13 Nov.	Ramsbury	288	
26 Nov.	Ramsbury	289	
3 Dec.	Ramsbury	290	
18 Dec.	Ramsbury	573	

1491

1 Jan.	Ramsbury	473-4	
18 Jan.	Ramsbury	292-3	
22 Jan.	Ramsbury	295, 475, 485	
28 Jan.	New Windsor	487	
1 Feb.	Ramsbury	538	
4-5 Feb.	Newbury	494, 496	
10 Feb.	Ramsbury	498	
26 Feb.	Ramsbury	574	
17 March	Sherborne	298	
19 March	Sherborne	575	
24 March	Sherborne	299	
28 March	Sherborne	489	
2 April	Ramsbury	576	
6-7 April	Ramsbury	488, 300	
16 April	Ramsbury	301	
18 April	Sonning	485	
17 May	Ramsbury	303-4	
24 May	Ramsbury	305	
28 May	Ramsbury	577	
24 June	London	310	(Convocation met
29 June	London	311	at St Paul's, 21
6 July	London	312	June-?)
15 July	Abingdon	502	
16 July	Ramsbury	483	
19 July	Ramsbury	504	
25 Aug.	Shaftesbury	314	
30-31 Aug.	Sherborne	315-6	
2 Sept.	Sherborne	317	
5 Sept.	Sherborne	318	
24 Sept.	Sherborne	578	
1 Oct.	Salisbury	320	
6 Oct.	Ramsbury	322	
10 Oct.	Ramsbury	323	(Parliament met at
18 Oct.	London	325	Westminster, 17 Oct.-
29 Oct.	London	327	4 Nov. 1491 & 26 Jan.-
10 Nov.	London	479	5 March 1492.)
12 Nov.	Sonning	328	(Convocation met at
24 Nov.	Sonning	329	St Paul's, ?-8 Nov.)

3 Dec.	Ramsbury	330
17 Dec.	Ramsbury	579
26 Dec.	Ramsbury	541
30 Dec.	Ramsbury	543

1492

31 Jan.	Ramsbury	336
1 Feb.	London	337
11 Feb.	London	338, 558
3 March	London	339
13 March	Ramsbury	341
15 March	Ramsbury	342
17 March	Ramsbury	580
19 March	Ramsbury	343
24 March	Ramsbury	345
26-7 March	Ramsbury	551, 346
3-4 April	Ramsbury	555, 348
7 April	Ramsbury	581
9 April (?)	Ramsbury	480-1
11 April	Ramsbury	347
21 April	Ramsbury	582
26 April	Ramsbury	349
28 April	Ramsbury	351
2 May	Wilton	352
23 May	Bradenstoke	354
8 June	Ramsbury	355
16 June	Ramsbury	583
27 June	London	360
30 June	London	361
16 July	Ramsbury	483
6 Sept.	Ramsbury	P.R.O., C.82/98/15: See
9 Sept.	Sonning	363 Appendix A
30 Dec.	Eltham	373

1493

12 Jan.	London	377
16 Feb.	London	384
20 Feb.	Sonning	559
2 March	Ramsbury	584
6-7 March	Ramsbury	390-2
20 March	Ramsbury	393
22-23 March	Ramsbury	P.R.O., C.82/104/17 (33):
26-27 March	Ramsbury	395-7 See Appendix A;
3 April	Ramsbury	398 585.
6 April	Ramsbury	586
11 April	Ramsbury	399
17 April	Ramsbury	400, 402-3
27 April	Ramsbury	404

| 29 April | Ramsbury | <u>406</u> |
| 1 June | Ramsbury | <u>587</u> |

Peter Courtenay, bishop of Winchester, died 20 September 1492 (P.R.O., C.82/102/8): licence to elect his successor, 19 January 1493; delivered 22 January (P.R.O., C.82/102/7(9)). Langton was translated from Salisbury to Winchester, 13 March (Reg. Langton, Winton., Fo. 1). Custody of temporalities had been granted to him 12 January and 14 February (P.R.O., C.82/103/12 (60)): delivered 16 February (<u>C.P.R., 1485-94</u>, pp.412, 427). Plenary restitution of temporalities, 25 June (P.R.O., C.82/107/3 (77)), upon receipt of bull of translation; delivered 27 June (<u>C.P.R., 1485-94</u>, p.432). By 8 July Langton was at Wolvesey palace (Reg. Langton, Winton., Fo. 2).

INDEX OF PERSONS AND PLACES

Ap David ap Gwyn, John, of St
Asaph dioc., 574
Ap Herry, John, chapl., r. of
Dorchester Holy Trinity, 2
Ap John:
Richard, of St Asaph dioc., 572
Thomas, of St Asaph dioc., 574
Ap Lothyum, John, chapl., r. of
Milston, 118
Appleton (Apylton), Berks., 372
Appulby, Thomas, monk of Reading,
431
Ap Richard:
Eli, v. of Kintbury, 256
John, cl., co-feoffee of Walter
Devoreux, lord of Ferrers,
468-9
Arborfield (Herberghfelde,
Erberghfeld), Berks., 440, 522,
527, 544, 552
Arthur, John, chapl., r. of
Chilton Foliat, 106
Arundel, earl of:
William fitz Alan, patron, 38,
47, 77
Thomas fitz Alan, patron, 147,
200, 218, 236, 369
Arundell:
M. John:
canon of Salisbury cath.:
prebendary of Beminster
Secunda, 246
prebendary of Durnford, 247,
427
r. of Sutton Courtenay, 242,
317
Thomas, r. of West Knighton, 387
Ashbury (Asshbury), Berks., 409
Ashe, John, r. of Sutton Veny, 562
See also Asshe
Ashmore (Asshemer, Ashmere), Dorset,
440, 521, 529, 544, 552
Ashton Keynes (Asshton), Wilts.,
342
Askerswell (Askyrswell, Askyrwell),
Dorset, 96, 114
Asserton, Wilts., free chapel,
407
Asshborn, Henry, of London,
patron, 299
See also Assheborne

Asshe:
John, alias Knowdeshill or
Knowdeshille, of Bath and Wells
dioc., vicar choral of
Salisbury cath., 579-80,
587
William, BA, 570
See also Ashe
Assheborne:
Henry, gent., patron, 93
M. Thomas, BCL, r. of Shaw, 59
See also Asshborn
Astley, lord, see Dorset,
Marquess of
Athelhampton (Athelhampston),
Dorset, free chapel, 241
Attekynson, Robert, chapl., r. of
Pusey, 60
Attewell, John, chaplain of
Chilton, 36
See also Atwell
Atwater, M. William, MA, r. of
Piddlehinton, 128
Atwell, M. John MA, r. of
Blandford St Mary, 331
See also Attewell
Atworth (Cottellisatworth alias
Atteworth parva), Wilts., 8
Audley (Audelay, Awdeley):
Edmund, bp. of Salisbury, 562
John, kt., lord Audley, 92
patron, 199
Austell, Thomas, canon of
Salisbury cath. and prebendary
of Teinton Regis, 427
Austen, Geoffrey, chapl., v. of
Kintbury, 256
Avebury, Wilts., 440, 523, 528,
544, 552
Avenell, Richard, monk of Bindon,
575, 578, 585
Avington (Avyngton), Berks., 440,
544, 552
Awbrey, Roger, of Hereford dioc.,
579
Aylberton or Aylburton, John,
monk of Malmesbury, 564, 566,
572
Aylward, William, cl., of
Winchester dioc.:
papal dispensation from

Aylward, William, (cont.)
  defect of age, 350
  v. of Puddletown, 351

Baase, William, v. of Bower Chalke,
  115
Baill, John, of Coventry and
  Lichfield dioc., 585
Baker:
  Hugh, v. of Chisledon, 175
  M. John, DTh:
    commissary for the approp-
      riation of Wanborough, 507
    v. of Chitterne All Saints,
      117
    v. of Melksham, 69
  M. Thomas, BC & CnL, 460
    prior of hospital of St John
      Baptist, Wilton,
        administrator of goods of
          John Hall, 466
  Walter, 580
Baldry, M. Richard:
  v. of Bishops Cannings, 224,303
  v. of Saffron Walden, London
    dioc., 224
Bale, Walter, of Exeter dioc., 563
Balinghen (Banelyngham), Therouanne
  dioc., 265
Ball, John, chapl., cantarist of
  chantry of St Michael de
  Mowndes, Bridport, 262
Balle, William, chapl., v. of
  Sydling St Nicholas, 138
Balteswell, Richard, cl.:
  r. of West Dean, 145
  ordained to pension from West
    Dean, 573-4, 579
Bampton, Richard, r. of Wootton
  Rivers, 277
Banaster, Elisha, priest, v. of
  Gussage All Saints, 14
    See also Banyster
Banbury, Walter, canon of Osney,
  566
Banys, Edward, of York dioc., 580
Banyster, William, chapl., v. of
  Damerham, 197
    See also Banaster

Barbour:
  Robert, of Exeter dioc., 566
  Walter, MA, r. of Codford St
    Peter, 92
Bardys, M. Adrian de, BCL:
  canon of Salisbury cath.:
    prebendary of Hurstborne and
      Burbage, 403
    prebendary of Ramsbury, 181,
      402, 427
  patron, 181
  r. of Marlborough St Peter, 72
  r. of Wroughton, 318, 400
Barford St Martin (Bereford),Wilts.,
  159
Bargh, John, cl., keeper of
  Sturthill free chapel, 222
Barker:
  Robert, chapl.:
    r. of Fifield Bavant, 139
      (Barkar)
    v. of Bower Chalke, 115, 381
  Thomas, parker of Sonning and
    keeper of 'Berewood', Berks.,
    559
Barkham (Berkham), Berks., 240
Barnaby:
  John, of York dioc., 580
    (Barneby), 581
  William, priest, cellarer of
    Bisham, 556
Barnard, M. John, MA, v. of Ashton
  Keynes, 342
Barnstaple, Devon, priory (Clun.),
  prior and conv., orders conferred
  to title, 563, 581
Barowe, Margaret, nun of Wilton,
  412
Barre:
  John, and Joan his wife, patrons,
    287
  Thomas, of Lincoln dioc., 584-5,
    587
Barry, William, v. of Sutton
  Benger, 354
Bartholomei, Michael, v. of
  Burstock, 279
Bartlot (Barlott), Simon, priest,
  cellarer of Ivychurch, 505

Birley (Byrley) (cont.):
  M. William, MA, 485, 487, 498
    v. of Hilton, 263
Bisham (Bursham, Burstellesham,
  Bustlesham, Bustlesham Montague),
  Berks., 224, 412
  church, taxation of, 442, 522,
    527, 546, 554
  priory (OSA), 514
    election of prior, 556-8
    prior, see Greve, William;
      Sewy, Richard
    prior and conv., 523
      collectors of clerical tenth,
        542-3
      orders conferred to title,
        556-8, 566, 568
      patrons, 237
    subprior and conv., 556-7
Bishops Cannings (Cannyngys
  Episcopi), Wilts., 224, 303
Bishop's Caundle (Cawndell),
  Dorset, 461
Bishops Lavington, Wilts., see
  West Lavington
Bishopstone (Bisshoppeston alias
  Ebbesborne Episcopi,
  Bysshopston), Wilts., 239, 440,
  523, 528, 544, 552
Bishop's Waltham, Hants., 507
Bisshop:
  Edward, of Duntish, Buckland
    Newton, Dorset, signification
    of contumacy, 455
  John, 571
Blacked, Thomas, chapl., r. of
  Donhead St Andrew, 177
Blakborn or Blakborne:
  John, OFM, 566
  Richard, canon of Bisham, 556
Blakden:
  Thomas, chapl., r. of Manningford
    Abbots, 178
  William, v. of Damerham, 197
Blakemore, Nicholas, r. of
  Chilmark, 148
Blaksore, Thomas of Worcester
  dioc., 587
Blandford Forum (Blandeford
  Forum), Dorset, 295
Blandford St Mary (Blanford
  marie, Blandford marie), Dorset,
  103, 331

Blebury, John, priest, monk of
  Reading, 431
Blewet or Blewette:
  Thomas, chapl., r. of Remenham,
    93
  Thomas, patron, 93
Blont (Blonte, Blunt), Walter, of
  Hereford dioc., 584-7
Blount, Simon, patron, 232
Blunsdon St Andrew (Blounesden,
  Blounesdon Andrewe, Blounsden,
  Blounsdon Andrews), Wilts.,
  121, 137, 207
Blunt, see Blont
Blynkynsop, Edmund, cl., keeper
  of Witherston free chapel, 216
Bochell, William, chapl., r. of
  Batcombe, 23
Bodmin (Bodemin), Cornwall,
  priory (OSA), prior and conv.,
  orders conferred to title, 565
Boket, M. William, r. of Marnhull,
  217
Bolney, Joan, nun of Wilton, 412
Bolton, M. William, canon of
  Salisbury cath. and prebendary
  of Major Pars Altaris, 228,
  427
Bonvile, lord, see Dorset,
  marquess of
Borde, Robert, chapl.:
  r. of Godmanstone, 189, 290
  r. of Winterborne Abbas, 290
Bordeall alias Bourdell, Richard,
  chapl., r. of North Poorton, 190
Boscombe (Bestcombe), Wilts., 140
  440, 461, 523, 528, 544, 552
Bosquyet, M. Richard, BCnL,
  proctor for M. John de Giglis,
  288
Bostok or Bostoke, M. John, BCnL:
  canon of Salisbury cath.:
    prebendary of Durnford, 269
    prebendary of Minor Pars
      Altaris, 270, 427
    residentiary, 69, 225, 427,
      429
  r. of Okeford Fitzpaine, 225
  v. of Bradford-on-Avon, 301
  v. of Melksham, 69, 95
Boteler alias Smyth, Thomas, 563

Bottell, Geoffrey, proctor for
Thomas Rydley, 363
Bothe:
Joan, nun of Wilton, 412
Robert, canon of Salisbury cath.
and prebendary of Charminster
and Bere, 141, 427
Botyll, John, chapl., v. of Compton
Chamberlayne, 107
Bourdell, see Bourdeall
Bourgchier, Fulk, lord of
FitzWarin, 155
Bowdon, M. Thomas, MA, v. of New
Windsor, 22
Bower, M. William, BCL, inductor
to St Peter's Marlborough, 304
Bower Chalke (Burchalke,
Burghchalke), Wilts., 115, 381
Bowyer alias Brynfyre, Simon, r.
of Dinton, 83
Boyer, Thomas, r. of Manningford
Bruce, 193
Bradeley, Thomas, OFM, 566
Bradenstoke (Bradenstok, Baddestoke),
Wilts., 354
priory (OSA), 36
prior, 514
See also Walshe, Thomas
prior and conv.:
orders conferred to title,
566-72, 578-80, 587
patrons, 267
taxation, 521, 523, 528
Bradford, Thomas, monk of
Abbotsbury, 568
Bradford Abbas, Dorset, 113
Bradford-on-Avon, Wilts., 301
Bradpole (Bradepole), Dorset, 31
Branch or Branche:
William, of Carlisle dioc., 567
M. William:
r. of Orcheston St George, 77
subdean of Salisbury cath., 71
427
Bray or Braye:
Clement, monk of Reading, 431
John, monk of Reading, 432
Richard, cl., canon of Salisbury
cath. and prebendary of
Yetminster Prima, 383
William, r. of Inkpen, 250
William, OFM of Salisbury, 563-4

Bremelham, Thomas, monk of
Malmesbury, 564
Bremhill (Bremle alias Bremell,
Bremyll), Wilts., 188, 461
Brenfyre, Thomas, chapl., v. of
Wootton Bassett, 182, 231
See also Bowyer
Brent, Robert, armiger, patron,
408
Brereton:
John, armiger, and Katherine his
wife, lady of Owermoigne,
patrons, 367
M. Robert:
r. of Alton, 370
r. of Owermoigne, 367
Brevynt, Philip, r. of Compton
Abbas, 316
Brewe, M. William, MD, cl.:
r. of Abingdon St Nicholas, 311,
357
r. of Milton, 356
Brice or Bryce, John, chapl., r.
of Melbury Sampford, 70, 227
Bridport (Birtporte, Birtteport,
Birtpote, Brudeporte), Dorset:
chantry of St Michael de
Mowndes, 67, 195, 262, 371
church, 67, 262, 371, 489
Brigge, John, 563-4
Brigger or Brygger, William, of
Thatcham, confession and
abjuration of heresy, 486-7
Brighmerston, Wilts., see Milston
Brightwalton, Berks., 440, 522,
527, 544, 552
Brinkworth (Brynkeworth,
Brynkworth), Wilts., 377
Bristol (Bristoll), Glos., 484n.
abbey (OSA), abbot and conv.,
patrons, 111
Blackfriars, orders conferred
to title, 571
Bristow or Bristowe:
John, priest, monk of Reading,
431
Thomas, monk of Abingdon, 584
Brixton Deverill (Brixston
Deverell, Bryxston Deverell),
Wilts., 125, 461
Brixworth, see Salisbury, cath.,
prebendaries

135

Broad Chalke (Chalke), Wilts.,
John Alwyn's chantry, 461
Broad Hinton (Henton), Wilts., 442,
523, 528, 546, 554
Broad Windsor (Brodwyndelsor),
Dorset, 461
Brocas, William, armiger, patron,
360
Brodesideling, Dorset, see Sydling
St Nicholas
Broke, M. William, BCL, of
Canterbury dioc., fellow of All
Souls Coll., Oxford, 581-2
Brome, William, chapl., v. of
Swindon, 99
Brone, Richard, MA, witness of
appropriation of Wanborough,
507
Brooke, lordship of, see
Willoughby, Robert
Broomhall (Bromehale, Bromehall,
Bromhale), Berks., priory (OSB,
nuns), prioress and conv., 422
exempt from clerical tenth, 439
taxation, 522, 527
Broughton Gifford (Broughton),
Wilts., 151
Broune:
John, 573
Peter, of Glasgow dioc., 569
Thomas, of Worcester dioc.,
580-1
William, and Christina his wife,
patrons, 189 (Browne), 290
See also Brown
Brounsop, William, chapl., r. of
Durweston, 312
Browkys, Robert de, co-heir of
lord Humphrey Stafford, earl of
Devon, 220
Brown or Browne:
John, cantarist of Glanvilles
Wootton, 171
John, cl., patron, 180
John, gent., patron, 180
Philip, of Hinton Waldrist,
confession and abjuration of
heresy, 419-20
William, and Christina his wife,
patrons, 189, 290 (Broune)
See also Broune

Brownyng (Brownyngs), William,
armiger, patron, 70, 91, 127,
158, 227
Bruern (Bruera), Oxon., abbey
(Cist.), abbot and conv.:
orders conferred to title,
570-2, 581, 584-5
patrons, 134, 405
Bryan:
Henry, MA, 563-6
John, abbot of Bindon:
convocation proctor, 517
dispensation to hold a
secular benefice, 449
r. of Tyneham, 122
Brydd, see Burde
Brydde, William, chapl., v. of
Bradford-on-Avon, 301
Brynfyre, see Bowyer
Buckfast (Bukfaste), Devon,
abbey (Cist.), abbot and conv.,
orders conferred to title, 580
Buckhorn Weston (Weston, Weston
Maundervile), Dorset, 162, 544,
552
Buckland (Buckelond, Bucland,
Buklande), Berks., 123, 163, 323,
458a, 509
Buckland (Buklande), John, monk
of Bindon, 575, 578, 585
Buckland Newton (Buklonde),
Dorset, 455
Budde, William, chapl.:
commissioner for gaol delivery
v. of Reading St Mary, 16, 344,
537
Bugge, John, OFM of Dorchester,
573
Bulbridge (Bulbrigge), Wilts., 461
Bull, Ralph, cl., chaplain of
Whelpley free chapel, 401
Bullington (Bolyngton), Lincs.,
priory (OGilb.), prior and conv.,
orders conferred to title, 574-6
Bullok:
Oswald, of Durham dioc., 580-1,
583
Richard, BCnL, r. of Lydiard
Tregoze, 94
Bullokys, Eleanor, widow, patron,
240

Burde alias Brydd, M. John, v. of
Reading St Mary, 16
See also Birde
Burges (Burgis):
John, of Durham dioc., vicar-
choral of Salisbury cath., 570,
574-6
Thomas, monk of Abingdon, 566
M. William, BCnL, r. of
Winterborne Steepleton, 79
Burgh, Edward, kt., and Anne his
wife, patrons, 273
Burlay or Burlech or Burlegh,
M. Richard:
canon of Salisbury cath. and
prebendary of Warminster,427
chaplain or keeper of Asserton
free chapel, 407
r. of Great Wishford, 408
Burley, Thomas, chapl., r. of Long
Bredy, 100
Burnell, Thomas, of Worcester
dioc., 570
Burnham, Bucks., abbey (OSA,
canonesses), abbess and conv.,
orders conferred to title,
573-4
Burstock (Bourghstoke, Burghstoke),
Dorset, 279, 461
Burton, Dorset, 441, 545, 553
Burton:
Robert, OFM, 566
M. Robert, MA, v. of Sherston,
320
Bury, George, acolyte, r. of
Shillingstone, 5
Bury St Edmunds, Suffolk, abbey
(OSB), abbot and conv., orders
conferred to title, 584-6
Buscot, Berks., 484n.
Bustard, M. William, of Lincoln
dioc., fellow of All Souls Coll.,
Oxford, 584-5
Buste, John, v. of Wargrave, 349
Butler, Thomas, see Ormond, earl
of
Byconyll, John, co-feoffee of
Humphrey, earl of Devon, lord of
Batcombe, patron, 23
Byrley, see Birley
Byrte, William, r. of Wareham St
Martin, 245

Cadigan, David, of St Davids dioc.,
580-1
Calixtus III, pope, 507
Calthrop, William, kt., patron,
112
Cam (Kam), Richard, monk of
Malmesbury, 568, 572, 577, 579
Cambridge, Cambs.:
hospital of St John the
Evangelist, master and
brothers, orders conferred
to title, 580
King's College, provost and
scholars, patrons, 115, 326,
381, 390
university, colleges in,
exemption from clerical
tenth, 439
Camera, see de Camera
Campyon, M. Thomas, r. of Lytchett
Matravers, 38
Camyll, William, v. of Swindon,
99
Canford Magna, Dorset, 267
Cannings, Wilts., All Saints, see
All Cannings
Cannings Episcopi, Wilts., see
Bishops Cannings
Canterbury, archbishop of, 265
See also Deane, Henry; Morton,
John
Carnebull, M. Henry, cl., canon
of Salisbury cath. and prebendary
of Yatesbury, 406
Carpenter:
George, of Woodstock, heretic,
419
M. Richard, of Hereford dioc.,
566
Carpenter alias Harford alias
Daniell, William, of Newbury,
confession and abjuration of
heresy, 497-8
Carre, Marcus, of Durham dioc.,
574-6
Carvar, see Kerver
Carvenell, M. Michael, r. of
Farnborough, 223
Carver:
John, OC, of Exeter dioc., 574
William, chapl., v. of Reading
St Mary, 344
See also Kerver

Casey, William, r. of Corscombe, 391
Casson or Cesson, Thomas, BA, of York dioc., 580-1
Castle Combe (Castelcombe), Wilts., 9, 499-500, 564-5, 576
Castle Eaton (Castell Eton alias Moysi), Wilts., 25
Catesby:
John, justice of gaol delivery, 463
William, esquire of the body of the king, patron, 507
Catmore (Catemer, Cattemere), Berks., 124
Cator (Cater), M. Alexander, BC & CnL, 460
commissioner for patronage inquisition, 119
proctor for Wilton abbey, 412
r. of Grasby, Lincoln dioc., 243
v. of Norton Bavant, 243
Catour, William, 116
Caviller, Robert, 587
Cawndell, Dorset, see Bishop's Caundle
Cayter, Edmund, canon of Bradenstoke, 566
Cely, Thomas, 568
Cerne, Dorset, 214
abbey (OSB), 487, 514
abbot, see Bemyster, Roger
abbot and conv.:
collectors of clerical tenth, 541, 543
orders conferred to title, 563, 571-2, 575, 577-8, 581, 587
patrons, 19, 100, 135, 209, 251, 261, 290, 328-9
Cerne, John, monk of Cerne, 571, 575, 578, 581
Cesson or Sissin or Sisson, William, of Lincoln dioc., 581, 584-5
See also Casson
Chadderton, M. Edmund or Edward:
archdeacon of Salisbury, 517
canon of Salisbury cath. and prebendary of Stratton, 427
convocation proctor, 517

Chaddleworth (Chadelworth, Chadlworth), Berks., 168, 183
Chalbury (Chetilbury), Dorset, 440, 521, 529, 544, 552
Chaldon Herring or East Chaldon (Chauedon Heryng alias Chaldon), Dorset, 46
Chalfield Magna, Wilts., see Great Chalfield
Chalke, Wilts., see Bower Chalke and/or Broad Chalke
Chamber:
John, v. of Milton Lilbourne, 330
John, ordained to title of his vicarage of Salisbury cath., 563-4
Chamberge, Dorset, see Kimmeridge
Chapman, Simon, of Norwich dioc., 580-1
Chardstock (Chardestoke), Dorset, 278
Charlton (Charleton), Wilts., 161
Chatres, M. Christopher, MA, v. of Bishops Cannings, 303
Chaundeler, M. Thomas, r. of Childrey, 299
Chawsey, John, of Stratford, patron, 211
Chayne, see Cheyne
Chekke, M. William, canon of Salisbury cath. and prebendary of Bedminster and Redclyffe, 334
Cherite, M. William, r. of Easton, 574
Cheselbourne (Cheselborn), Dorset, 215
Chettle (Chetell, Chetille), Dorset, 440, 544, 552
Cheyne (Chayne):
M. Edward, DC & CnL:
canon of Salisbury cath. and prebendary of Beminster Secunda, 65, 427
convocation proctor, 517
dean of Salisbury cath., 65, 286, 427-30, 517, 560
r. of Castle Eaton, 25
r. of Stalbridge, 20
John, kt. (styled armiger in 1476), 291.

138

Cheyne (Chayne) (cont.):
  co-feoffee of Humphrey, earl of
    Devon, lord of Batcombe, patron,
    23
  patron, 56, 253
  and Margaret his wife, patrons,
    190, 238, 305
  Roger, armiger, 494
Chicklade (Chikelade, Chiklade),
  Wilts., 287
Chieveley (Cheveley), Berks., 157,
  441, 545, 553
Child Okeford, Dorset, 54
Childe (Chylde), Thomas, chapl.:
  r. of Woodsford, 261, 329
  v. of Milborne St Andrew, 325
Childrey (Chelrey), Berks., 299
Chilmark (Chyldemarke, Chylmarke),
  Wilts., 148
Chilton (Chylton), Berks., 36, 170
Chilton Foliat (Chilton Folyet,
  Chilton Folyott), Wilts., 106
Chippenham, Wilts., chantry, 306,
  500
Chipping Campden (Camden), Glos.,
  chantry, 552
Chippynge Lamborne, Berks., see
  Lambourn
Chisledon (Cheseldene, Cheseldeyn,
  Chuseldene, Chuseldon), Wilts.,
  175, 440, 523, 528, 544, 552
Chitterne (Cetter) All Saints,
  Wilts., 117, 461
Chitterne St Mary (Cectra mariae),
  17
Chivelay, John, monk of Reading,
  431
Cholderton (Chaldryngton),
  Wilts., 353
Cholsey, Berks., 280, 363
Cholsey, Robert, monk of Reading,
  573
Christ Church, Twynham, Hants.,
  priory (OSA), prior and conv.:
  orders conferred to title, 570
  patrons, 295, 338, 351
Christian Malford (Cristenmalford),
  Wilts., 354
Church, M. Roger, DCnL, of
  Canterbury dioc., 584-5
Churchill, Thomas, v. of Portesham,
  266

Church Knowle (Knolle), Dorset,
  50
Chute, Wilts., 91
Chypnam, M. William, r. of Tubney,
  129
Chyverell Magna, Wilts., see Great
  Cheverell
Cirencester (Cirencestre), Glos.,
  abbey (OSA), abbot and conv.,
    patrons, 21, 180, 254, 330,
    364, 380
Clareys, John, v. of Fifehead
  Magdalen, 111
Clarke, John, chapl., r. of Newton
  Toney, 84
  See also Clerk
Clatford, Wilts., alien cell, prior,
  458a, 462
Cleiser, David, of St Andrews dioc.,
  584, 586-7
Clerk or Clerke:
  John, 583
  ____, r. of Hilperton
  Richard, lawman of Faringdon
    ward, London, 463
  Thomas, chapl.:
    r. of Denchworth, 134, 405
    r. of Padworth, 165
  M. Thomas, BCL, 485, 487, 498,
    504
  William, of Worcester dioc., 572
  See also Clarke
Clerkenwell, Middlesex, see London,
  Clerkenwell
Cleve or Clyff, John, chapl., r.
  of Whaddon, 281, 555
Clewer (Clewar), Berks., chantry,
  360
Cliffe or Clyff, John, monk of
  Abingdon, 583-4
Clifford, John, r. of Poole Keynes,
  552
Clifton or Clyfton, John, monk of
  Reading, 431, 573
Clyffe Pypard (Clyve Pypard, Clyve
  Pyppard), Wilts., 229
Clyve, M. Michael, DCL or DCnL,
  master of coll. of St Katherine,
    Wanborough, and proctor for
    archd. of Wilts., and for
    bp. of Winchester, 507

Codford St Mary (Codforde Marie, Codford Marye), Wilts., 112

Codford St Peter (Codforde Peter, West Codforde), Wilts., 92

Codryngton (Cotryngton), John, monk of Abingdon, 585-7

Cok, William, of York dioc., 580

Cokethorpe, Oxon., 504

Cokke, see Cooke

Cokkys:
James, r. of Langton Herring, 24
M. Laurence, DCnL, priest:
canon of Salisbury cath. and prebendary of Netheravon, 1, 423, 427
chancellor to bp. Langton:
director of monastic elections, 412, 416, 431, 505, 556ff.
present at heresy trials, 485, 487, 493-4, 496,502
proctor for chapter of Salisbury cath., 429
commissioner for visitation, 423
convocation proctor, 517
official of the consitory, heresy trial, 460
patron, 110
r. of Fisherton Anger, 293
r. of Winterborne Bassett, 34, 294
vicar general, 1, 423

Coksey, Thomas, kt., patron, 193

Coldale, M. John, DTh:
r. of Upwey, 321
v. of Buckland, 162, 323

Cole, John, chapl., commissioner for delivery of criminous clerks, 457

Colerne, Wilts., 392

Coleshill (Colleshull, Colleshyll), Berks., 322

Colmore, Thomas, of Exeter dioc., 581

Colnet, M. Richard, BCL, notary, cl., of Canterbury dioc., recorder for the appropriation of Wanborough, 507

Colney, Thomas, 116

Coloma, see de Coloma

Colstane (Constane), Richard, of Carlisle dioc., 569-71

Colyngborn or Colyngborne, John, abbot of Hyde, Winchester, commissary for Lionel Wydeville, bp. of Salisbury, 507

Colyns, M. Richard, MA, v. of Longbridge Deverill, 219

Colyshull, Lady Elizabeth, as co-heir of Lord Humphrey Stafford, earl of Devon, patron, 220

Comaland, Alice, abbess of Wilton, 412

Combe:
John, monk of Malmesbury, 564
M. William, BCL:
r. of Shaw, 59
v. of Puddletown, 338, 351

Comnor or Comnore, Thomas, monk of Abingdon, 573, 583

Compton, Berks., 332

Compton Abbas (Compton Abbatis, Compton Abbess), Dorset, 316, 440, 521, 529, 544, 552

Compton Bassett (Compton Basset juxta Calne), Wilts., 461

Compton Beauchamp, Berks., 440, 522, 527, 544, 552

Compton Chamberlayne (Compton Chamberleyn), Wilts., 107, 159, 528, 544, 552

Coniwey, David, canon of Oxford St Frideswide, 566

Cooke or Cokke, John of Lincoln dioc., 567-8

Coole, John, BA, fellow of All Souls Coll., Oxford, 584-5

Corbet or Corbett:
John, r. of Iwerne Minster, 319
Richard, kt., co-feoffee of Walter Devoreux, Lord Ferrers, kt., 467-9

Corfe Castle (Corffe Castell), Dorset, 489

Cornish, John, monk of Abingdon, 584

Cornwayle, Thomas, kt., co-feoffee of Walter Devoreux, Lord Ferrers, kt., 467-9

Corringdon, John, canon of Salisbury cath. and prebendary

Corringdon, John (cont.)
  of Alton, 427
Corscombe, Dorset, 391
Corsley (Corselay, Corseley,
  Corslay), Wilts., 30
Corton (Corston, Croston),
  Wilts., 440, 523, 528, 544, 552
Cosham, _____, 463
Coston, William, priest, canon of
  Bisham, 556-7
Cosyn, Malcolm, canon of Salisbury
  cath. and prebendary of
    Netherbury in Ecclesia, 427
    See also Cousyn
Coterell, James, v. of Ramsbury,
  181
Cottellisatworth, Wilts., see
  Atworth
Cotteswold, John, of Lincoln
  dioc., 585
Cotton, William, chapl., keeper or
  chaplain of Asserton free
  chapel, 407
Courtenay, Peter, bp. of Winchester,
  169, 318
Cousyn, M. William, clerk, canon
  of Salisbury cath. and
    prebendary of Major pars
      Altaris, 337
      See also Cosyn
Cove, Richard, v. of Ashton
  Keynes, 342
Cowleston, Wilts., see East
  Coulston
Coxwell, Berks., see Great Coxwell
Coyn or Coyne, William, chapl., r.
  of Ham, 15, 169
Crampelay or Cramplay or Crampley,
  M. William:
    r. of Codford St Peter, 92
    v. of Blandford Forum, 295
Cranborne (Cranneborn), Dorset, 389
Crich or Criche or Cryche, Henry,
  578, 584, 586
Cricklade (Crikelade, Crikkelade,
  Criklade, Criklayd, Crykelade),
  Wilts.:
    hospital or priory of St John
      the Baptist, 404, 461
    St Sampson's ch., 307, 500,
      528, 544, 552
Crofton or Croston, Dorset, 441,
  545, 553

Crokeshank, John, chapl., v. of
  Alvediston, 390
Crokkar or Crokker, Henry, chapl.,
  v. of West Overton, 149, 260
Cromer, Alexander, of Canterbury
  dioc., 566
Croppe, John, of Bath and Wells
  dioc., 563
Croser, Thomas, canon of
  Marlborough, 576-7
Crosse:
  M. John, proctor for M. James
    Stanley, 382
  Walter, chapl., r. of Wootton
    Fitzpaine, 236
Croston, Dorset, see Crofton
Croxton, Leics., abbey (Prem.),
  abbot and conv., orders conferred
    to title, 568
Croyden, Surrey, archiepiscopal
  residence, 534
Cruce, John, of Exeter dioc., 566
Crunwear (Cronewer), Wales, 87
Cryche, Dorset, see Steeple
Cumnor (Comnore), Berks., episcopal
  residence, 566
Curteys (Curtays, Curtayse):
  John, chapl.:
    r. of Whaddon, 97
    v. of Melksham, 95, 302
  Richard, r. of Denchworth, 134
Cusse, John, 567, 570-2

Dade, William, chapl., r. of
  Owermoigne, 367
Dagnall, Thomas, of St Davids dioc.,
  566
Dalaware, William, 578-80
Daldre, William, justice of gaol
  delivery, 463
Dale:
  Eugenius, of Norwich dioc., 579
  Richard, proctor for Richard
    Waren, 168
  M. Robert, MA, of Bath and Wells
    dioc., fellow of Merton Coll.,
      Oxford, 575
Damerham, (Domerham), Hants., 197
Dane, John, kt., guardian or
  keeper of Edward Trussell during
    minority, 226

141

Daniell, see Carpenter
Darell:
  Edward, armiger, patron, 82
  George, kt., 82
Dartford (Derteforde, Dertford),
  Kent, priory (OP, nuns),
    prioress and conv.:
      patrons, 139, 243
      taxation, 523, 528
Davell, Thomas, r. of Sopworth, 102
David, Philip, chapl., v. of
  Cricklade St Sampson, 307, 552
    See also ap David
Davy:
  Henry, of Bangor dioc., 585
  Lewis, chapl., v. of Coleshill,
    322
  Thomas, canon of Salisbury cath.
    and prebendary of Blewbury,
    427
Davyd, M. John, alias Kidwely:
  r. of Hamstead Marshall, 87
  r. of St Teilo's, Crunwear,
    St Davids dioc., 87
  See also ap David
Davyson, M. John:
  dean of Salisbury cath., 427,
    507
  r. of Mildenhall, 48
Dawne, George, canon of Salisbury
  cath. and prebendary of
  Ruscombe Southbury, 427
Day:
  M. John, DTh, present at heresy
    trials, 485, 487, 494, 496,
    504
  Robert, chapl., priest:
    canon of Salisbury cath.:
      prebendary of Axford, 61, 427
      prebendary of Grantham
        Australis, 205
      prebendary of Ratfyn, 62
      present at heresy trial, 496,
        498
    r. of Eaton Hastings, 166
    r. of Marlborough St Peter, 72,
      204
    r. of Welford, 203
Dean, Wilts., see West Dean
Dean, forest of, 563
Deane, Henry, archbp. of
  Canterbury, 562

de Camera, Lucas, OFM of Salisbury,
  563
de Coloma, Gerard, OFM of
  Salisbury, 568
de la Gowche or de la Gownche,
  see Lagowche
de la Herne, see Herne
Delamar, M. Mathew, chapl., v. of
  West Overton, 260
De la Warr, lord, see Weste,
  Thomas
de Meyndek ap Pell, of St Asaph
  dioc., 574
Denby or Denbye, M. John, MA:
  r. of Melbury Osmond, 91, 127
  r. of West Dean, 145, 552
    non-resident, 552
  v. of Chute, 91
Denchworth (Dengeworthe,
  Denscheworth), Berks., 134, 405
Denham, John or William, of
  Durham dioc., 566, 574, 576
Denton, John, of Fyfield, armiger,
  patron, 372
Derby, countess of, see Beaufort,
  Lady Margaret
Derby, Nicholas, 567
Deremonte, Maurice, chapl., r. of
  Buckhorn Weston, 162
Devenyshe, William, r. of Langley
  Burrell, 273
Deverell Langbrig, Wilts., see
  Longbridge Deverill
Devizes (Devises), Wilts., 491
Devon, earl of: Humphrey Stafford:
  lord of Battecombe, 23
  patron, 220
Devoreux:
  John, kt., co-feoffee of Walter
    Devoreux, Lord Ferrers, kt.,
    467-9
  Walter, Lord Ferrers, kt., 467-
    9
Dewhirst, Elisha, chapl., v. of
  Basildon, 310
Dewlish (Develiche), Dorset, see
  Milborne St Andrew
Dewsaver or Dusavir, Richard,
  chap., r. of Askerswell, 96,
  114
Diar, Thomas, Exeter dioc., 565
Dinton (Dynton), Wilts., 83

East Hagbourne (Hakborne), Berks.,
380
East Hendred (Estehenreth,
  Esthenrede, Esthenreth), Berks.:
    ch., 440, 461, 484n., 503-4,
      522, 527, 544, 552
    manor chapel of St John the
      Baptist, 153
East Lavington, Wilts., see
  Market Lavington
East Lulworth (Este Lulleworth),
  Dorset, 28
Easton (Eston), Wilts., priory,
  (Trin.):
    prior, see Marshall, William
    prior and conv.:
      exemption from clerical
        tenth, 439
      orders conferred to title,
        563, 573-4, 579, 585
      patrons, 13, 110, 282, 315
      taxation, 523, 528
Easton Grey (Eston Gray,
  Estongrey), Wilts., 362, 584-7
East Shefford (Este Shifforde),
  Berks., 64
Eaton Hastings (Eton Hastyngys
  alias Water Eton), Berks., 166
Ebbesborne Episcopi, Wilts., see
  Bishopstone
Ebbesborne Wake (Ebisborne),
  Wilts., 90
Ederose, Wilts., priory (OSA),
  see Ivychurch
Edington (Edingdon, Edyngdon,
  Edyngton), Wilts., collegiate
    ch., 32, 39-40, 42-5, 47, 514
    rector, see Hulle, Bro.
      William
    rector and conv.:
      appropriators of Buckland,
        509
      orders conferred to title,
        564-5, 568, 572
      patrons, 123, 163, 322-3
      taxation, 522-3, 527
Edmond:
  John, r. of Stourton, 238
  Roger, chapl., r. of Tidmarsh,
    230
  See also Edmundys
Edmunde, Robert, 582

Edmundys (Edmonde, Edmondys),
  M. Richard, MA, of Bath and
    Wells dioc., fellow of
      Merton Coll., Oxford, 577,
        584-6
Edward I, king, 116
Edward IV, king, 92, 467
Edward, John, of Newbury,
  confession and abjuration of
    heresy, 490-1, 494
Egilsfelde or Eglesfeld, Bro.
  Robert, preceptor of Beverley,
    locumtenens for the prior of
      Hospitallers in England,
        patron, 124, 274, 326
Elizabeth of York, queen, papal
  bull concerning her marriage
    with Henry VII, 471-2
Ellis (Elys), M. Geoffrey, BCL:
  canon of Salisbury cath. and
    prebendary of Coombe and
      Harnham, 27, 427
  r. of Enborne, 56
  See also Elys
Elmelay, Thomas, r. of Batcombe,
  23
Elsiner, Richard, chapl., r. of
  Woolhampton, 352
Eltham, Kent, 373
Elton, Robert, of Newbury,
  confession and abjuration of
    heresy, and relapse, 492-4
Elwell, Elizabeth, prioress of
  Wilton, 412
Elworton, William, monk of
  Abingdon, 566
Ely, bp. of, see Morton, John
Elyngdon, Wilts., see Wroughton
Elyot (Eliott, Elyott):
  John, chapl., r. of Swanage, 47,
    147
  Robert, chapl.:
    r. of Stourton, 238
    v. of Bishopstone, 239
  M. William, BCL, cl.:
    canon of Salisbury cath. and
      prebendary of Bishopstone,
        44, 427
    keeper of the free chapel of
      St Stephen, Little Mayne,
        309
    provost of St Edmund's coll.,
      Salisbury, patron, 107

144

Elys:
  John, chapl., r. of Silton, 187
  Geoffrey, chapl., r. of
    Winterbourne Earls, 589
  See also Ellis
Empstar or Empster, Thomas,
  chapl., r. of Sulham, 80, 185
Emwell, M. John:
  canon of Salisbury cath. and
    prebendary of Coombe and
    Harnham, 27
  r. of Berwick St John, 12
  r. of Stalbridge, 20
  r. of West Dean, 26
Enborne (Eneborne), Berks., 56,
  440, 522, 527, 544, 552
Enford (Endford, Enforde), Wilts.,
  458, 458n
Englefeld, Thomas, gent., 255
Englefield, Berks., 255
Englisshe, Edward, r. of
  Radipole, 19
Erbefelde, Richard, Bonhomme
  of Edington, 568
Erbery or Yerbery, Richard,
  Bonhomme of Edington, 565, 572
Erchefonte, Wilts., see Urchfont
Erle, Richard, armiger, 291
Esshing or Essyng, Peter, chapl.,
  r. of Wootton Fitzpaine, 218,
  236
Estbury, John, armiger, patron,
  11
Estekyngton, Wilts., priory (OSB,
  nuns), see Kington St Michael
Esteney, John, abbot of
  Westminster, 507
Esterby, John, priest, diocs.,
  Salisbury and York,
    present at monastic elections,
    505, 556
Esterfeld, John, cl.:
  present at heresy trial, 494,
    496
  r. of Newbury, 160, 494, 496
Esthorp, M. Brian, MA. present
  at heresy trial, 502
  v. of South Newton, 394
Estmonde (Estemonde, Estmond):
  John, cl., portioner or keeper
    of the free chapel or portion
    of Haxton, 155

Estmonde (cont.):
  M. John, MA, 583-4
  M. Richard, DTh, r. of Broughton
    Gifford, 151
  William, chapl. or cantarist of
    Chippenham chantry, 306
Eton, Bucks., college, provost and
  coll., patrons, 128
Everard, John, chapl., cantarist
  of Clewer, 360
Everleigh (Everley), Wilts., 196
Evers, M. George, notary, proctor
  for Edward Newland, 326
Evesham, Robert, monk of Malmesbury,
  564
Evottys, Thomas, priest, canon of
  Bisham, 556
Ewike, William, MA, present at
  heresy trial, 504
Ewlawe, M. Richard, chapl., r. of
  Hatford, 120
Exchequer, treasurer and barons of,
  436, 439, 451-2, 463, 518-9, 524,
  530, 543
Exeter, archd. of, see Hopton, M.
  David
Eye, Oxon., 473
Eysey (Eysy), Wilts., 440, 523,
  528, 544, 552
Eyston, John, armiger, patron, 153

Fabell, Roger, r. of Manningford
  Abbots, 178
Faringdon (Faryndon, Faryngdon),
  Berks., 484n., 487
Farlay, Wilts., priory (Clun.),
  See Monkton Farleigh
'Farlegh', Winchester dioc., 507
Farleigh, Wilts., see Monkton
  Farleigh
Farleigh Wallop (Farlegh Walop),
  Hants., 136
Farley, Roger, monk of Malmesbury,
  564
Farlingham, Jone, of Hinton
  Waldrist, heretic, 419
Farmer, M. Robert, BCnL, r. of
  Manston, 395
Farnborough (Farnburgh), Berks.,
  223

Favell, John, see Towkar
Fayrfax, Guy, kt., as feoffee of
    Henry Percy, earl of
    Northumberland, patron, 225
Felde, William, priest, monk of
    Reading, 431
Felley (Falley), Notts., priory
    (OSA), prior and conv., orders
    conferred to title, 570-2
Ferne, Robert, OP, 566
Ferreis or Ferys, John, armiger,
    patron, 121, 137
Ferrers of Groby, Lord, see
    Dorset, Marquess of
Ferrour, John, chapl., r. of
    Chicklade, 287
Feteplas, Richard, armiger,
    patron, 64
Fifehead Magdalen (Fyfhide, St
    Mary Magdalene Fyfhyde),
    Dorset, 111
Fifehead Neville (Fyfehednevill),
    Dorset, 368
Fiffeld or Fiffelde, William,
    monk of Abingdon, 584-5
Fifield Bavant (Fyfhide Bavente,
    Fyfhyde Bavente), Wilts., 139
Finchampstead (Fynchampstede),
    Berks., 152
Fisher, Henry, of Carlisle dioc.,
    563
    See also Fyssher
Fisherton Anger (Fyssherton
    Anger), Wilts., 293, 466
Fittleton (Fydelton), Wilts.,
    82
FitzAlan, see Arundel, earls of
Fitzherbert, _____ (clerk of the
exchequer), 451, 463
Fitzhugh, Alice, Lady Fitzhugh,
    relict of Henry Fitzhugh,
    patron, 132
FitzWarin, Lord, see Bourgchier,
    Fulk
Flaxley (Flaxlay in forest of
    Dean), Glos., abbey (Cist.),
    abbot and conv., orders
    conferred to title, 564
Florence, Richard, of Norwich dioc.,
    581-2

Flynte:
    John, monk of Sherborne, 571
    575
    Thomas, of Winchester dioc.,
        vicar-choral of Salisbury
        cath., 570, 576
Fontmell Magna (Fountemele,
    Fountmele), Dorset, 186
Forde, Joan, see Vorde
Fordington, Dorset, prebend of,
    142, 588
Forster (Forstere):
    M. John, MA, canon of Slaisbury
        cath.:
        prebendary of Fordington and
            Writhlington, 142, 288
        prebendary of Grantham
            Borealis, 143
    John, of Bath and Wells dioc.,
        572-5
    John, lawman of Faringdon ward,
        London, 463
    See also Foster
Fosse, Robert, chapl., v. of
    Chitterne St Mary, 17
Foster or Forster, Richard, chapl.:
    v. of Clyffe Pypard, 229
    v. of Rowde, 7, 229
Fowell, M. William, of Exeter
    dioc., 569
Fox:
    Matthew, chapl., v. of Wroughton,
        345
    Nicholas, chapl., r. of Sopworth,
        376
    M. Richard, DCL, canon of
        Salisbury cath.:
        prebendary of Bishopstone,
            44
        prebendary of Grantham
            Borealis, 39, 427
    M. Thomas, chapl., r. of Tubney,
        129, 249
Foxley (Foxlay) Wilts., 3
Frampton, James, armiger, patron,
    37
Fremott, Geoffrey, chapl., r. of
    Fifehead Neville, 368
Frilsham (Fridelesham,
    Frydelesham), Berks., 336, 440,
    522, 527, 544, 552

Frithelstock (Frithelstoke),
Devon, priory (OSA), prior and
conv., orders conferred to
title, 563
Frome, Henry, monk of Sherborne,
568
Frome Belett, Dorset, 440, 521,
529, 544, 552
Frome St Quintin, Dorset, 101
Frome Vauchurch (Frome Vouchurche
alias Neggechurche, Negchurch),
Dorset, 220, 440, 521, 529,
544, 552
Froxfield (Froxfeld), Wilts., 282
Frye, John, of Martock, Bath and
Wells dioc., 563-4
Frynde, M. John, v. of Colerne,
392
Frythay, Stephen, cantarist of St
Michael de Mowndes chantry,
Bridport, 371
Fulham, Middlesex, residence of bp.
of London, 444, 448, 531, 547
Fyfield (Fifeld), Berks., 372
Fylell, Hugh, chapl., r. of Inkpen,
250
Fynde, John, of London dioc., 581
Fynymor or Fynymore:
M. William, MA, keeper or r. of
Tubney, 249
William, of Worcester dioc.,
565
Fynys, John, 580
Fyssher, Hugh, r. of Wareham St
Michael, 198
See also Fisher
Fyttok, John, of Bath and Wells
diioc., vicar-choral of
Salisbury cath., 584

Gamlyn, Edward, cantarist of
Godmanston chantry in St
Thomas's, Salisbury, 286
Garbrandi, Henry, chapl., v. of
Norton, 386
Garde, M. George:
r. of Leigh, London dioc., 202
v. of New Windsor, 202
Gardyner, Thomas, 563
Garet, John, chapl., v. of
Somerford Keynes, 213

Garnet, John, 563-5
Gartham, M. Richard, r. of
Corsley, 30
Gascoyn (Gaskyn), Robert, 585-7
Gawlare or Gawler, Robert, cl. or
chapl.:
r. of Melbury Osmond, 127, 158
r. of Winterborne Zelston,
385
Gay, Thomas, r. of Frilsham, 336
Gedney, William, r. of Melbury
Sampford, 70
Geffray:
M. David, r. of Holwell, 21
Thomas, r. of Foxley
See also Jeffrey
Gelys, William, of Exeter dioc.,
580
Gent, John, r. of Winterborne
Abbas, 209
Gente, M. Robert, BCnL, r. of
Langton Herring, 24, 154
Genys, John, r. of Wootton
Fitzpaine, 218.
George, William, chapl., cantarist
of St Mary's chantry in
Lambourn ch., 11
Gerard, John, 571
Gerbarde, William, armiger,
patron, 150
Gielles, Thomas, chapl., r. of
Winterborne Monkton, 399
Gifford, William, MTh, witness at
appropriation of Wanborough, 507
Giglis or Gylys, M. John (de), DC &
CnL, clerk, canon of Salisbury
cath.:
prebendary of Fordington and
Writhlington, 288
prebendary of Major pars
Altaris, 228, 289
Gilbert:
Joan, nun of Wilton, 412
John, chapl., v. of Fifehead
Magdalen, 111
Gile (Gyle):
Henry, 570
M. Henry, BCL, cantarist of
Godmanston chantry in St
Thomas's ch., Salisbury, 297
366
John, alias Smyth, 576, 578-80

Gille, William, r. of Grittleton, 308

Glanvilles Wootton (Wotton Glamvile), Dorset, chantry, 171, 235

Glastonbury, Somt., abbey (OSB): abbot, 477
abbot and conv., patrons, 197, 217, 219, 276, 308

Glastonbury (Glastenbury), John, monk of Reading, 431

Gloos, Robert, r. of Tidmarsh, 314

Gloucetour or Glowceter, Thomas, chapl.:
commissioner for gaol delivery, 537
r. of Wallingford St Mary Major, 53, 537

Gloucestre, William, monk of Reading, 431

Gobarde, William, chpl., r. of Church Knowle, 50

Goddard, Richard, of Newbury, confession and abjuration of heresy, 486-7

Goddysgrace, Robert, chapl., r. of Teffont Evias, 221

Godelonde, Alice, nun of Wilton, 412

Godeyere, William, apparitor, 428
See also Godyer

Godhyn, William, v. of Ashbury, 409

Godmanstone, Dorset, 105, 189, 290

Godyer or Godyere:
Robert, see Basset
M. Walter, of London dioc., fellow of Oriel Coll., Oxford, 580
See also Godeyere

Gogh, Thomas, keeper of the hosp. of St John the Baptist, Cricklade, 404

Gokewell (Gokwell), Lincs., priory (Cist. nuns), prioress and conv., orders conferred to title, 584-6

Gold, John, 573

Goldesmyth, Thomas, chapl., v. of Charlton, 161

Goldewegge, M. Thomas, v. of Sturminster Newton, 276

Goldewell, Nicholas, canon of Salisbury cath. and prebendary of Shipton, 427

Goryng, John, armiger, as feoffee of Henry Percy, earl of Northumberland, patron, 225

Gotfrith, M. Nicholas, BC & CnL:
bp.'s commissary in the archdeaconries of Dorset and Salisbury:
commissioner for delivery of criminous clerks, 418
commissioner for visitation, 424
collector of charitable subsidy, 445, 447
commissioner for patronage inquisition, 119
election of the abbess of Wilton, 412
election of the dean of Salisbury, 427
president of the consistory, heresy trial, 460
r. of Broughton Gifford, 151
r. of Odstock, 150, 445, 447

Gowche, John de la, see Lagowche

Gowrton, Thomas, chapl., r. of Chilton, 170

Grace, John, monk of Reading, 431

Grasby (Gravesby), Lincs., 243

Grattelyng, Cristina, nun of Wilton, 412

Graunt, Nicholas, canon of Bradenstoke, 587

Gray (Grey):
Robert, armiger, patron, 96, 114
William, 567

Great Chalfield (Estchalfelde alias Chalfelde Magna), Wilts., 167

Great Cheverell (Chiverell Magna, Chyverell Magna), Wilts., 291

Great Coxwell, Berks., 461, 484n.

Greatham (Gretham), Durham, hosp., master and brothers, orders conferred to title, 584-6

Great Wishford (Wyshfford), Wilts., 408

Gregory, Richard, OP, 566

Grenall, see Grynall

Grenehode, Robert, chapl., r. of Lytchett Matravers, 38

Greve, William, priest, prior of Bisham, 556ff.

Grevell, Thomas, of Worcester dioc., 568

Grey, Thomas, see Dorset, marquess of

Grittleton (Grutlyngton), Wilts., 308

Grivville, Thomas, r. of Shaftesbury St Martin, 283

Grobam, Richard, 578

Groby, Lord Ferrers of, see Dorset, marquess of

Gryce, John, chapl., r. of Langley Burrell, 273

Grymelby, Agnes, nun of Wilton, 412

Grynall (Grenall, Grenehall):
  Edward, chapl., r. of Winterborne Zelston, 55, 264
  Nicholas, armiger, of Northants., patron, 55, 264
  ____, and Joan his wife, patrons, 385

Gulbey, Martin, r. of West Chelborough, 214

Gunthorp or Gunthorpe, M. John, cl.:
  canon of Salisbury cath.:
    prebendary of Alton, 427
    prebendary of Bitton, 365
    dean of Wells cath., 365

Gussage All Saints (Gussuch All Saints alias Gussuch Regis), Dorset, 14

Gussage St Michael (Gussuge), Dorset, 191

Gyan, William:
  canon residentiary of Salisbury cath. and prebendary of Torleton, 427, 429
  warden of the choristers, Salisbury cath., 355

Gybault, Nicholas, r. of Wareham Holy Trinity, 81

Gybbys, Alice, abbess of Shaftesbury, 590

Gybson, William, of Leicester, patron, 78

Gydding, M. William:
  commissioner for gaol delivery, 537
  v. of Wantage, 537

Hacborn or Hakeborne, John, priest, monk of Reading, 431

Hakbourne, Berks., see Hagbourne

Hakkar, William, 566

Halesowen, Worcs., abbey (Prem.), abbot and conv., orders conferred to title, 584-7

Hall (Halle):
  John, of Fisherton Anger, litigation, 466
  Nicholas, armiger, 291
  William, of Lincoln dioc., 563
  William, of Worcester dioc., 581

Ham (Hamme), Wilts., 15, 169

Hamden, M. Edmund, DTh, r. of Sutton Courtenay, 317

Hammond, Henry, OP of Salisbury, 584
  See also Hanont

Hammoon (Hammohun), Dorset, 174

Hampden, Margery, widow, heiress and lady of Fisherton, patron, 293

Hampstead, see Hamstead

Hampton:
  John, gent., 291
    royal commissioner for inquisition into escapes of of criminous clerks, 463
  Richard, cantarist of St Michael de Mowndes chantry, Bridport, 262

Hamstead Marshall (Hampstede Marshall), Berks., 87, 440, 522, 527, 544, 552

Hancok or Hancoke, Richard, chapl.:
  r. of Winterborne Farringdon, 298
  r. of Winterborne Steepleton, 79
  v. of Sydling St Nicholas, 130, 138

Hanney, Berks., 484n.

Hannington (Hanendon, Hanyngdon), Wilts., 64, 440, 523, 528, 544, 552

Hanot or Hamonde, William. of
   Exeter dioc., 580-1
Hanyngton, William, keeper or
   coportioner of tithes of
   Welneley, 168
Hardegate or Hardgate, Thomas, of
   York dioc., 576, 578
Hardy, Richard, chapl., cantarist
   of St Michael de Mowndes chantry,
   Bridport, 195, 371
Hardyng (Harding):
   Richard, of Durham dioc., 580-1
   Thomas, of Exeter dioc., 566
Hare, M. Thomas, proctor for
   William Parkar, 372
Harecourt (Harecowrte):
   George, canon of Salisbury cath.
      and prebendary of Preston, 427
   Katherine, relict of Richard
      Harecourt, kt., patron, 145,
      183
   Richard, kt.:
      lord of Wytham, 183
      patron, 18, 26
   Simon, cl., canon of Salisbury
      cath. and prebendary of
      Preston, 388
Harford (Harforde, Herford):
   John, canon of Maiden Bradley,
      564
   Roger, priest, monk of Reading,
      431, 566
   William, see Carpenter, William
Harington, Lord, see Dorset,
   marquess of
'Harlyng', 426
Harper, William, a blind man, 486
Harris (Harrys):
   John, r. of Newton Toney, 84
   John, 573, 579, 585
   Richard, chapl., r. of West
      Knighton, 387
   Richard, 571, 574-5, 578
   Thomas, canon of Maiden Bradley,
      567
Harrison, John, cantarist of the
   chantry of the Holy Trinity,
   Hungerford, 284
Harryson, Robert, chapl., r. of
   Huish, 172
Harryngton, Christopher, chapl.,
   r. of Manston, 395

Harsenape, Thomas, chapl., r. of
   Binfield, 364
Harthorn, Robert, chapl., v. of
   Warfield, 268
Harward, M. William:
   commissioner for gaol delivery,
      537
   v. of Abingdon St Helen, 537
Harwell (Harewell), Berks., 131
Haselden, John, armiger, patron, 5
Haselwiche, John, r. of Long
   Bredy, 135
Hastings (Hastingys, Hastyngis):
   Edward, kt., Lord Hastings,
      Botreaux, and Hungerford:
      executor of William
         Hastings, patron, 92
      patron, 200
   Katherine, widow, executor of
      William Hastings, patron, 92
   William, kt., Lord Hastings, 92
Hatford, Berks., 120
Haton or Hatton, John, chapl., r.
   of Teffont Evias, 98, 221
Haughmond (Haghmon, Hamonde,
   Hamone), Salop., abbey (OSA),
   orders conferred to title,
   563-4, 566
Haukyns, M. Thomas, MA, of
   Hereford dioc., fellow of All
   Souls Coll., Oxford, 584-7
   See also Hawkyns
Hauson or Hawson:
   John, of Durham dioc., vicar-
      choral of Salisbury cath., 563
   Richard, chapl.:
      r. of Balinghen, Therouanne
         dioc., 265
      r. of Ditchampton, 265
   Richard, cl., proctor for
      Richard Hauson, 265
Hawardyn:
   M. Humfry, r. of Barford St
      Martin, 159
   William, chapl., r. of Barford
      St Martin, 159
Hawkchurch (Haukechurche), Devon,
   238
Hawkyns, John, chapl., r. of
   Barkham, 240
   See also Haukyns

150

Hawsok, Elizabeth, nun of Wilton,
412
Hawtre, Edward, chapl.:
canon of Salisbury cath. and
prebendary of Preston (called
'M.'), 388
r. or keeper of the chapel cure
of St John the Baptist in East
Hendred manor, 153
Haxton (Hakelston), Wilts., free
chapel or portion, 155
Hayne, Alice, nun of Wilton, 412
Haynes:
M. John, MA, of Exeter dioc.,
fellow of All Souls Coll.,
Oxford, 584-5, 587
William, chapl., r. of Farnborough,
223
Hayward (Hawarde, Haywarde,
Heyward):
M. Richard, DCL:
canon of Salisbury cath. and
prebendary of Lyme and
Halstock, 397, 427
commissioner for the
appropriation of Wanborough,
507
official of the consistory
of the bp. of Winchester,
507
r. of Hazelbury Bryan, 398
William, chapl., r. of Melbury
Sampford, 227
Hazelbury Bryan (Haselbere
briand), Dorset, 398, 398n.
Heddington (Hedyndon), Wilts.,
313
Hede, M. Thomas, BCL, of Worcester
dioc., 585
v. of Colerne, 392
Hedley (Hedlay):
M. Thomas, BCL, r. or keeper of
St Mary's chapel, Atworth, 8
Thomas, chapl., r. of Little
Chalfield, 179
William, OFM of Salisbury, 564
Henbury, M. Thomas, chapl., r. of
Sulham, 185
Hendelay or Henlay, Thomas, priest,
keeper or subprior of Leominster,
resident at Reading abbey, 431

Hendred, East, Hendred, West, see
East Hendred, West Hendred
Henry III, king, grant to bps. of
Salisbury, 463
Henry VI, king, 507
Henry VII, king, 400, 413, 431-4,
451-2, 455, 463, 475, 505, 556
mandates:
collection of clerical tenth,
436ff., 540ff., 548ff.
collection of clerical
subsidy, 518ff.
convocation, 515ff., 539
papal bull concerning his
marriage with Elizabeth of
York, 471-2
patron, 87, 146, 265, 358,
589
Henster, M. William, v. of
Cholsey, 363
Henstoke, Richard, r. of All
Cannings, 384
Henton, Wilts., see Broad Hinton
Herberghfelde, Berks., see
Arborfield
Hereford, bp. of, 507
Herne, John de la, chapl., r. of
Woodsford, 329
Hethcottys (Hethcote, Hethcotys),
Ralph, BCnL, priest:
canon of Salisbury:
prebendary of Bitton, 43,
427
prebendary of Chardstock,
40
prebendary of Hurstbourne
and Burbage, 373, 403
prebendary of Ramsbury, 402
convocation proctor, 517
present at election of abbot
of Reading, 431
present at heresy trial, 487
proctor for M. John Reynold,
326
r. of Buckland, 123, 163, 509
r. of Wroughton, 400
Hether, William, v. of New Windsor,
22
Hewes, John, armiger, patron, 93
See also Hewys
Hewlet, John, chapl., r. of
Brixton Deverill, 125

Heworth, William, chapl., v. of
Minety, 4
Hewster, M. William, MA, v. of
Cholsey, 280
Hewys, Thomas, of St Asaph dioc.,
567
See also Hewes
Heyes, Robert, brother of the hosp.
of St John the Baptist, Oxford,
507
Heytesbury, Lord, see Hungerford,
Robert
Hichman, George, of Worcester
dioc., 568-71
Higges or Higgys, William:
v. of Clyffe Pypard, 229
v. of Rowde, 229, 361
Higham, M. William, DTh, canon of
Salisbury cath. and prebendary
of Durnford, 247, 269
Highmore, Richard, of Carlisle
dioc., 574
See also Hyghmor
Highwroth, Wilts., 487
Hignell:
Alice or Alis, of Newbury,
confession and abjuration of
heresy, 495-6
Richard, of Newbury, confession
and abjuration of heresy,
486-7
Hill (Hille, Hyll, Hylle):
John, r. of Lydiard Tregoze, 94
Margaret, nun of Wilton, 412
M. Richard, BCnL:
bp. of London, 246, 471
letters calling a
convocation, 539
letters for collection of
a minor subsidy, 547
canon of Salisbury cath. and
prebendary of Beminster
Secunda, 65, 246
dean of the chapel royal, 65
proctor for John ap Herry, 2
Robert, monk of Milton, 568
Thomas, priest, monk of
Reading, 431
Hilling, see Hyllyng
Hilmarton (Helmerton), Wilts., 237
Hilperton (Hylperton), Wilts.,
458n, 555

Hilston, John, prior of Hurley,
convocation proctor, 517
Hilton (Helton), Dorset, 263, 461
Hilton, William, of York dioc.,
580
Hinton, Somerset, charterhouse,
419n.
Hinton House, Berks., 419n.
Hinton Martell (Hynton Martyn),
Dorset, 109
Hinton Waldrist (Hynton), Berks.,
419, 419n., 420
Hobart, James, royal attorney, 463
Hobbis, Thomas, chapl., r. of
Tollard Royal, 252
Hobill or Hobyll, M. John, MA,
fellow of New Coll., Oxford,
573-4
Hodgys, M. Walter, BC & CnL, of
Winchester dioc., commissioner
for appropriation of Wanborough,
507
Hody:
Alexander, BA, r. of Great
Wishford, 408
William, kt.:
patron, 210
witness to royal letters, 451,
463
Holande, Nicholas, r. of Godmanstone,
105
Holder, Thomas, chapl., r. of
Mildenhall, 48, 133
Holes, M. Thomas, BCL:
canon of Salisbury cath. and
prebendary of Ratfyn, 208
keeper of Witherston free
chapel, 216
present at election of prior of
Ivychurch, 505
present at heresy trial, 502
r. of Dinton, 83
Holme:
Anastasia, nun of Wilton, 412
John, of London dioc., vicar
choral of Wells cath., 563
Thomas, r. of Chilton Foliat,
106
Holte, Richard, proctor for M.
Edmund Hamden, 317
Holwell (Hollewall), Dorset, 21

152

Holyday, Robert, of Worcester
dioc., 572
Homet, Lord, see Hungerforde,
Robert
Hoper:
John, 563
William, v. of Bremhill, 188
Hopkyns:
Pascasius, of Exeter dioc.,
566
Thomas:
ordained, 579
v. of West Hendred, in
dispute with the prior and
conv. of Wallingford, 483
Hopton, M. David, priest:
archd. of Exeter, 427
canon of Salisbury cath.:
prebendary of Beminster Prima,
427
prebendary of Bitton, 333
Horseman or Horsman, William,
chapl.:
present at heresy trial,
498, 504
r. of Baverstock, 285
Horsley, William, chapl., r. of
Alton, 370
Horton, John, abbot of Stanley,
convocation proctor, 517
Hoskyns or Heskyn, John, OP of
Bristol, 566, 571
Hosplete, see Osplete
Hoton, Thomas, canon of Salisbury
cath. and prebendary of Slape,
427
Houchynson, William, OP in Oxford
university, 567
See also Huchenson
Howchyns, William, of Worcester
dioc., 563
See also Huchyns
Howell:
John, BCL or BCnL, present at
heresy trial, 494, 496
Richard, of St Asaph dioc., 574
William, of St Davids dioc., 574
Howse, John, r. of Donhead St
Andrew, 177
Howton, Roger, r. of Church
Knowle, 50

Hoy, John, chapl. of Blunsdon St
Andrew, 121
Huchenson, John, chapl., r. of
Biddestone, 296
See also Houchynson
Huchyns, Maurice, 564
See also Howchyns
Huddesfeld, William, kt., patron,
312
Huddeston, Gilbert, r. of Letcombe
Bassett, 258
Hues, William, collector for
indulgence for repair of St Mary-
le-Strand, 454
Huish (Hewysshe alias Howes,
Huysshe), Wilts., 172, 440, 523,
528, 544, 552
Hull, Henry, co-feoffee of Humphrey,
earl of Devon, lord of Batcombe,
patron, 23,
Hullavington (Hunilavyngton),
Wilts., 440, 523, 528, 544, 552·
Hulle, Bro. William:
convocation proctor, 517
r. of Edington, 324, 517
r. of Poulshot, 324
Hulse, Roger, MA, present at
heresy trial, 502
Hulverdale or Hulvyrdale, M.
William:
v. of Harwell, 131
v. of Winterborne St Martin,
410
Hungerford, Berks., Holy Trinity
chantry, 284, 461
Hungerford (Hungerforde,
Hungerffforde):
Margaret, Lady Hungerforde
and Botreaux, widow of
Robert, Lord Hungerforde,
kt., 291
Robert, kt., Lord Hungerford,
Heytesbury, and Homet, 291
patron, 48, 133
Walter, kt.:
lord of Teffont, patron, 98,
221
patron, 292
Hunte, Thomas, priest, canon of
Bisham, 556
Huntley, Richard, of Worcester
dioc., 567, 570

Iwerne Minster (Ewerne, Ywern),
  Dorset, 319

James _____, literate, proctor
  for M. Robert Shirborn, 299
Jamys, Richard, chapl., cantarist
  of chantry in Glanvilles
  Wootton ch., 235
Jeffrey, David, chapl., r. of
  Abingdon St Nicholas, 357
  See also Geffray
Jenyn, M. John, of Bath and Wells
  dioc., 567
Jervys, William, canon of
  Bradenstoke, 587
John, M. Lewis, BC & CnL:
  chapl. or r. of Chilton, 36,
    170
  r. of Wallingford St Mary
    Major, 53
Johnson:
  John, of York dioc., 567
  Thomas, 579-81
  See also Jonson
Jokyns, William, r. of Wareham St
  Peter, 57
Jolyff, M. John, 567
Jonyngys, William, canon of
  Maiden Bradley, 567, 571
Jonys (Jonis):
  David, chapl. or cl., BA:
    keeper of the hospital of
      St John the Baptist,
      Cricklade, 404
    v. of Sutton Benger, 379
  Philip, 583
  M. William, BCnL:
    collector of charitable
      subsidy, 446-7
    commissary, commissioner for
      collection of minor subsidy,
      533, 536
    commissary-general and
      sequestrator in archdeaconries
      of Berks. and Wilts.,
        commissioner for
          visitation, 425
    commissioner for patronage
      inquisition, 120
    r. of Marlborough St Peter,
      304

Jonys (Jonis) (cont.):
  r. of Steeple, 32
  v. of Cricklade, 307, 447
  William, r. or chapl. of
    Shaftesbury Holy Trinity, 86
Jonson, Thomas, proctor for M.
  Richard Baldry, 224
  See also Johnson
Joyce, M. Richard, MA, r. of
  Sunningwell, 85
Jule, Thomas of Exeter dioc., 564
Jurdan, Isabella, nun of Wilton,
  412

Kam, Richard, see Cam
Karon, Ralph:
  r. of East Shefford, 64
  r. of Hannington, 64
Kelnar, John, cantarist of the
  chantry of St Michael de Mowndes,
  Bridport, 67
Kelsay or Kelsey, M. Richard, BCL:
  commissioner for delivery of
    criminous clerks, 418
  present at the election of the
    abbot of Reading, 431
  r. of Upton Lovell, 76
  subdean of Salisbury cath., 71,
    259, 418
Kempe:
  Robert, r. of Tollard Royal, 252
  Thomas, bp. of London, 202:
    letters for calling
      convocation, 515-6
    letters for collection of a
      charitable subsidy, 444, 448
    letters for collection of two
      minor subsidies, 531
    mandate for keeping feast of
      the Transfiguration, 448
Kenardington (Kennerston,
  Kennerton), Kent, 584-5
Kendall or Kendale:
  John, co-feoffee of Humphrey,
    earl of Devon, lord of the
    manor of Batcombe, patron,
    23
  Brother John, prior of the
    hospital of St John of
    Jerusalem in England,
    patron, 274, 352, 387

155

157

Leche, M. John:
  r. of Brixton Deverill, 125
  v. of Bishops Cannings, 224
  v. of Saffron Walden, London
    dioc., 224
Lechelade, John, monk of Abingdon,
  566
Lee:
  John, priest, r. of Winterborne
    Steepleton, 45
  John, of Coventry and Lichfield
    dioc., 580-2
  M. Thomas, DTh, keeper or r. of
    the chapel cure of St John the
    Baptist in East Hendred
    manor, 153
  Thomas, r. of Tockenham, 192
Leeds (Ledes), Kent, priory (OSA),
  prior and conv., orders
  conferred to title, 576
Legate or Legatt, Robert, OC, in
  Oxford univ., 566-7
Legge, M. Robert alias Palyngton,
  r. of Blandford St Mary, 103
Leigh (Lygh), Essex, 202
Leigh Delamere (Legh, Ligh
  Delamer, Lygh), Wilts., 108,
    440, 523, 528, 544,
    552
Lemes, Cornelius, OC, 573
Leominster (Lemyster), Herefs.,
  priory (OSB), 431
Leomister, Leompster, or
  Leomyster:
    John, priest, monk of
      Reading, 431-2
    Richard, priest, monk of
      Reading, 431, 566
    William, monk of Reading, 573
Letcombe Bassett (Ledecombe
  Bassett, Letcombe Basset,
    Letcombbasset), Berks., 258,
    440, 522, 527, 544, 552
Letcombe Regis, Berks., 484n.
Lethome, John, of York dioc., 581
Lever, William:
  commissioner for gaol delivery,
    537
  v. of North Moreton, 359, 537
Lewes, Sussex, priory (Clun.),
  prior and conv., patrons, 34,
    294

Lewes, John, of Bath and Wells
  dioc., 570
Lewis, William, 571
Ley:
  John, armiger, patron, 171, 235,
    275
  Robert, of Corsley, armiger,
    patron, 30
Leyett, Thomas, gent., patron,
  368
Leyfonde, Roger, r. of Leigh
  Delamere, 108
Leyott, John, chapl., r. of
  Fifield Bavant, 139
Leystone, William, chapl., v. of
  Chisledon, 175
Lichefeld or Lichfeld, M. Richard,
  DCnL or DCL:
    canon of Salisbury cath. and
      prebendary of Wilsford and
      Woodford, 375
    canon residentiary of St Paul's
      cath. and official and
      keeper of the spiritualities
      of the city and dioc.
      of London sede
        vacante, 224, 534
          See also Lychefeld
Liddington (Ludyngton), Wilts.,
  442, 523, 528, 546, 554
Lincoln, bp. of, 243, 507
  inductor, 41-2, 78, 143, 205
    See also Russell, John
Lingfield (Lyngefelde), Surrey,
  471
Little Chalfield (Westchalfeld),
  Wilts., 179
Little Mayne (Lytelmayn, Lytilmayn),
  Dorset, free chapel of St
  Stephen, 309
Littleton Drew (Lytelton Drewe),
  Wilts., 461
Llantarnam (Llanthernam),
  Monmouthshire, abbey (Cist.),
  abbot and conv., orders
  conferred to title, 576
Llanthony, Glos., priory (OSA),
  prior and conv., orders
  conferred to title, 567,
    570-1, 579
      See also 'Langton'

Lloyd or Lloyde:
  David, of St Davids dioc.,
    575
  John, r. of a moiety of Child
    Okeford, 54
  Richard, chapl., v. of
    Steventon, 327
Loco Regali, see Rewley
Lokar, Richard, of Exeter dioc.,
    563
Lokkesley or Lokley, John, chapl.,
    r. or chapl. of Blunsdon St
    Andrew, 121, 137
London:
  186, 199, 226, 240-2, 244, 253,
    259, 310-2, 325, 327, 337-9,
    360-1, 377, 384, 452, 466, 479,
    515, 534, 558
    bp. of, 202, 246
      See also Hill, Richard;
        Kempe, Thomas
  Clerkenwell priory (OSA, nuns),
    prioress and conv., patrons,
    103, 331
  coll. of St Laurence Poultney,
    master and coll., orders
    conferred to title, 566
  dioc., keeper of spiritualities
    sede vacante, see Lichefeld,
    M. Richard
  Fleet Street (Fletestrete,
    Fletestrette):
    episcopal residence, 85,
      87, 454, 463, 519
    friary (OC), 427
  hospital of St Mary of
    Bethlehem without Bishopsgate,
    456
  hospital of St Mary without
    Bishopsgate (Bisshopesgate,
    Bisshoppesgate), prior
    and conv., orders
    conferred to title,
    581-2
  hospital of St Thomas of Acon,
    465
  Minories (Franciscan nuns),
    522, 527
  St Mary le Strand (Stronde)
    without Temple Bar, 454
  St Mary over the Res, see
    Southwark

London (cont.):
  St Paul's cath., 224, 444, 515,
    518, 531, 539-40, 547-8
London:
  John, priest, subprior of
    Reading, 431-2
  Roger, canon of St Frideswide,
    Oxford, 566
Long Bredy (Langebredy, Langebrydy,
  Langbredy), Dorset, 100, 135
Longbridge Deverill (Deverell
  Langbrig), Wilts., 219
Long Crichel (Longecrichill),
  Dorset, 253
Longe:
  Henry, armiger, royal commissioner
    for inquisition into escapes
      of criminous clerks, justice
        of the liberty of the city
          of Salisbury, 463
  Nicholas, proctor for William
    Brydde, 301
  Robert, r. of Wingfield, 233
Longleat (Longa leta), Wilts.,
  priory (OSA), prior and conv.,
  orders conferred to title,
  564-5
Long Newton, Glos., 440, 523,
  528, 544, 552
Lovell:
  Francis, viscount, patron, 507
  Henry, kt., Lord Morley
    (Morlay), patron, 76
  Thomas, kt., lord of Cholderton,
    patron, 353
  William, r. of Teffont Evias,
    98
  M. William, BCL, of Durham
    dioc., 568
Lucas, Robert, of York dioc., 566
Lucy, William, lord of Compton
  Chamberlayne, patron, 159
    See also Luke, William
Ludlowe:
  John, 291
  William, armiger, 291
Ludwell, William, chapl., r. of
  Frome St Quintin, 101
Luke, William, and Alice his wife,
  patrons, 207
    See also Lucy, William
Lutterworth, Leics., 78

Lychefeld, M. John, DCL, r. of
Brinkworth, 377
See also Lichefeld
Lychet, John, monk of Abbotsbury,
568, 571
Lydiard Tregoze (Lydyarde
Traygose), Wilts., 94
Lye, M. Gilbert, r. of Allington,
136
Lygh, Robert, armiger, 291
Lyllyngston, Richard, of Castle
Combe, confession and
abjuration of heresy, 499–
500
Lyllyngton, William:
orders, 567–8
r. of Studland, 340
Lymbry, M. John, r. of Hawkchurch,
328
Lymyn', Richard, v. of Sherborne,
commissary to deliver criminous
clerks, 457
Lynde, John, chapl., v. of
Stapleford, 315
Lyndeley, John, of York dioc., 566
Lynell, Hugh, v. of Chieveley, 157
Lyngen', John, kt., co-feoffee of
Walter Devoreux, Lord Ferrers,
467–9
Lynton, William, proctor for M.
William Elyot, 309
Lytchett Matravers (Lichet
Mawtravers, Lychet Mawtravers),
Dorset, 38

Machon, M. Richard, r. of
Brinkworth, 377
Mades, M. Thomas, cl., canon of
Salisbury cath. and prebendary
of Chardstock, 201
Magdalene Coll., Oxford, see
Oxford, Magdalen Coll.
Maiden Bradley (Mayden bradley,
-legh, -leigh, -leygh)., Wilts.,
priory (OSA), 514
prior and conv.:
collectors of clerical
tenth, 542–3
orders conferred to title,
563, 567, 571
prior, convocation proctor,
517

Makkys, Thomas, 570–3
Malmesbury (Malmesbery), Wilts.:
abbey (OSB), abbot and conv.:
abbot, see Olveston, Thomas
collectors of clerical
subsidy, 519, 524, 526, 530
orders conferred to title,
564–8, 572–4, 577, 579–81,
584–7
patrons, 377, 386
churches:
St Mary Westport, 440, 523,
528, 544, 552
St Paul, 500
Maltus, William, OP of Salisbury,
570
Manningford Abbots (Mannyngford
Abbatis, Manyngforde Abbatis),
Wilts., 178, 440, 523, 528,
544, 552
Manningford Bruce (Mannyngford
Brewes, Manyngforde Brewes),
Wilts., 193, 440, 523, 528,
544, 552
Manston, Dorset, 395
Marchall:
John, canon of Osney, 566
William, OFM, 566
See also Marshall
Marchaunt, William, canon of
Ivychurch, imprisoned for
divers felonies, 505
Mareis, Thomas, chapl., cantarist
of the chantry of St Michael de
Mowndes, Bridport, 67, 195
Margam (Morgan), Glamorgan,
abbey (OCist.), abbot and conv.,
orders conferred to title,
567
Margrave, Thomas, of York dioc.,
566
Market Lavington (Estlavyngton),
Wilts., 271
Marlande, M. Adam, r. of Buckland,
123
Marlborough (Marleborowh,
Marleburgh, Merleburgh), Wilts.:
peculiar jurisdiction,
official, 355
priory (OGilb.), prior and
conv., orders conferred to
title, 564, 576–7
St Peter, 72, 204, 304, 461

Marlborough (cont.):
  chantry of St Katherine, 461
Marlow (Great), (Marlawe magna),
  Bucks., 556
Marnhull (Marnhall), Dorset, 217
Marrall, Thomas, of Coventry and
  Lichfield dioc., 563-4, 566
Marshall (Mershall):
  Richard, of Durham dioc., 584-6
  Robert, OP of Salisbury, 568,
    570
  Robert, of Durham dioc., 580-2
  William, prior of Easton:
    dispensation to hold a secular
      benefice in commendam with
      the priory, 433
    v. of Stapleford, 110, 315
    See also Marchall
Marten, Richard, 580
Martock (Mertoke), Somerset, 563
Martyn (Martin):
  M. Edmund, DC & CnL:
    keeper of Athelhampton free
      chapel, 241
    present at heresy trial, 487
    r. of Chaldon Herring or East
      Chaldon, 46
    r. of Swanage, patron of
      Swanage vicarage, 33, 47
  John, chapl., presented to
    Tyneham but rejected by bp.,
    122
  John, r. of Fisherton Anger
  M. Thomas, DCnL, v. of North
    Moreton, 359
  William, r. of Up Cerne, 6
  William, armiger, patron, 241,
    298
Mason:
  John, r. of North Wraxall, 232
  Thomas, of Lincoln dioc., 585
Massy, John, chapl., r. of
  Odstock, 150
Mateii, John junior, and Joanna
  his wife and John his son, 119
Mathewe:
  Roger, monk of Cerne, 575, 587
  William, literate, proctor for
    M. Thomas Pope, 328
Mathu, Stephen chapl., v. of East
  Lulworth, 28
Maudevile, Thomas, 575

Mauntell, John, 563
Mawghthill or Mawghthille, Robert
  567-8, 570
Mawrice, William, r. of Englefield,
  255
Maydeman, John, r. of Great
  Cheverall, 291
Mayhowe (Mayhewe):
  John, DCnL, present at heresy
    trial, 487
  M. Richard, DTh, president of
    Magdalen Coll., Oxford, 507
Medewe, Henry, v. of Warfield, 268
Melbury Osmond (Melbery Osmonde,
  Melbury Osmund), Dorset, 91, 127,
    158, 440, 521, 529, 544, 552
Melbury Sampford (Melbury
  Samforde), Dorset, 70, 227
Melcombe Horsey (Melcombe
  Turges), Dorset, 173
Melksham (Melkesham, Milkesham,
  Mylkesham), Wilts., 69, 95, 302
Membury, Wilts., free chapel, 461
Menger, John, chapl., r. of
  Pilsden, 210
Merefeld, Thomas, v. of Swanage,
  33
Mersh, Henry, canon of Ivychurch,
  505
Merton (Marton), Hants., priory
  (Aug.), prior and conv.,
    patrons, 28, 213
Merton Coll., Oxford, see Oxford,
  Merton Coll.
Mervyn:
  John, armiger, co-feoffee of
    Robert Hungerford, kt., Lord
    Hungerford, patron, 48, 133,
    291
  Walter, 291
Metford, Robert, justice of gaol
  delivery, 463
Meyndek ap Pell, Geoffrey de, of
  St Asaph dioc., 574
Michell (Michaell, Mychell):
  M. John, MA:
    r. of Castle Eaton, 25
    r. of Tarrant Rushton, 305
  John, of Exeter dioc., 574-5
  M. Thomas, MA:
    orders, 567, 570-2
    r. of Heddington, 313

Michell (cont.):
  William, v. of Canford Magna,
    267
Middelton (Mylton):
  Geoffrey, hermit, 450, 464
  John, monk of Milton, 568, 571,
    578
Milborne St Andrew (Milbon St
  Andrew alias Dereliche),
  Dorset, 325
Mildenhall (Mildenhale,
  Myldenhale), Wilts., 48, 133,
  300
Miles, M. David, BCnL, r. of
  Wareham St Peter, 57
  See also Milys
Million, Thomas, v. of Urchfont,
  35
Milston (Brighmerston alias
  Mildeston, Brightmerston alias
  Mildeston), Wilts., 119
Milton (Mylton), Berks., 49, 356
Milton (Middleton, Middilton,
  Myddelton, Mylton), Dorset,
  abbey (OSB.), 487
    abbey and conv.:
      abbot, convocation
        proctor, 517
      collectors of clerical
        subsidy, 519-20, 524,
        526, 530
      orders conferred to title,
        567-8, 570-1, 578, 584,
        586-7
      patrons, 130, 138, 470
      visitation, 517
Milton Lilbourne (Milton Lilbon,
  Mylton Lilbon), Wilts., 330
Milverton, M. John, r. of Enborne,
  56
Milys (Miles), M. William:
  commissioner for gaol delivery,
    537
  v. of Steventon, 327, 537
Minchin Buckland, Somerset, priory
  (domus Sancti Johannis Baptiste)
  (OSA, nuns), prioress and conv.,
    orders conferred to title,
    563-4
Minety (Mynty), Wilts., 4
Mitton or Mytton, William, chapl.:
  r. of Finchampstead, 152

Mitton or Mytton (cont.):
  r. of Upton Lovell, 76
Mody:
  Edmund, gent., patron, 273
  John, armiger, lord of Foxley,
    patron, 3
Moleyns, Katherine, nun of
  Shaftesbury, prioress of
  Kington St Michael, 480-2
Molle, John, 567-8
Mompesson:
  M. Henry, BC & CnL, r. of
    Mildenhall, 133, 300
  John, armiger:
    co-feoffee of Robert
      Hungerforde, kt., Lord
      Hungerforde, patron, 48,
      133
    justice of the liberty of city
      of Salisbury, 463
    patron, 48, 133, 159
    royal commissary for
      inquisition into escapes
      of criminous clerks, 463
Mone, M. Thomas, r. of Tyneham,
  122
Monk Bretton, Yorks., priory (OSB),
  prior and conv., orders
  conferred to title, 566
Monke, Robert, chapl., r. of
  Shaftesbury St Martin, 283
Monkton Farleigh (Farlay,
  Farlegh), Wilts.:
  ch., 440, 523, 528, 544, 552
  priory (Clun.), prior and conv.:
    orders conferred to title,
      568-9
    patrons, 10, 88, 102, 296,
      306, 313, 376
    prior, convocation proctor,
      517
Montacute, Somerset, priory (Clun.),
  prior and conv., orders
  conferred to title, 563-4
Monyngton, Thomas, armiger,
  co-feoffee of Walter Devoreux,
  Lord Ferrers, kt., 467-9
Mordy, Thomas, OC, 573
More, see Northmoor
More or Moore:
  Richard, v. of Milborne St
    Andrew, 325

162

More or Moore (cont.):
  William, monk of Sherborne, 568
  William, monk of Malmesbury, 564
Moreland, M. Adam, v. of Buckland,
  323
    See also Morland
Moreman, Thomas, of Exeter dioc.,
  563
Moren, John, cantarist of St
  Katherine's chantry in St
    Edmund's coll. ch., Salisbury,
    29
Mores, M. William, BCL, of Bath
  and Wells dioc., incumbent of
  Porlock, 584
Moressh, Thomas, r. of Fittleton,
  82
Moreton (Morton), Dorset, 37
Morgan:
  Geoffrey, chapl., r. of Oaksey,
  10
  M. John, DCnL, r. of West Dean,
  26
  M. Owen:
    commissioner for gaol delivery,
    537
    r. of Wallingford St Leonard,
    66, 537
  M. Philip, v. of Chieveley, 157
  William, v. of Froxfield, 282
Morland (Moreland):
  Hugh, proctor for M. William
    Morland, 180
  M. William, cl., r. of Binfield,
    180, 364
    See also Moreland
Morley:
  Lord, see Lovell, Henry
  Thomas, chapl., r. of Blundsdon
    St Andrew, 137
Mortemer, John, of Harlyng,
  charitable subsidy in favour of,
  426
Mortlake, Surrey, archiepiscopal
  residence, 444
Morton:
  John, archbishop of Canterbury:
    decree for keeping feast of
      the Transfiguration on 7
      August, 448
    letters calling for a
      convocation, 515, 539

Morton (cont.):
    letters for levying &c.
      taxation, 444-8, 531-4, 547
    mandate for publication of
      papal bull concerning the
      marriage of Henry VII and
      Elizabeth of York, 471
    patron, 180
  Robert, monk of Abingdon, 573,
    583
  M. Robert:
    canon of Salisbury cath. and
      prebendary of Horton, 51,
      427
    bp. of Worcester, 51
Mose, William, BA, of Bath and
  Wells dioc., 563
Mouncell, Luke, chapl., r. of
  Swyre, 146
Mounteforde, Edmund, kt., patron
  of Remenham, 93
Moysi, Wilts., see Castle Eaton
Muchelney, Somerset, abbey (OSB),
  abbot and conv., orders
  conferred to title, 567
Mugwurthy, M. Thomas, BCL, of
  Exeter dioc., 580
Mutte, Reginald, r. of Catmore,
  124
Mychell, see Michell
Mylborne, Thomas, kt., patron, 265
Mytton, see Mitton

Nele, Richard, 564
Nessingwik or Nessingwike, M.
  William, BCnL, priest:
    canon of Salisbury cath.:
      canon residentiary, 418, 427,
      429
      prebendary of Faringdon, 427
    commissioner for delivery of
      criminous clerks, 418
Neuborough, Thomas, gent., patron,
  312
    See also Newburgh
Neulond or Newlond, William,
  monk of Cerne, 571, 575, 578,
  587
    See also Newland

North Wroxall (Northwraxalle,
North Wraxhale), Wilts., 232
Norton, Wilts., 386
Norton Bavant (Norton Bavent),
Wilts., 243
Notley, Bucks., abbey (OSA),
abbot and conv., orders
conferred to title, 574, 576,
585
Notte, Christopher, chapl.:
r. of Biddestone, 88, 296
r. of Great Cheverell, 291

Oaksey (Woxci), Wilts., 10
Oder, John, chapl., v. of
Swanage, 33
Odlande, John, chapl.:
cantarist of Godmanston chantry
in Salisbury St Thomas, 286
r. of Chicklade, 287
Odstock (Odestoke, Odstoke),
Wilts., 150, 445
Odyngesley, William, v. of Latton, 254
Offynton, Berks., see Uffington
Ogan, Thomas, r. of Shillingstone, 5
Ogyll, George, of Durham dioc.,
566
Okeforde Skylling, Dorset, see
Shillingstone
Okeford Fitzpaine (Okeford
Phippayn), Dorset, 225
Okey, Thomas, v. of Norton, 386
Old Windsor (Wyndesor, Wyndesour),
Berks., 442, 522, 527, 546, 554
Olveston:
Thomas, abbot of Malmesbury,
convocation proctor, 517
Thomas, monk of Malmesbury, 584
Oram, John, of Bath and Wells
dioc., 569
'Orcharde', Exeter dioc., 563
Orchardeshurne in Durweston,
Dorset, 312
Orcheston (Orsheton), Wilts., 77
Oriel Coll., Oxford, see Oxford,
Oriel Coll.
Ormond, earl of, Thomas Butler:
lord of Rampisham, patron, 74
Lord Rochford, patron, 202
Orums, Thomas, chapl., v. of
Cranborne, 389

Osmington (Osmyngton, Osmynton),
Dorset, 461, 470
Osney, Oxon., abbey (OSA), abbot and
conv., orders conferred to title,
563-70, 573-5, 579-81, 583-7
Osplete (Hosplete), M. John, MA,
chapl.:
keeper of hospital of St John
the Baptist, Shaftesbury, 194
r. of Cheselbourne, 215
r. of Gussage St Michael, 191
Overton, Wilts., see West Overton
Owermoigne (Owermoyne, Owremoyne),
Dorset, 367
Owston (Oselveston), Leics., abbey
(OSA), abbot and conv., orders
conferred to title, 585
Oxford, Oxon.:
Blackfriars, 566
city or university, 439, 507,
567, 574
hosp. of St John the Baptist,
507
priory of St Frideswide (OSA.),
prior and conv.:
orders conferred to title,
566-7, 569-71, 580-3, 587
patrons, 66
university:
All Souls Coll., warden and
fellows, orders conferred
to title, 566
Exeter Coll., r. and fellows,
patrons, 126
Magdalen Coll., president and
scholars:
appropriation of Wanborough
chantry, 451-2, 507-8
orders conferred to title,
567, 584-6
patrons, 129, 249, 409
Merton Coll., warden,
scholars, and brothers:
orders conferred to title,
573, 575, 584-6
patrons, 156
New Coll., warden and fellows,
orders conferred to title,
566, 570, 573-4, 576, 580-2
Oriel Coll., provost and
fellows, orders conferred
to title, 580-2, 586-7

Oxford, Oxon (cont.):
  Queen's Coll., provost and
    scholars:
      orders conferred to title,
        580-2
      patrons, 393
Oxforde:
  Francis, canon of St Frideswide,
    Oxford, 566
  John, canon of Osney, 566

Pacye, Thomas, alias Strobull,
  see Strobull, Thomas
Padworth, Berks., 165, 440, 522,
  527, 544, 552
Page:
  Richard, chapl., v. of Urchfont,
    35
  Richard, canon of Ivychurch:
    elected prior, 505-6, 591
    orders, 570, 572-3
Pakkar, William, OP, 570
Palle, Christopher, 567-8
Palmer:
  Henry, chapl., r. of Moreton, 37
  Henry, r. of Biddestone, 88
  John, of Exeter dioc., 566
  William, chapl., r. of Everleigh,
    196
Palyngton, M. Robert, see Legge,
  M. Robert
Panavilioni, Claudius, chapl., r.
  of Tarrant Rushton, 305
Parkar, William, BCnL, r. of
  Appleton, 372
Parsons, M. David, BC & CnL,
  commissioner for patronage
  inquisition, 120
Pashe, M. Thomas, r. of Sutton
  Courtenay, 242
Patrik (Patrikke) alias Stephynson,
  M. Andrew, MA:
    orders, 584-7
    r. of Easton Grey, 362
Patwyn, Thomas, of Norwich dioc.,
  568-9
Pavy:
  M. Hugh:
    archd. of Wilts.:
      appropriation of Wanborough,
        507

Pavy (cont.):
    patron, 4
    bp. of St David's, 87
  Thomas, r. of North Poorton, 190
Payn:
  Henry, r. of Silton, 187
  Richard, cl., canon of Salisbury
    cath. and prebendary of Minor
    pars altaris, 270
Pell, ap, see Meyndek, Geoffrey de
Pendeley, John, v. of East
  Hagbourne, 380
Pendleton, Thomas,chapl., v. of
  Latton, 254
Penfold, Nicholas, 571
Penne, Thomas, canon of Bradenstoke,
  587
Pentridge (Pentrich alias
  Petrynch, Pentryche), Dorset,
  73, 440, 521, 529, 544, 552
Pepyr, Robert, r. of Moreton, 37
Percy, Henry, see Northumberland,
  earl of
Pere, William, of Bath and Wells
  dioc., 563
Peret or Perot, Philip, monk of
  Abbotsbury, 568, 575
Perkyns, John, armiger, patron,
  152
Peronyll, Richard, of York dioc.,
  566
Perot, see Peret
Person or Persons, M. David, BC &
  CnL:
    proctor for M. Hugh Pavy,
      archd. of Wilts., 507
    proctor for the president and
      scholars of Magdalen Coll.,
      Oxford, 507
Peryngcorte de Castelcombe,
  Robert, 576
Pese, John, canon of Salisbury
  cath. and prebendary of
  Grimston, 427
Pest, William, vicar-choral of
  St George's, Windsor, commissary
  for gaol delivery, 537
Petegrewe, John, literate,
  proctor for hospital of St
  Thomas of Acon, London, 465
Petipace, Henry, fellow of
  Vaux Coll., Salisbury, 573, 584-6

Petir, M. William, r. of Wytham, 18

Peverell, John, r. of Askerswell, 96

Pevesay or Pevesey, M. Robert, MA:
  r. of Ebbesborne Wake, 90
  succentor of Salisbury cath., 89-90
  v. of Preshute, 355

Pewsay:
  Agnes, nun of Wilton, 412
  Elizabeth, nun of Wilton, 412

Phelipes, M. John, BCL, r. of Swanage, 147

Philip, Raginald, of St David's dioc., 581

Philipes or Philippes, M. Rouland, MA, of Worcester dioc., 586-7

Philipis, Robert, v. of Somerford Keynes, 213

Philippis, Thomas, chapl., subdean of Salisbury cath., 259

Piddlehinton (Pydelhynton), Dorset, 128

Piers:
  John, of Chichester or Bath and Wells dioc., fellow of New Coll., Oxford, 581-2
  Roger, monk of Sherborne, 571, 575

Pierson, M. John, r. of Bishopstone, patron of Bishopstone vicarage, 239

Pilsdon (Pyllesdon), Dorset, 210

Pilton, John, monk of Malmesbury, 584

Pirrot, Walter, 563

Plubell, William, r. of Berwick St Leonard, 343

Plympton, Devon, priory (OSA), prior and conv., orders conferred to title, 566, 569, 575

Pokeswell, Humfry, gent., patron, 312

'Pole', ch. or chapel, 487

Pole:
  Joan, nun of Wilton, 412
  Roger, chapl., r. of Frilsham, 366

Ponyngys, Eleanor, countess of Northumberland, patron, 312

Poole, M. William, BCnL, r. of Winterbourne Bassett, 294

Poole (Pole), Dorset, ch. or chapel, 489

Poole Keynes (Pole), Glos., 440, 523, 528, 544, 522

Poore, Richard, bp. of Salisbury, grant from Henry III, 463

Pope:
  M. Thomas:
    canon of Salisbury cath., 328
    r. of Hawkchurch, 328
    See also Calixtus III, Innocent VIII, Sixtus IV

Porlock (Putlok), Somerset, 584

Porte, William, v. of Aldermaston, 164

Porter, Thomas, r. of Cheselbourne, 215

Portesham, Dorset, 266

Portesham, John, monk of Abbotsbury, 575

Portland, M. William, MA, of Norwich dioc., fellow of All Souls Coll., Oxford, 567

Porton, Wilts., see Idmiston

Potterne (Pottern), Wilts., 461

Poucherdon, Thomas, monk of Sherborne, 571, 575

Poughley (Poghley, Poughlay), Berks., priory (OSA), prior and conv.:
    orders conferred to title, 570-1, 573-5, 580-2, 584
    prior Thomas, convocation proctor, 517
    taxation, 439, 522, 527
    visitation, 514

Poulshot (Pollesholte, Paulesholte), Wilts., 324, 461

Poulton (Pulton), Glos., priory (OGilb.), prior and conv., orders conferred to title, 569-71

Powerstoke, John, r. of Chaldon Herring or East Chaldon, 46

Preshute (Presshute, Preschute alias Preshute cum capella, Prestechute, Prestchute, Preschutt), Wilts., 355, 440, 458n, 461-2, 523, 528, 544

167

Preston:
  M. John, BCnL, r. of Ham, 15
  Matilda, widow, patron, 187
  M. Robert, v. of West Overton, 149
Prilacy, Hugh, 574
Priour, William, of Newbury,
  confession and abjuration of
  heresy, 486-7
Puddletown (Pedelton, Pedeltown),
  Dorset, 338, 351
Pulley, M. John Richard, r. of
  Appleton, 372
Puncknowle (Penkenoll, Ponknoll),
  Dorset, 398n., 440, 521, 529,
  544, 552
Purcer, John, late of Salisbury,
  tailor, indicted, delivered, as
  a criminous clerk, 463
Purdewe, Henry, of Winchester dioc.,
  vicar-choral of Salisbury cath.,
  567-8, 570, 576
Purley, Berks., 440, 522, 527, 544,
  552
Pusey (Pewsay), Berks., 60, 461
Pykton, Richard, of London dioc.,
  583
Pykyn, Thomas, v. of Preshute,
  355
Pymbarde, John, chapl., cantarist
  of chantry in Reading St Mary,
  116
Pynnok or Pynnoke, John, bonhomme
  of Edington, 565, 568, 572

Queen's Coll., Oxford, see Oxford,
  Queen's Coll.

Radclyff:
  Edmund, of Coventry and
    Lichfield dioc., 573
  William, monk of Abingdon, 566
Rading (Radyng, Reding):
  Edmund, monk of Reading, 431
  Henry, monk of Reading, 431,
    568-9
  John, monk of Reading, 431
  Robert, monk of Reading, 431,
    573
Radipole (Radepole, Radepoll),
  Dorset, 19, 251

Rampisham (Rampsham), Dorset, 74
Rampsham, Peter, abbot of
  Sherborne, priest:
    canon of Salisbury cath. and
      prebendary of Sherborne, 427
    convocation proctor, 517
Ramsbury (Rammesbury, Remmeybury,
  Remysbury), Wilts.:
    ch., 181, 461
    episcopal residence, 91, 113-
    4, 117-8, 121, 123, 129-30,
    132-3, 140, 146, 157, 159, 167,
    173, 177, 180, 203, 208, 218,
    225, 228, 234, 249-50, 263,
    281-2, 184-90, 292-3, 300-1,
    303-5, 322-3, 330, 336, 341-3,
    345-9, 351, 355, 390-3, 396-
    400, 402, 404, 406, 450, 458,
    464, 470, 473-6, 481, 483,
    485, 487, 498, 504, 509-10,
    512, 516, 524-5, 532, 538,
    541, 543, 551, 555, 567-9,
    572-7, 579-87, 590
    free chapel of Membury, see
      Membury
Randolffe, William, r. of
  Baverstock, 285
Rawlyn, Henry, clerk, prebendary
  of Urchfont, 58
Rawlyns, William, co-feoffee of
  William Trussel, 78
Ray, John, BA, 563
Rayn, William, of York dioc., 569
Raynes, M. Thomas, vicar-choral
  of the free chapel of St George,
  Windsor, commissioner for
  gaol delivery, 537
Raynold or Reynold, M. John, BCL:
  r. of Beeford, York dioc., 326
  r. of Shaftesbury St Peter, 341
  r. of Stour Provost, 326
Reading (Rading, Radyng, Redyng),
  Berks., 463
  abbey (OSB):
    abbey and conv.:
      abbot, see Thorne, John (1);
        Thorne, John (2)
      collectors of clerical
        subsidy, 519, 524
      orders conferred to title,
        566, 568-9, 573, 580-2,
        584-6

Stephins, John, chapl., cantarist
of John Sewarde's chantry in
Holy Trinity ch., Dorchester,
75
Stephyn, John, of Exeter dioc.,
566
Stephyns, M. Thomas, r. of
Abingdon St Nicholas, 244
Stephynson, M. Andrew, see Patrik
Stere, Augustine (Augustyn), of
Speen, confession and
abjuration of heresy, 486-7
Sterengare, John, of Hinton
Waldrist, heretic, 419
Sterr, M. Thomas, MA, r. of
Holwell, 21
Steventon (Stephynton, Stevynton),
Berks., 327, 501, 537
Stevynton, John, chapl., r. of
Wingfield, 233
Stillington, Robert, bp. of Bath
and Wells, 588
Stokfissh or Stokfisshe, William,
vicar-choral of Salisbury cath.,
427
Stokton, John, third prior of
Reading, 431
Stokys (Stoykys), M. John, MA:
r. of Milton, 49, 356
r. of Tarrant Hinton, 52
r. of Trowbridge, 358
Stoner, Robert, priest, precentor
and novice-master of Bisham,
556-7
Store, M. Ralph, notary public,
proctor for William Wilton, 217
Story, Andrew, OC, 573-4
Stour Provost (Stoureprewis
alias Stourepreaulx), Dorset,
326
Stourton, Wilts., 238
Stourton (Storton):
John, kt., Lord Stourton,
patron, 6
Raginald, kt., 291
William, Lord Stourton, kt.,
patron, 162, 370
Stowell, Robert, co-feoffee of
Humphrey, late earl of Devon,
lord of the manor of Batcombe,
patron, 23

Strangwysche, Edward, of York
dioc., 566
Strata Marcella, Montgom., abbey
(OCist.), abbot and conv.,
orders conferred to title, 572
Stratford Toney, Wilts., 211
Stratton St Margaret (Stretton
St Margaret), Wilts., 156, 461
Streatley (Streteley, Stretley),
Berks., 440, 461, 522, 527,
544, 552
Strobull (alias Pacye), Thomas,
chapl.:
r. of Sopworth, 102, 376
r. of Sherston, 320
Strode, Joan, nun of Wilton, 412
Stong:
John, 567-9
Thomas, cl., v. of Hilmarton,
237
Studland (Stodelonde), Dorset,
340
Sturminster Newton (Sturmyster
Newton), Dorset, 276
Sturthill (Sterthyll), Dorset,
free chapel, 222
Styleman, M. Antony, gent.,
proctor for M. Thomas Waget,
292
Suffolk, duke of, John de la Pole,
patron, 120
Sulham, Berks., 80, 185, 440, 522,
527, 544, 552
Sulhamstead Abbots (Sulhamstede
Abbatis), Berks., 440, 522,
527, 544, 552
Sunning, see Sonnyngys, John
Sunningwell (Sunyngwell), Berks.,
85
Sutton:
M. Henry, MD:
canon of Salisbury cath.:
canon residentiary, 427,
429
prebendary of Chisenbury
and Chute, 63, 458
prebendary of Ratfyn, 62,
427
dispute over tithes in
Chisenbury, 458
master or warden of Vaux Coll.,
Salisbury, 325

Sutton (cont.):
John, of Exeter dioc., 566
John, monk of Abingdon, 584
Thomas, MA, r. of Stanton St
Quintin, 132
Sutton Benger, Wilts., 379, 354,
461
Sutton Courtenay (Sutton Courteney,
Sutton Courtney), Berks., 242,
317, 467-9
Sutton Veny (Fennysutton),
Wilts., 562
Sutton Waldron (Sutton Walrand,
Sutton Walrond), Dorset, 199
Salwell, Thomas, monk of Durham,
566
Swan or Swane, John, alderman of
London, co-feoffee of William
Trussell, 78, 226
Swanage (Swanwych, Worthe and
Swanwiche), Dorset, 33, 47, 147
Swanne, Richard, chapl., chapl. or
cantarist of Chippenham chantry,
306
Swettok, Robert, of Ashwell,
Rutland, patron, 78
Swindon (Swyndon), Wilts., 99
Swine (Swyna), Yorks., priory
(OCist. nuns), prioress and
conv., orders conferred to
title, 567
Swyre, Dorset, 146
Sydenham, Maurice, of Bath and
Wells dioc., 566
Sydling St Nicholas (Brodesideling,
Brodesidelyng, Brodesydelyng),
Dorset, 130, 138
Sylke:
John, v. of Bradpole, 31
M. William, DCnL, r. of Milton,
49
Sylle, Richard, of York dioc., 566
Symon, M. Thomas, r. of West
Wittenham, 126
Sympmyngys, John, chapl., r. of
Leigh Delamere, 108
Symson, William, chapl., r. of
Stanton St Quintin, 132
Syngle, William, r. of Hinton
Martell, 109
Syon, Middlesex, abbey
(Bridgettine), abbess and conv.,

Syon (cont.):
patrons, 31
Sysson, Thomas, of York dioc.,
566

Taberer, John, r. of Rampisham,
74
Tailour (Taylour, Taylor,
Tayllour, Taillour):
John, priest:
r. of Fosley, 3
v. of Minety, 4
M. John, canon of Salisbury
cath. and prebendary of
Hurstbourne and Burbage,
373, 427
Simon, cantarist of Swayne's
chantry in St Thomas',
Salisbury, 272
Thomas, chapl. of Norridge St
Michael the Archangel chapel,
275
Thomas, of Newbury, fuller,
confession and abjuration
of heresy, 484-5
William, 568, 571-2, 577
William, chapl., commissary
for delivery of criminous
clerks, 457
Tallay, David, canon of Talley,
581
Talley (Tallay), Carmarth., abbey
(Prem.), abbot and conv., orders
conferred to title, 581
Tame, John, armiger, patron, 207
Tanner, John, of Steventon,
confession and abjuration of
heresy, 501-2
Tapnaile (Taple), John, of
Exeter dioc., 567-9
Tarrand, Nicholas, of Carlisle
dioc., 567
Tarrant (Tarent, Tarraunt),
Dorset, abbey (OCist. nuns):
abbess and conv., orders
conferred to title,
567-8, 572
taxation, 439, 521, 529
Tarrant Hinton (Tarrent Hynton),
Dorset, 52

177

Walkar (cont.):
  v. of Wargrave, 349
Walker, John, r. of St Mary's in
  Breadstreet, Wilton, 118
Walle, William, chapl., v. of
  Rowde, 361
Wallingford (Walyngford,
  Walyngforde), Berks.:
  churches:
    St Leonard, 66, 440, 522,
      527, 537, 544, 552,
    St Mary Major, 53, 440,
      522, 527, 537, 544,
      552
    St Peter, 440, 522, 527,
      537, 544, 552
  gaol, 463, 537
  priory (OSB), prior and conv.:
    collectors of clerical
      tenth, 550-1
    dispute over vicar's
      portion in West Hendred,
      483
    patrons, 53
    prior, John, convocation
      proctor, 517
      See also Zouche,
        Antony
  royal free chapel in the
    castle, dean and coll. or
    fellows, patrons, 131
Walop, Richard, armiger, of
  Farleigh Wallop, Winchester
  dioc., patron, 136, 184
Walshe, Thomas, prior of
  Bradenstoke:
  convocation proctor, 517
  present at heresy trial,
  504
Walston or Woleston, Robert, monk
  of Malmesbury, 584-5
Walter:
  John, chapl., r. of Compton
    Abbas, 316
  William, 579
Waltham, Holy Cross, Essex, abbey
  (OSA), abbot and conv., patrons,
  22, 202
Walton, M. Thomas or M. William,
  MA, r. of Wytham, 18, 183

Wanborough (Wamberge, Wamburgh,
  Wanbrow), Wilts., coll. or
  chantry or chapel of St
    Katherine, 451-2,
    507-8
Wantage (Wantynge), Berks.:
  ch., 487, 537
  gaol, 537
Warburton, M. Geoffrey:
  r. of Balinghen, Therouanne
    dioc., 265
  r. of Ditchampton, 265
Wareham (Warham), Dorset:
  Holy Trinity, 81
  St Martin, 243, 346, 440, 521,
    529, 544, 552
  St Michael, 198
  St Peter, 57
Waren or Waryn:
  Richard, chapl.:
    keeper or co-portioner of the
      tithes of Woolley, 168
    r. of All Cannings, 384
  Thomas, patron, 106
  Thomas, r. of Buckhorn Weston,
    162
Warfield (Warfeld), Berks., 268
Wargrave (Wergrave), Berks., 349
Wargrave, William, priest, monk
  of Reading, 431
Warlond, John, chapl., v. of
  Canford Magna, 267
Warminster (Wermister), Wilts.,
  461
Warner, M. Thomas, BCL, r. of
  Wytham, 183
Warwikhill, John, of Glasgow
  dioc., 584
Wasing (Wavesyng), Berks., 257
Water Eton, Berks., see Eaton
  Hastings
Watson:
  Nicholas:
    r. of Melbury Osmond, 91
    v. of Chute, 91
  Owain, chapl., v. of Bishopstone,
    239
  M. Richard, of Carlisle dioc.,
    569
  Thomas, of Coventry and
    Lichfield dioc., 581

Weston (cont.):
  John, literate, proctor for
    M. Robert Pevesey, 355
West Overton, Wilts., 149, 260,
  441, 545, 553
Westporte, Wilts., see Malmesbury
Westrope, John, v. of Winterbourne
  Stoke, 206
West Stafford, Dorset, 440, 521,
  529, 544, 552
West Wittenham (West Wyttenham),
  Berks., 126
Westwod or Westwode:
  Robert, monk of Abingdon, 573,
    577, 584
  Robert, v. of Longbridge
    Deverill, 219
Wethers, M. John, of Bath and Wells
  dioc., fellow of Magdalen Coll.,
  Oxford, 567
Weybayhous, Dorset, see Upwey
Whaddon (Wadden, Whadden),
  Wilts., 97, 281, 555
Wheler, John, 570
Whelpley, Wilts., free chapel, 401
Wherwell (Wharwell), Hants.,
  abbey (OSB nuns), abbess and
  conv., patrons, 196, 332
Whipham, William, late of
  Reading, cutler, indicted and
    imprisoned as a criminous
      clerk, 463
Whissyng (Whyssyng), Robert
  (Richard), 568-71
Whiston, William, of Lincoln
  dioc., 570, 572, 574
Whitacre, John, proctor for
  John Newman, 52
Whitby, Richard:
  canon residentiary of Salisbury
    cath., 427, 429
  proctor for Edward Cheyne,
    429-30
  treasurer of Salisbury cath.
    and prebendary of Calne, 427,
    429
White (Whyte):
  Elizabeth, nun of Wilton, 412
  John, canon of Bradenstoke,
    566, 569
  William, OP of Salisbury, 570
Whitell, Richard, OP, 566

Whithed or Whithede:
  John, 570-1, 577
  Richard, of Newbury, infected
    with heresy by Robert Elton,
    492
Whithorne, John, chapl., r. of
  Letcombe Bassett, 258
Whittemor, John, monk of
  Dunkeswell, 572
Whittok, Thomas, r. of Hammoon,
  174
Whittpoll, Richard, of Worcester
  dioc., fellow of New Coll.,
  Oxford, 580
Whyssyng, see Whissyng
Whytyng, John, of Hereford dioc.,
  564
Wickham (Wilsford and Wyckham,
  Wykeham), Berks., 522
Wilde:
  Richard, OP of Oxford univ., 567
  M. Walter, BCnL, v. of Sturminster
    Newton, 276
Wilkyns, Gilbert, chapl., r. of a
  moiety of Child Okeford, 54
Wilkynson:
  Edmund, chapl., r. of Ham, 169
  Henry, proctor for William
    Leystone, 175
Willey, James, of York dioc., 566
William, Thomas, of Exeter dioc.,
  575
Williams:
  Morgan, of St David's dioc.,
    581
  Thomas, of Llandaff dioc., 567
Willisford or Willisforde or
  Wilsford, M. Edmund, MA, of
    Exeter dioc., fellow of Oriel
    Coll., Oxford, 580-2
Willoughby (Wiloughby, Wylloughby):
  Cecily, abbess of Wilton, 12,
    412-7
  M. Edward, MA:
    canon of Salisbury cath. and
      prebendary of Grantham
      Borealis, 143-4
    r. of Berwick St John, 12
    r. of Chilmark, 148
  Robert, lord of Brook (Broke),
    patron, 407

183

York (cont.):
  patron, 32, 45, 50, 79, 192, 248
Yprus, William, chapl., r. of
  Iwerne Minster, 319
Ywern, Dorset, <u>see</u> Iwerne Minster

Zouche:
  Antony, prior of Wallingford,
    483
  John, kt., Lord Zouche, patron,
    25

SUBJECT INDEX

Priors; prioresses, see Heads of
religious houses
Prisons, see Gaols
Processions, 420, 485, 487, 489,
491, 493, 496, 498, 500, 504
Proctors:
for appropriations, 469, 507
for collections, 456, 465
for convocations, 516-7
for decanal election, 427, 429-30
for institutions, 52, 112, 115,
168, 175, 180, 198, 217, 239,
265-7, 288, 299, 301, 303,
309, 317, 326, 328, 331, 355,
363, 372, 377, 382, 391, 397,
for matters related to conventual
elections, 412, 431, 505,
556-7
for pensions, 215, 292, 331
for professions of obedience,
224
Procurations, see under
Archdeacons
Proxy, see Proctors
Pulpits, see Ecclesiastical
articles
Punishments, see Penance
Pyxes, see Ecclesiastical
articles

Queens, 471-2

Registers of other bps., references
to, 452, 461, 466
Registrars, see under Bishops:
officers
Religious:
institutions to benefices, 122,
314, 324
ordinations, 563-87 passim
See also Friars; Religious
houses
Religious houses, 427, 470, 485,
487, 502
appropriated, 461, 507-8
appropriations to:
disputed, 483
vacated, 509
collectors for clerical
taxation, see Taxation

Religious houses (cont.):
elections, 412-7, 431-4,
505-6, 556-8
exempt from taxation, 439
exempt from ordinary, 477-9
heads, see under Heads of
religious houses
patrons of benefices, 2-410
passim, 461, 470
visitations of, 512-4
See also Colleges; Collegiate
churches; Hospitals
Renegade monk, 475
Resignations of benefices, see
under Benefices
Royal clerks, see Kings: officers
Rye, 419

Sacraments, heretical beliefs
about, 488
baptism, 484, 501
confession, 484, 486, 488,
492, 497
eucharist, 419, 459, 484,
486, 490, 492, 497, 501,
503
holy orders, 459, 484, 486,
488, 492, 497, 501, 503
matrimony, 484
Seneschals, bp.'s, see Bishops:
officers
Sentences, of bp., in tithes
dispute, 458
See also Commissions; Decrees;
Grants; Letters; Licenses;
Mandates; Monitions;
Petitions; Significavits
Sermons, 419, 487, 489, 496, 499
Sheriffs, see Kings: officers
Significavits, 455
See also Commissions; Decrees;
Grants; Letters; Licenses;
Mandates; Monitions;
Petitions; Sentences
Subdeacons, ordinations, 563-87
passim
Subdeans, see under Cathedrals:
dignities
Succentors, see under Cathedrals:
dignities

197